A JOURNEY
TOWARD HEAVEN

A JOURNEY TOWARD HEAVEN

A Daily Devotional from the
Sermons of Jonathan Edwards

Edited by
Dustin W. Benge

Reformation Heritage Books
Grand Rapids, Michigan

A Journey toward Heaven
© 2012 Dustin W. Benge

Published by
Reformation Heritage Books
2965 Leonard St. NE
Grand Rapids, MI 49525
616-977-0889 / Fax 616-285-3246
e-mail: orders@heritagebooks.org
website: www.heritagebooks.org

Printed in the United States of America
12 13 14 15 16 17/10 9 8 7 6 5 4 3 2 1

Library of Congress Cataloging-in-Publication Data

Edwards, Jonathan, 1703-1758.
 A journey toward heaven : a daily devotional from the sermons of Jonathan Edwards / edited by Dustin W. Benge.
     p. cm.
 Includes bibliographical references and index.
 ISBN 978-1-60178-192-5 (alk. paper)
 1. Devotional calendars. 2. Congregational churches—Sermons. 3. Sermons, American. I. Benge, Dustin W. II. Title.
 BV4811.E295 2012
 242'.2—dc23
                              2012032244

For additional Reformed literature, request a free book list from Reformation Heritage Books at the above address.

In heartfelt appreciation to

JIMMY BURCHETT

my friend,
my brother,
my co-laborer in the gospel.

"Iron sharpeneth iron" (Prov. 27:17).

FOREWORD

By any measure of scriptural standards, Jonathan Edwards has to rank among the most important mentors of biblical piety in the history of Christianity. His writings that deal with this subject—some clearly intended for public reflection, like the classic *The Religious Affections,* which began as a series of sermons; others meant for more personal study, like the *Personal Narrative*, originally written for Aaron Burr Sr., his future son-in-law—contain tremendous wisdom for the living of the Christian life. Similar to John Calvin and the Frenchman's English Puritan heirs, the great motif of Edwards's life from his conversion in the early 1720s until his death in 1758 was how to live the moments and days that he was given to the glory of God. During the 1740s, in the wake of the Great Awakening, he also came to see that a significant part of his calling under God was to serve as a public guide and literary mentor to other Christian pilgrims imbued with the same passionate desire. Gifted with intellectual brilliance, deep dealings with the triune God, and living at a time of great spiritual advances, Edwards was ideally suited to serve as such a mentor. In fact, certain distinctive spiritual themes in his work warrant talking about Edwardsean spirituality as a distinct school of piety. And evangelical piety in the latter half of the "long" eighteenth century is very much one that is dominated by questions and matters that deeply interested Edwards. Moreover, unlike others in church history who, while adequate theological and spiritual guides in their own day have little to connect them to later generations, Edwards speaks across the centuries, as this book of Edwardsean daily readings well reveals.

Read day after day throughout the year, this group of selections from such a profound author of biblical spirituality will undoubtedly help many would-be Christian pilgrims. It is very much a labor of love. It is a privilege to know its editor, Dustin Benge, and of his desire to help Edwards speak to our day. May the living God fulfill all of his hopes for this work and that for the honor of Christ Jesus.

—Michael A. G. Haykin

PREFACE

I was like many high school students, in that the first sermon I read by Jonathan Edwards was "Sinners in the Hands of an Angry God," which was preached on July 8, 1741, in Enfield, Connecticut. I was enraptured and devastated by the vivid images Edwards painted of the horrors of the lost condition and ultimate destiny of man apart from salvation in Jesus Christ. It wasn't until my college years that I purchased the two-volume works of Jonathan Edwards published by Banner of Truth. I began to work through these volumes, devouring every word, while beholding a beauty and loveliness of God that I had never seen before. I was particularly caught up in the profound way Edwards spoke through his sermons to his own congregation in Northampton as well as those beyond his own flock. Whether Edwards was writing in his *Miscellanies*, composing books and treatises for publication, or simply reflecting and meditating in a country field, it was all done that he might stand before his congregation each week and deliver God's Word through the means of preaching. Reflecting on the preaching event, Edwards said in his 1742 work, *Some Thoughts Concerning the Present Revival of Religion in New England*,

> I should think myself in the way of my duty, to raise the affections of my hearers as high as possibly I can, provided that they are affected with nothing but truth, and with affections that are not disagreeable to the nature of the subject. I know it has long been fashionable to despise a very earnest and pathetical way of preaching; and they only have been valued as preachers, who have shown the greatest extent of learning, strength of reason, and correctness of method and language. But I humbly conceive it has been for want of understanding or duly considering human nature, that such preaching has been thought to have the greatest tendency to answer the ends of preaching; and the experience of the present and past ages abundantly confirms the same. Though, as I said before, clearness of distinction, illustration, and strength of reason, and a good method in the doctrinal handling of the truths of religion, is in many ways needful and profitable, and not to be neglected; yet an increase in speculative knowledge in divinity is not what is so much

needed by our people as something else. Men may abound in this sort of light and have no heat. How much has there been of this sort of knowledge, in the Christian world, in this age! Was there ever an age, wherein strength and penetration of reason, extent of learning, exactness of distinction, correctness of style, and clearness of expression, did so abound? And yet, was there ever an age, wherein there has been so little sense of the evil of sin, so little love to God, heavenly-mindedness, and holiness of life, among the professors of the true religion? Our people do not so much need to have their heads stored, as to have their hearts touched; and they stand in the greatest need of that sort of preaching which has the greatest tendency to do this.[1]

Week after week, the clear purpose for which Edwards preached was that men might have "their hearts touched." As far as he was concerned, it was through preaching that God raised the affections of sinners and brought them to know the truth of the gospel. It was also through preaching that God conforms a converted soul into the image of Christ. If we are to know the true heart of Jonathan Edwards, we must read and know his sermons.

For several years, I searched for a book of daily readings by Jonathan Edwards. Edwards himself never wrote or compiled such a book. I desired to find a book of daily readings that went beyond the pithy sayings and anecdotes of most modern-day devotional writings. I found a few books that looked promising but still lacked in depth and substance. Therefore, while in the midst of my seminary years at The Southern Baptist Theological Seminary in Louisville, Kentucky, I set out to compile the type of Edwards daily devotional that I would like to read. I began combing through numerous miscellanies, treatises, and other works. However, I never seemed to capture the true essence of Edwards's words that would speak personally to the heart; this led me to his sermons. Consequently, what you have before you is a project that began as a personal endeavor but concludes as an ardent desire to see the words of Edwards in the hands of a much wider audience. It is my most sincere hope and prayer that you will find these daily readings from the sermons of Jonathan Edwards challenging and edifying, touching your hearts for the glory of God as you desire to grow in holiness and conformity to Christ.

---

1. Jonathan Edwards, *The Works of Jonathan Edwards*, ed. Edward Hickman (Edinburgh: The Banner of Truth Trust, 1997), 1:391.

A grateful heart and much appreciation must be extended to Dr. Michael A. G. Haykin. His help, advice, and assistance in seeing this work through to publication has been invaluable. I would also like to thank my parents, Wayne and Vera Benge, for their never-ending support, love, and prayers. It has been their training and encouragement that has directed me to seek Christ above all other satisfactions. Thanks, too, to all those dear friends who read over these words providing suggestions and an editing eye: Molli Hall, Heather Burchett, Cameron Debity, Kathy Barnett, and Jeff and Andrea Cavanaugh. Finally, to Jimmy Burchett, who, like Aaron and Hur—who held up the arms of Moses in the midst of battle (see Ex. 17:12)—continues to hold me up by his unceasing prayers, love, and kindness. It is to him that I devote this book. If I could speak for Jonathan Edwards I think he would say it would be his most sincere prayer, as well as mine, that as you read these pages that your hearts would be lifted to new heights of joy and affection for our triune God as you continue your journey toward heaven.

—Dustin W. Benge

CHOSEN BY GOD

According as he hath chosen us in him before the foundation of the world, that we should be holy and without blame before him in love: having predestinated us unto the adoption of children by Jesus Christ to himself, according to the good pleasure of his will.

—EPHESIANS 1:4–5

True Christians are chosen by God from the rest of the world. God does not utterly cast off the world of mankind. Though they are fallen and corrupted and there is a curse brought upon the world, yet God chooses a certain number for Himself. This election supposes that the persons chosen are found among others. The word "election" signifies a choosing out. The elect are favored by electing grace among the rest of mankind, with whom they are found mixed together as the tares and the wheat. They are found among them in the same sinfulness and in the same misery, and are alike partakers of original corruption. They are among them in being destitute of anything in them that is good, in enmity against God, in being in bondage to Satan, in condemnation to eternal destruction, and in being without righteousness, so that there is no distinction between them prior to election. No foreseen excellency in the elected is the motive that influences God to choose them. Election is only from His good pleasure. There is no distinction already existing in them that causes God to choose them rather than the rest. God does not choose men because they are excellent, but He makes them excellent because He has chosen them. It is not because God considers them as holy that He chooses them, but He chooses them that they might be holy.

§ From "Christians a Chosen Generation, a Royal Priesthood, a Holy Nation, a Peculiar People," p. 937

THE MERCY OF GOD

Have mercy upon us, O LORD, have mercy upon us: for we are exceedingly filled with contempt.
— PSALM 123:3

It is God's manner to make men sensible of their misery and unworthiness before He appears in His mercy and love to them. The mercy of God, which He shows to a sinner when He brings him home to the Lord Jesus Christ, is the greatest and most wonderful exhibition of mercy and love of which men are ever the subjects. There are other things in which God greatly expresses His mercy and goodness to men, many temporal favors. The mercies that God bestowed upon His people of old: His advancing Joseph in Egypt, His deliverance of the children of Israel out of Egypt, His leading them through the Red Sea on dry land, His bringing them into Canaan, and driving out the heathen from before them, His delivering them from time to time from the hands of their enemies, were great mercies. But they were not equal to saving His people from the guilt and dominion of sin. As God would prepare men for the bestowment of those less mercies by making them sensible of their guilt and misery, so especially will He so do before He makes known to them this great love of His in Jesus Christ. When God designs to show mercy to sinners He first brings them to reflect upon themselves and consider and be sensible what they are and what condition they are in. This is God's manner of dealing with men when He gives them other great and remarkable mercies and manifestations of His favor. It is a confirmation that it is His method of proceeding with the souls of men, when about to reveal His mercy and love to them in Jesus Christ.

⟡ From "God Makes Men Sensible of Their Misery before He Reveals His Mercy and Love," p. 834

DEPENDENT UPON GOD

For by grace ye are saved through faith; and that not of your-selves: it is the gift of God.
— EPHESIANS 2:8

There is an absolute and universal dependence of the redeemed on God. The redeemed are in everything directly, immediately, and entirely dependent on God: they are dependent on Him for all, and are dependent on Him every way. The redeemed have all their good of Him. God is the great author of it. He is the first cause of it; and not only so, but He is the only proper cause. It is of God that we have our Redeemer. It is God that has provided a Savior for us. Jesus Christ is not only of God in His person, as He is the only begotten Son of God, but He is from God, as we are concerned in Him and in His office of Mediator. He is the gift of God to us: God chose and anointed Him, appointed Him His work, and sent Him into the world. As it is God that gives, so it is God that accepts the Savior. He gives the purchaser, and He affords the thing purchased. It is of God that Christ becomes ours, that we are brought to Him and are united to Him. It is of God that we receive faith to close with Him, that we may have an interest in Him: "For by grace are ye saved through faith; and that not of yourselves: it is the gift of God" (Eph. 2:8). It is of God that we actually receive all the benefits that Christ has purchased. It is God that pardons and justifies and delivers from going down to hell; and into His favor the redeemed are received when they are justified. So it is God that delivers from the dominion of sin, cleanses us from our filthiness, and changes us from our deformity.

֍ From "God Glorified in Man's Dependence," pp. 3–4

SIN AGAINST GOD

How then can I do this great wickedness, and sin against God?
— GENESIS 39:9

God is a being infinitely lovely, because He hath infinite excellency and beauty. To have infinite excellency and beauty is the same thing as to have infinite loveliness. He is a being of infinite greatness, majesty, and glory, and therefore He is infinitely honorable. He is infinitely exalted above the greatest potentates of the earth and the highest angels in heaven, and therefore He is infinitely more honorable than they. His authority over us is infinite, and the ground of His right to our obedience is infinitely strong, for He is infinitely worthy to be obeyed Himself, and we have an absolute, universal, and infinite dependence upon Him. So sin against God, being a violation of infinite obligations, must be a crime infinitely heinous, and so deserving of infinite punishment. Nothing is more agreeable to the commonsense of mankind than that sins committed against anyone must be proportionally heinous to the dignity of the being offended and abused. This was the aggravation of sin that made Joseph afraid of it in Genesis 39:9: "How then can I do this great wickedness, and sin against God?" This was the aggravation of David's sin, in comparison with which he esteemed all others as nothing, because they were infinitely exceeded by it: "Against thee, thee only, have I sinned" (Ps. 51:4). The eternity of the punishment of ungodly men renders it infinite, and it renders it no more than infinite and therefore renders no more than proportional to the heinousness of what they are guilty of. If there be any evil or faultiness in sin against God, there is certainly infinite evil.

﹩ From "The Justice of God in the Damnation of Sinners," p. 66

THE PERFECTION OF GOD

Be still, and know that I am God.
— PSALM 46:10

God is an absolutely and infinitely perfect being, and it is impossible that He should do amiss. As He is eternal and receives not His existence from any other, He cannot be limited in His being, or any attribute, to any certain determinate quantity. If anything has bounds fixed to it, there must be some cause or reason why those bounds are fixed just where they are. It will follow that every limited thing must have some cause; therefore, the being that has no cause must be unlimited. It is most evident by the works of God that His understanding and power are infinite. For He that hath made all things out of nothing and upholds and governs and manages all things every moment, in all ages, without growing weary, must be of infinite power. He must also be of infinite knowledge; for if He made all things and upholds and governs all things continually, it will follow that He knows and perfectly sees all things, great and small, in heaven and earth, continually at one view, which cannot be without infinite understanding. Being thus infinite in understanding and power, He must also be perfectly holy; for unholiness always argues some defect, some blindness. It is impossible that wickedness should consist with infinite light. God being infinite in power and knowledge, He must be self-sufficient and all-sufficient. Therefore it is impossible that He should be under any temptation to do anything amiss, for He can have no end in doing it. When any are tempted to do amiss, it is for selfish ends. But how can an all-sufficient Being, who wants nothing, be tempted to do evil for selfish ends? So God is essentially holy, and nothing is more impossible than that God should do amiss.

§ From "The Sole Consideration, That God Is God, Sufficient to Still All Objections to His Sovereignty," pp. 107–8

CHRIST DEFEATED SATAN

Having spoiled principalities and powers, he made a shew of them openly, triumphing over them in it. —COLOSSIANS 2:15

In the work of redemption, Christ has appeared above Satan. Though Satan never exalted himself so high as he did in procuring these sufferings of Christ; yet, Christ laid the foundation for the utter overthrow of his kingdom. He slew Satan, as it were, with his own weapon; the spiritual David cut off this Goliath's head with his own sword, and He triumphed over him in His cross: "Having spoiled principalities and powers, he made a shew of them openly, triumphing over them in it" (Col. 2:15). Then the wisdom of Christ appeared gloriously above the subtlety of Satan. Satan, that old serpent, used a great deal of subtlety to procure Christ's death. And doubtless, when he had accomplished it, he thought he had obtained a complete victory, being then ignorant of the contrivance of our redemption. But so did the wisdom of Christ order things that Satan's subtlety and malice should be made the very means of undermining the foundations of his kingdom. And so He wisely led him into the pit that he had dug. In this also Christ appeared gloriously above the guilt of men, for He offered a sacrifice that was sufficient to do away all the guilt of the whole world. Though the guilt of man was like the great mountains, whose heads are lifted up to the heavens, yet His dying love and His merits appeared as a mighty deluge that overflowed the highest mountains, or like a boundless ocean that swallows them up, or like an immense fountain of light that with the fullness and redundancy of its brightness swallows up men's greatest sins, as little [dust] motes are swallowed up and hidden in the disk of the sun. In this Christ appeared above all the corruption of man, in that hereby He purchased holiness for the chief of sinners.

🔖 From "Christ Exalted," p. 215

LOVE YOUR NEIGHBOR

He that hath pity upon the poor lendeth unto the LORD; and that which he hath given will he pay him again.

—PROVERBS 19:17

God tells us that He will look upon what is done in charity to our neighbors as done unto Him and what is denied unto them as denied unto Him: "He that hath pity on the poor lendeth to the LORD" (Prov. 19:17). God has been pleased to make our needy neighbors His receivers. He in His infinite mercy has so interested Himself in their case that He looks upon what is given in charity to them as given to Himself; and when we deny them what their circumstances require of us, He looks upon it that we rob Him of His right. Christ teaches us that we are to look upon our fellow Christians in this case as Himself, and that our giving or withholding will be taken as if we so behaved ourselves toward Him. Christ says to the righteous on His right hand, who has supplied the wants of the needy, "Inasmuch as ye have done it unto one of the least of these my brethren, ye have done it unto me" (Matt. 25:40). In like manner He says to the wicked who did not show mercy to the poor, "Inasmuch as ye did it not to one of the least of these, ye did it not to me" (Matt. 25:45). Now what stronger enforcement of this duty can be conceived? Is it possible that Jesus Christ looks upon our kind and bountiful, or unkind and uncharitable, treatment of our needy neighbors as such a treatment of Himself?

֍ From "Christian Charity," p. 166

ETERNAL PRAISE

And I heard as it were the voice of a great multitude, and as the voice of many waters, and as the voice of mighty thunderings, saying, Alleluia: for the Lord God omnipotent reigneth.

— REVELATION 19:6

It may be a matter of great comfort that you are to spend your eternity with the saints in heaven where it is so much their work to praise God. The saints know what cause they have to praise God and oftentimes are ready to say they long to praise Him more and that they never can praise Him enough. This may be a consolation to you, that you will have a whole eternity in which to praise Him. They greatly desire to praise God better. This, therefore, may be your consolation, that in heaven your heart will be enlarged and you will be enabled to praise Him in an immensely more perfect and exalted manner than you can do in this world. You will not be troubled with such a dead, dull heart with so much coldness, so many clogs and burdens from sin, and from an earthly mind; with a wandering, unsteady heart; with so much darkness and so much hypocrisy. You will be one of that vast assembly that praise God so fervently that their voice is "as the voice of many waters, and as the voice of mighty thunderings" (Rev. 19:6). You long to have others praise God, to have everyone praise Him. There will be enough to help you and join you in praising Him and those that are capable of doing it ten thousand times better than the saints on earth. Thousands and thousands of angels and glorified saints will be around you, all united to you in dearest love, all disposed to praise God, not only for themselves but for His mercy to you.

꙳ From "Praise, One of the Chief Employments of Heaven," p. 917

HAPPINESS AND REST

Incline your ear, and come unto me: hear, and your soul shall live; and I will make an everlasting covenant with you, even the sure mercies of David.
— ISAIAH 55:3

Happiness and rest are what all men pursue. But the things of the world, wherein most men seek it, can never afford it; they are laboring and spending themselves in vain. But Christ invites you to come to Him and offers you this peace, which He gives His true followers, and that so much excels all that the world can afford (see Isa. 55:2–3). You that have hitherto spent your time in the pursuit of satisfaction in the profit or glory of the world or in the pleasures and vanities of youth have this day an offer of that excellent and everlasting peace and blessedness that Christ has purchased with the price of His own blood. As long as you continue to reject those offers and invitations of Christ and continue in a Christless condition, you never will enjoy any true peace or comfort but will be like the prodigal, who in vain endeavored to be satisfied with the husks that the swine did eat. The wrath of God will abide upon you, and misery will attend you wherever you go that you never will be able to escape. Christ gives peace to the most sinful and miserable that come to Him. He heals the broken in heart and binds up their wounds. But it is impossible that they should have peace while they continue in their sins (see Isa. 57:19–21). There is no peace between God and them, for as they have the guilt of sin remaining in their souls and are under its dominion, so God's indignation continually burns against them, and therefore there is the reason why they travail in pain all their days.

᪥ From "The Peace Which Christ Gives His True Followers," p. 92

PRONE TO SIN

Be sober, be vigilant; because your adversary the devil, as a roaring lion, walketh about, seeking whom he may devour.

—1 PETER 5:8

The heart of man is naturally prone to sin; the weight of the soul is naturally that way, as the stone by its weight tends downward. And there is very much of a remaining proneness to sin in the saints. Though sin is mortified in them, yet there is a body of sin and death remaining; there are all manner of lusts and corrupt inclinations. We are exceedingly apt to get into some ill path or other. Man is so prone to sinful ways that without maintaining a constant strict watch over himself, no other can be expected than that he will walk in some way of sin. Our hearts are so full of sin that they are ready to betray us. That to which men are prone, they are apt to get into before they are aware. Sin is apt to steal in upon us unaware. Besides this, we live in a world where we continually meet with temptations; we walk in the midst of snares; and the devil, a subtle adversary, is continually watching over us, endeavoring, by all manner of wiles and devices, to lead us astray into by-paths: "I am jealous over you…. I fear, lest by any means, as the serpent beguiled Eve through his subtlety; so your minds should be corrupted from the simplicity that is in Christ" (2 Cor. 11:2–3); "Be sober; be vigilant; because your adversary the devil, as a roaring lion, walketh about, seeking whom he may devour" (1 Peter 5:8). These things should make us the more jealous of ourselves.

§ From "Christian Cautions, or the Necessity of Self-Examination," p. 175

THE WORK OF THE SPIRIT

Therefore thus saith the Lord GOD; behold, mine anger and my fury shall be poured out upon this place, upon man, and upon beast, and upon the trees of the field, and upon the fruit of the ground; and it shall burn, and shall not be quenched.
— JEREMIAH 7:20

Men in a natural condition may have convictions of the guilt that lies upon them and of the anger of God and their danger of divine vengeance. Such convictions are from the light of truth. That some sinners have a greater conviction of their guilt and misery than others is because some have more light, or more of an apprehension of truth, than others. And this light and conviction may be from the Spirit of God. The Spirit convinces men of sin, but yet nature is much more concerned in it than in the communication of that spiritual and divine light. It is from the Spirit of God only as assisting natural principles, and not as infusing any new principles. Common grace differs from special in that it influences only by assisting of nature, and not by imparting grace or bestowing anything above nature. The light that is obtained is wholly natural, or of no superior kind to what mere nature attains to, though more of that kind is obtained than would be obtained if men were left wholly to themselves. Or, in other words, common grace only assists the faculties of the soul to do more fully what they do by nature, as natural conscience or reason will by mere nature make a man sensible of guilt and will accuse and condemn him when he has done amiss. Conscience is a principle natural to men, and the work that it does naturally, or of itself, is to give an apprehension of right and wrong and to suggest to the mind the relation that there is between right and wrong, and a retribution. The Spirit of God, in those convictions that unregenerate men sometimes have, assists conscience to do this work in a further degree than it would do if they were left to themselves.

§ From "A Divine and Supernatural Light," p. 13

FLY FOR REFUGE TO CHRIST

For what is our hope, or joy, or crown of rejoicing? Are not even ye in the presence of our Lord Jesus Christ at his coming?
— 1 THESSALONIANS 2:19

It is the will of God that men should have true hope and comfort conferred upon them in no other way than by Jesus Christ. It is only by Him that sinners have comfort at their conversion, and it is by Him only that the saints have renewed hope and comfort after their declensions. And therefore the way to obtain this comfort is to look to Him, to fly for refuge to Him. And in order to do this, persons have need to be brought to a sense of their necessity of Him. And that they may be so, it is needful that they should be sensible of their calamity and misery, that they should be in trouble and be brought to see their utter helplessness in themselves. And not only natural men, but Christians also, who are fallen into sin and are in a dead and senseless frame, need something to make them more sensible of their necessity of Christ. Indeed, the best are not so sensible of their need of Christ but that they need to be made more sensible; but especially those who are in ill and dead frames and a declining state need trouble and humbling to make them sensible of their need of Christ and to prepare their minds for a renewed confiding application to Christ as their only remedy. The godly in such a case are sick with a sore disease, and Christ is the only physician who can heal them; and they need to be sensible of their disease, that they may see their need of a physician. They, as well as natural men, need to be in a storm and tempest to make them sensible of their need to fly to Him who is a hiding place from the wind and a covert from the tempest.

§ From "Hope and Comfort Usually Follow Genuine Humiliation and Repentance," p. 844

HUMILIATION AND SUFFERING

Wherefore God also hath highly exalted him, and given him a name which is above every name: that at the name of Jesus every knee should bow, of things in heaven, and things in earth, and things under the earth; and that every tongue should confess that Jesus Christ is Lord, to the glory of God the Father.

— PHILIPPIANS 2:9–11

The exaltation of Christ is given Him in reward for His humiliation and sufferings. This was stipulated in the covenant of redemption, and we are expressly told in Philippians 2:8–11 that it was given Him in reward for His sufferings: "And being found in fashion as a man, he humbled himself, and became obedient unto death, even the death of the cross. Wherefore God also hath highly exalted him, and given him a name which is above every name: that at the name of Jesus every knee should bow, of things in heaven, and things in earth, and things under the earth; and that every tongue should confess, that Jesus Christ is Lord, to the glory of God the Father." God sees that He who appeared in such a low estate among mankind, without form or comeliness, having His divine glory veiled, should appear among men a second time, in His own proper majesty and glory, without a veil, to the end that those who saw Him here at the first, as a poor, frail man, not having anywhere to lay His head, subject to much hardship and affliction, may see Him the second time in power and great glory, invested with the glory and dignity of the absolute Lord of heaven and earth; and that He who once tabernacled with men and was despised and rejected of them may have the honor of arraigning all men before His throne and judging them with respect to their eternal state!

§ From "The Final Judgment, or the World Judged Righteously by Jesus Christ," p. 193

SECRET THINGS BROUGHT TO LIGHT

*For God shall bring every work into judgment, with every
secret thing, whether it be good, or whether it be evil.*
— ECCLESIASTES 12:14

The Scripture declares that God will bring every work into judgment, with every secret thing, whether it is good or whether it is evil. It is fit that all the concerns and all the behavior of mankind, both public and private, should be brought at last before God's tribunal and finally determined by an infallible judge. But it is especially requisite that it should be thus, as to affairs of very great importance. Now the mutual concerns of a Christian minister and his church and congregation are of the vastest importance: in many respects, of much greater moment than the temporal concerns of the greatest earthly monarchs and their kingdoms or empires. It is of vast consequence how ministers discharge their office and conduct themselves toward their people in the work of the ministry and in affairs appertaining to it. It is also a matter of vast importance how a people receive and entertain a faithful minister of Christ and what improvement they make of His ministry. These things have a more immediate and direct respect to the great and last end for which man was made and the eternal welfare of mankind, than any of the temporal concerns of men, whether private or public. And therefore it is especially fit that these affairs should be brought into judgment and openly determined and settled, in truth and righteousness, and that to this end ministers and their people should meet together before the omniscient and infallible Judge.

§ From "Farewell Sermon," p. 202

HELPLESS CREATURES

Break forth into joy, sing together, ye waste places of Jerusa-
lem: for the LORD hath comforted his people, he hath redeemed
Jerusalem.
— ISAIAH 52:9

There is naturally in men an exceeding insensibility of their dependence on God and a great disposition to ascribe those things that they enjoy to themselves or to second causes. This disposition reigns in natural men. They are wholly under the power of it. Therefore they need to be taught their own helplessness, utter insufficiency, and utter unworthiness. Otherwise, if hope and comfort should be bestowed upon them, they would surely ascribe all to themselves, or the creature, and so would be lifted up by it and would not give God the glory. Therefore it is God's manner first to humble sinners before He comforts them. And all this self-confident disposition is not extirpated out of the hearts of the godly, and especially when they get into ill frames does it prevail. And it is very requisite that, before any remarkable comfort is bestowed upon them, they should be the subjects of renewed humbling. They need renewably to see what helpless creatures they are, that so, when light is bestowed, they may be sensible how it is owing to God, and not to themselves or any other; and that they may, by their troubles and humblings, be prepared the more to admire God's power and mercy and free and rich grace to them. While men are continued in fullness in a fruitful land, they will not learn their own helplessness, and therefore God will cast them out of this fullness into a wilderness.

§ From "Hope and Comfort Usually Follow Genuine Humiliation and Repentance," p. 845

DEPEND NOT ON ANOTHER DAY

Take therefore no thought for the morrow: for the morrow shall take thought for the things of itself. Sufficient unto the day is the evil thereof.
— MATTHEW 6:34

Men act as though they depend on another day. They will do so if they set their hearts on the enjoyments of this life. I mean not, if they have any manner of affection to them. We may have some affection to the enjoyments of this world; otherwise they would cease to be enjoyments. If we might have no degree of rejoicing in them, we could not be thankful for them. Persons may in a degree take delight in earthly friends and other earthly enjoyments, but by setting our hearts on these things, by placing our happiness on them and letting out the current of our affections after them by turning and fixing our inclinations so much upon them that we cannot well enjoy ourselves without them, so that very much of the strength of the faculties of our minds is employed and taken up about these things, we show that we have our dependence on another day. The man who does this acts as though he depended on another day, yea many other days, in the world; for it is most evident that if the enjoyments of this world be of such a nature that they are not to be depended on for one day more, they are not worth the setting of our hearts upon them or the placing of our happiness in them. We may rejoice in the enjoyments of the world, but not in such a manner as to place the rest of our souls in them. We should conduct ourselves as those who have not the foundation of their joy shaken, though some appurtenances have failed. Our happiness as to the body of it, if I may so speak, should yet stand as on an immovable foundation.

⑤ From "Procrastination, or The Sin and Folly of Depending on Future Time," p. 238

NATURAL MEN ARE FULL OF SIN

For from within, out of the heart of men, proceed evil thoughts, adulteries, fornications, murders, thefts, covetousness, wickedness, deceit, lasciviousness, an evil eye, blasphemy, pride, foolishness.
—MARK 7:21-22

The hearts of natural men are exceedingly full of sin. If they had but one sin in their hearts, it would be sufficient to render their condition very dreadful. But they have not only one sin, but all manner of sin. There is every kind of lust. The heart is a mere sink of sin, a fountain of corruption, whence issues all manner of filthy streams. There is no one lust in the heart of the devil that is not in the heart of man. Natural men are in the image of the devil. The image of God is erased out, and the image of the devil is stamped upon them. God is graciously pleased to restrain the wickedness of men, principally by fear and respect to their credit and reputation and by education. And if it were not for such restraints as these, there is no kind of wickedness that men would not commit, whenever it came in their way. Men have not only every kind of lust and wicked and perverse dispositions in their hearts, but they have them to a dreadful degree. There is not only pride, but an amazing degree of it: pride whereby a man is disposed to set himself even above the throne of God itself. The hearts of natural men are mere sinks of sensuality. Man is become like a beast in placing his happiness in sensual enjoyments. The heart is full of the most loathsome lusts. The souls of natural men are more vile and abominable than any reptile. If God should open a window in the heart, so that we might look into it, it would be the most loathsome spectacle that ever was set before our eyes.

⟐ From "Natural Men in a Dreadful Condition," pp. 818–19

LOVE TO MEN IS CONTRARY TO ENVY

Let us walk honestly, as in the day; not in rioting and drunkenness, not in chambering and wantonness, not in strife and envying.

— ROMANS 13:13

Christian love disposes us to hearken to the precepts that forbid envy, and to the gospel motives against it, by its own immediate tendency. The nature of charity or Christian love to men is directly contrary to envy. For love does not grudge, but rejoices at the good of those who are loved. And surely love to our neighbor does not dispose us to hate him for his prosperity or be unhappy at his good. And love to God also has a direct tendency to influence us to obey His commands. The natural, genuine, uniform fruit of love to God is obedience, and therefore it will tend to obedience to those commands wherein He forbids envy as much as others, yea, to them more especially, because love delights to obey no commands so much as those that require love. And so love to God will dispose us to follow His example, in that He has not begrudged us our manifold blessings, but has rejoiced in our enjoyment; and it will dispose us to imitate the example of Christ in not begrudging His life for our sakes, and to imitate the example He set us in the whole course of His life on earth. A spirit of Christian love disposes to the same also indirectly, by inclining us to humility. It is pride that is the great root and source of envy. It is because of the pride of men's hearts that they have such a burning desire to be distinguished and to be superior to all others in honor and prosperity and that makes them so uneasy and dissatisfied in seeing others above them. But a spirit of love tends to mortify pride and work humility in the heart. Love to God tends to this, as it implies a sense of God's infinite excellence, and therefore tends to a sense of our comparative nothingness and unworthiness. Love to men tends to a humble behavior among men, as it disposes us to acknowledge the excellencies of others, and that the honors bestowed on them are their due, and to esteem them better than ourselves and thus more deserving of distinction than we are.

§ From "Charity Inconsistent with an Envious Spirit," pp. 120–21

RESIDENTS OF HEAVEN

Unto thee lift I up mine eyes, O thou that dwellest in the heavens.
— PSALM 123:1

There, even in heaven, dwells the God from whom every stream of holy love, yea, every drop that is, or ever was, proceeds. There dwells God the Father, God the Son, and God the Spirit, united as one, in infinitely dear and incomprehensible, mutual, and eternal love. There dwells God the Father, who is the Father of mercies, and so the Father of love, who so loved the world as to give His only begotten Son to die for it. There dwells Christ, the Lamb of God, the Prince of peace and of love, who so loved the world that He shed His blood and poured out His soul unto death for men. There dwells the great Mediator, through whom all the divine love is expressed toward men and by whom the fruits of that love have been purchased, and through whom they are communicated, and through whom love is imparted to the hearts of all God's people. There dwells Christ in both His natures, the human and the divine, sitting on the same throne with the Father. And there dwells the Holy Spirit—the Spirit of divine love, in whom the very essence of God, as it were, flows out and is breathed forth in love, and by whose immediate influence all holy love is shed abroad in the hearts of all the saints on earth and in heaven. There, in heaven, this infinite fountain of love—this eternal Three in One—is set open without any obstacle to hinder access to it, as it flows forever. There this glorious God is manifested and shines forth in full glory, in beams of love. And there this glorious fountain forever flows forth in streams, yea, in rivers of love and delight, and these rivers swell, as it were, to an ocean of love, in which the souls of the ransomed may bathe with the sweetest enjoyment, and their hearts, as it were, be deluged with love!

⚕ From "Heaven, a World of Charity, or Love," pp. 327–28

A MEASURE LIKE GOD

*The LORD thy God in the midst of thee is mighty; he will save,
he will rejoice over thee with joy; he will rest in his love, he will
joy over thee with singing.*
— ZEPHANIAH 3:17

When God sanctifies a soul and causes His Holy Spirit to dwell in it, He gives a principle of love and goodness that is more extensive; it makes them to be in a measure like God in His goodness. But as men are in themselves and by nature, their benevolence is confined to a few that they are in some way or another related to or concerned with, so that they love them from self-love. Their love does not extend beyond self; their love extends so far as self, in some respect, is extended, and no farther. It is well for us that it is not so with God. If the love and benevolence of God were so interested and mercenary, we might despair of ever having the benefit of it; for what profit or advantage can we be of to God? What can He get from us, or by anything that we can do for Him? And if God exercised His love to none but those from whom He had received some kindness and from whom He had a prospect of some benefit, as is wont to be with us, how miserable would we be! The love of man extends no farther than it is drawn. It is well for us that it is not so with God, for we have nothing to draw His love. The love of God extends the objects in whom He sees no beauty or loveliness; it extends to them and gives them beauty and makes them lovely. If the goodness and love of God extended to none but those whom it finds amiable, we would have nothing of it.

⸹ From "It Is Well for Us That God Is Not as We Are," pp. 17–18

OBJECTS OF PITY

If it be of works, then it is no more grace.

—ROMANS 11:6

Many persons who profess to believe say that they cannot merit anything and will say in their prayers that they are unworthy of the least of God's mercies. Yet, at the same time, they entertain in their hearts such a thought that it would be hard if God should have no respect to what they do and should nevertheless stand by and see them perish, refuse to hear their cries, and not show any pity to them. They do not think it is contrary to strict justice to do so, yet they think it is contrary to His mercy. They think that if God does not have mercy upon them and pity them, He will be unmerciful. He will show Himself to be hardhearted and not to be as merciful as He declares Himself in His Word to be. They think they do enough to draw the pity of any merciful being toward them. But you may consider that it would not be at all to the glory of God's mercy if your services should draw His mercy to you, for it is the glory of God's mercy that it is free and bestowed without being paid for or without any good works or religious performances to buy it. That mercy is more glorious that is given altogether freely and purely for nothing than that which is purchased and bought with a price. Mercy that is bought is justice. But it is the glory of God's mercy that He has mercy on whom He will have mercy and that He pities souls, not because they have done a great deal to deserve His pity, but only because they are miserable and helpless, and cannot deserve anything at all or do anything that is good. God pities persons because they are objects of pity, that is, because they are extremely miserable in that they are extremely sinful and wholly without righteousness and strength.

🕭 From "God Doesn't Thank Men for Doing Those Things He Commands," pp. 47–48

TRUE PEACE IS ONLY FOUND IN CHRIST

Peace I leave with you, my peace I give unto you: not as the world giveth, give I unto you.

— JOHN 14:27

He that is in Christ is in a safe refuge from everything that might disturb him: "And a man shall be as an hiding place from the wind, and a covert from the tempest: as rivers of water in a dry place, as the shadow of a great rock in a weary land" (Isa. 32:2). And hence, they that dwell in Christ have that promise fulfilled to them, which we have in the eighteenth verse of the same chapter: "And my people shall dwell in a peaceable habitation, and in sure dwellings, and in quiet resting places." And the true followers of Christ have not only ground of rest and peace of soul, by reason of their safety from evil, but also on account of their sure title and certain enjoyment of all that good of which they stand in need, living, dying, and through all eternity. They are on a sure foundation for happiness, are built on rock that can never be moved, and have a fountain that is sufficient and can never be exhausted. The covenant is ordered in all things and sure, and God has passed His Word and oath: "That by two immutable things in which it was impossible for God to lie, we might have strong consolation, who have fled for refuge to lay hold on the hope set before us" (Heb. 6:18). The infinite Jehovah is become their God, who can do everything for them. He is their portion who has an infinite fullness of good in Himself: "I am thy shield and thy exceeding great reward" (Gen. 15:1). As great a good is made over to them as they can desire or conceive of and is made as sure as they can desire. Therefore they have reason to put their hearts at rest and be at peace in their minds. He has bequeathed peace to the souls of His people, as He has procured for them and made over to them the spirit of grace and true holiness, which has a natural tendency to the peace and quietness of the soul. The soul by His means is brought to rest and ceases from restlessly inquiring, as others do.

§ From "The Peace Which Christ Gives His True Followers," p. 90

IRREVERENT SPIRIT IN WORSHIP

They have defiled my sanctuary in the same day, and have profaned my sabbaths.
— EZEKIEL 23:38

Persons who come to the house of God, into the holy presence of God, attending the duties and ordinances of His public worship, pretending with others, according to divine institution, to call on the name of God, to praise Him, to hear His Word, and commemorate Christ's death, and who yet, at the same time, are wittingly and allowedly going on in wicked courses or in any practice contrary to the plain rules of the Word of God, therein greatly profane the holy worship of God and defile the temple of God and those sacred ordinances on which they attend. By attending ordinances, and yet living in allowed wickedness, they show great irreverence and contempt of those holy ordinances. When persons who have been committing known wickedness, as it were the same day, and attend the sacred solemn worship and ordinances of God, and then go from the house of God directly to the like allowed wickedness—they hereby express a most irreverent spirit with respect to holy things and in a horrid manner cast contempt upon God's sacred institutions and on those holy things that we are concerned with in them. They show that they have no reverence of that God who has hallowed these ordinances. They show a contempt of that divine authority that instituted them. They show a horribly irreverent spirit toward that God into whose presence they come, and with whom they immediately have to do in ordinances, and in whose name these ordinances are performed and attended. They show a contempt of the adoration of God, of that faith and love and that humiliation, submission, and praise that ordinances were instituted to express. What an irreverent spirit does it show that they are so careless after what manner they come before God! They take no care to cleanse and purify themselves in order that they may be fit to come before God!

§ From "A Warning to Professors," pp. 186–87

DEGREES OF HAPPINESS AND GLORY

But this I say, he which soweth sparingly shall reap also sparingly;
and he which soweth bountifully shall reap also bountifully.
— 2 CORINTHIANS 9:6

There are different degrees of happiness and glory in heaven. As there are degrees among the angels, thrones, dominions, principalities, and powers, so there are degrees among the saints. In heaven are many mansions, and of different degrees of dignity. The glory of the saints above will be in some proportion to their eminency in holiness and good works here. Christ will reward all according to their works. He that gained ten pounds was given authority over ten cities, and he that gained five pounds over five cities (see Luke 19:17). "He which soweth sparingly shall reap also sparingly; and he which soweth bountifully shall reap also bountifully" (2 Cor. 9:6). And the apostle Paul tells us that, as one star differs from another star in glory, so also it shall be in the resurrection of the dead (see 1 Cor. 15:41–42). Christ tells us that he who gives a cup of cold water unto a disciple in the name of a disciple shall in no wise lose his reward; but this could not be true if a person should have no greater reward for doing many good works than if he did but few. It will be no damp to the happiness of those who have lower degrees of happiness and glory that there are others advanced in glory above them, for all shall be perfectly happy, every one shall be perfectly satisfied. Every vessel that is cast into this ocean of happiness is full, though there are some vessels far larger than others; and there shall be no such thing as envy in heaven, but perfect love shall reign through the whole society.

§ From "The Portion of the Righteous," p. 902

DEVILS KNOW GOD'S POWER

Thou believest that there is one God; thou doest well: the devils also believe, and tremble.

— JAMES 2:19

The devils know God's almighty power: they saw a great manifestation of it when they saw God lay the foundation of the earth, and they were much affected with it. They have seen innumerable other great demonstrations of His power: as in the universal deluge, the destruction of Sodom, the wonders of Egypt, at the Red Sea, and in the wilderness; causing the sun to stand still in Joshua's time; and many others. And they had a very affecting manifestation of God's mighty power on themselves, in casting all their hosts down from heaven into hell, and have continual affecting experience of it, in God's reserving them in strong chains of darkness and in the strong pains they feel. They will hereafter have far more affecting experience of it when they shall be punished from the glory of God's power with that mighty destruction, in expectation of which they now tremble. So the devils have a great knowledge of the wisdom of God. They have had unspeakably more opportunity and occasion to observe it in the work of creation and in the works of providence than any mortal man has ever had and have been themselves the subjects of innumerable affecting manifestations of it, in God's disappointing and confounding them in their most subtle devices in so wonderful and amazing a manner. So they see and find the infinite purity and holiness of the divine nature in the most affecting manner, as this appears in His infinite hatred of sin and in what they feel of the dreadful effects of that hatred. They know already by what they suffer and will know hereafter to a greater degree, and far more affecting manner, that such is the opposition of God's nature to sin, that it is like a consuming fire, which burns with infinite vehemence against it.

🕭 From "True Grace Distinguished from the Experience of Devils," pp. 46–47

FELLOWSHIP IN GLORY

To him that overcometh will I grant to sit with me in my throne, even as I also overcame, and am set down with my Father in his throne.
—REVELATION 3:21

The saints in heaven are received to a fellowship or participation with Christ in the glory of that dominion to which the Father hath exalted Him. The saints, when they ascend to heaven as Christ ascended and are made to sit together with Him in heavenly places and are partakers of the glory of His exaltation, are exalted to reign with Him. They are through Him made kings and priests and reign with Him and in Him over the same kingdom. As the Father hath appointed unto Him a kingdom, so He has appointed to them. The Father has appointed the Son to reign over His own kingdom, and the Son appoints His saints to reign in His. The Father has given to Christ to sit with Him on His throne, and Christ gives to the saints to sit with Him on His throne, agreeably to Christ's promise in Revelation 3:21. Christ, as God's Son, is the heir of His kingdom, and the saints are joint heirs with Christ. This implies that they are heirs of the same inheritance, to possess the same kingdom, in and with Him, according to their capacity. Christ, in His kingdom, reigns over heaven and earth; He is appointed the heir of all things, and so all things are the saints'. "Whether Paul, or Apollos, or Cephas, or the world, or life, or death, or things present, or things to come," all are theirs; because they are Christ's, and united to Him (see 1 Cor. 3:21–23).

❧ From "True Saints, When Absent from the Body, Are Present with the Lord," p. 30

THE OPPOSITION OF THE DEVIL

And [God] hath put all things under [Christ's] feet, and gave
him to be the head over all things to the church.

— EPHESIANS 1:22

God had appointed His Son to be the heir of the world, but the devil has contested this matter with Him and has strove to set himself up as god of the world. And how exceedingly has the devil exalted himself against Christ! How did he oppose Him as He dwelt among the Jews, in His tabernacle and temple! And how did he oppose Him when on earth! And how has he opposed Him since His ascension! What great and mighty works has Satan brought to pass in the world! How many Babels has he built up to heaven in his opposition to the Son of God! How exceeding proud and haughty has he appeared in his opposition! How have he and his instruments (see Dan. 10:21; 12:1) and sin, affliction, and death, of which he is the father, raged against Christ? But yet Christ, in the work of redemption, appears infinitely above them all. In this work He triumphs over them, however they have dealt proudly; and they all appear under His feet. In this the glory of the Son of God, in the work of redemption, remarkably appears. The beauty of good appears with the greatest advantage when compared with its contrary evil. And the glory of that which is excellent then especially shows itself when it triumphs over its contrary and appears vastly above it, in its greatest height. The glory of Christ, in this glorious exaltation over so great evil, that so exalted itself against Him, the more remarkably appears, in that He is thus exalted out of so low a state. Though He appeared in the world as a little child, yet how does He triumph over the most gigantic enemies of God and men!

᪥ From "Christ Exalted," pp. 216–17

GOD IS READY TO HEAR PRAYERS

O taste and see that the LORD *is good: blessed is the man that trusteth in him.*
— PSALM 34:8

Why is God so ready to hear the prayers of men? Because He is a God of infinite grace and mercy. It is indeed a very wonderful thing that so great a God should be so ready to hear our prayers, though we are so despicable and unworthy; that He should give free access at all times to everyone, should allow us to be importunate without esteeming it an indecent boldness, should be so rich in mercy to them that call upon Him that worms of the dust should have such power with God by prayer; that He should do such great things in answer to their prayers, and should show Himself, as it were, overcome by them. This is very wonderful when we consider the distance between God and us, and how we have provoked Him by our sins, and how unworthy we are of the least gracious notice. It cannot be from any need that God stands in of us; for our goodness does not extend to Him. Neither can it be from anything in us to incline the heart of God to us; it cannot be from any worthiness in our prayers, which are in themselves polluted things. But it is because God delights in mercy and condescension. He is herein infinitely distinguished from all other gods; He is the great fountain of all good, from whom goodness flows as light from the sun. We have a glorious Mediator who has prepared the way, that our prayers may be heard consistently with the honor of God's justice and majesty. Not only has God in Himself mercy sufficient for this, but the Mediator has provided that this mercy may be exercised consistently with the divine honor. Through Him we may come to God for mercy; He is the way, the truth, and the life; no man can come to the Father but by Him.

§ From "The Most High a Prayer-Hearing God," p. 116

RAGING WAVES OF WRATH

*And [who] said, hitherto shalt thou come, but no further: and
here shall thy proud waves be stayed?*
—JOB 38:11

There is a certain measure that God hath set to the sin of every wicked man. God says concerning the sin of man, as He says to the raging waves of the sea: "Hitherto shalt thou come, but no further" (Job 38:11). The measure of some is much greater than of others. Some reprobates commit but a little sin in comparison with others, and so are to endure proportionally a smaller punishment. There are many vessels of wrath, but some are smaller and others greater vessels; some will contain comparatively but little wrath, others a greater measure of it. Sometimes, when we see men go to dreadful lengths and become very heinously wicked, we are ready to wonder that God lets them alone. He sees them go on in such audacious wickedness, and keeps silence, nor does anything to interrupt them, but they go smoothly on, and meet with no hurt. But sometimes the reason God lets them alone is because they have not filled up the measure of their sins. When they live in dreadful wickedness they are but filling up the measure that God hath limited for them. This is sometimes the reason why God suffers very wicked men to live so long; because their iniquity is not full ("The iniquity of the Amorites is not yet full" [Gen. 15:16]). For this reason also God sometimes suffers them to live in prosperity. Their prosperity is a snare to them, and an occasion of their sinning a great deal more. Wherefore God suffers them to have such a snare because He suffers them to fill up a larger measure. So, for this cause, He sometimes suffers them to live under great light and great means and advantages, at the same time to neglect and misimprove all. Every one shall live until he hath filled up his measure.

§ From "Wrath upon the Wicked to the Uttermost," p. 122

AVOIDING SIN

Only take heed to thyself, and keep thy soul diligently, lest thou forget the things which thine eyes have seen, and lest they depart from thy heart all the days of thy life: but teach them thy sons, and thy sons' sons.
— DEUTERONOMY 4:9

It is very evident that we ought to use our utmost endeavors to avoid sin, which is inconsistent with needlessly doing those things that expose and lead to sin. And the greater any evil is, the greater care, and the more earnest endeavors does it require to avoid it. Those evils that appear to us very great and dreadful, we use proportionally great care to avoid. And therefore the greatest evil of all requires the greatest and utmost care to avoid it. Sin is an infinite evil, because it is committed against an infinitely great and excellent Being, and so is a violation of infinite obligation; therefore, however great our care be to avoid sin, it cannot be more than proportional to the evil we would avoid. Our care and endeavor cannot be infinite, as the evil of sin is infinite, but yet it ought to be to the utmost of our power. We ought to use every method that tends to the avoiding of sin. This is manifest to reason. And not only so, but this is positively required of us in the Word of God: "Take diligent heed to do the commandment and the law, which Moses the servant of the LORD charged you, to love the LORD your God, and to walk in all his ways, and to keep his commandments, and to cleave unto him, and to serve him with all your heart and with all your soul" (Josh. 22:5); "Take ye therefore good heed unto yourselves…lest ye corrupt yourselves" (Deut. 4:15–16); "Take heed to thyself, that thou be not snared" (Deut. 12:30); "Take heed and beware of covetousness" (Luke 12:15); "Let him that thinketh he standeth take heed lest he fall" (1 Cor. 10:12). These and many other texts of Scripture plainly require of us the utmost possible diligence and caution to avoid sin.

§ From "Temptation and Deliverance," pp. 227–28

SPIRITUAL SACRIFICES

Ye also, as lively stones, are built up a spiritual house, an holy priesthood, to offer up spiritual sacrifices, acceptable to God by Jesus Christ.

—1 PETER 2:5

Christians are a priesthood with respect to their offerings to God. The principal part of the work of the priests of old was to offer sacrifice and to burn incense. As the priests of old offered sacrifice, so the work of Christians is to offer up spiritual sacrifices to God. Christians offer up their own hearts to God in sacrifice; they dedicate themselves to God. The Christian gives himself to God freely as of mere choice. He does it heartily; he desires to be God's, and to belong to no other. He gives all the faculties of his soul to God. He gives God his heart, and it is offered to God as a sacrifice. A sacrifice, before it can be offered, must be wounded and slain. Therefore, the heart of a true Christian must first be wounded by a sense of sin, of the great evil and danger of it, and is slain with godly sorrow and true repentance. When the heart truly repents, it dies unto sin. Repentance is compared unto a death in the Word of God: "Knowing this, that our old man is crucified with him, that the body of sin might be destroyed, that henceforth we should not serve sin. For he that is dead is freed from sin. Now if we be dead with Christ, we believe that we shall also live with him. Likewise reckon ye also yourselves to be dead indeed unto sin, but alive unto God through Jesus Christ our Lord" (Rom. 6:6–9). As Christ, when He was offered, was offered broken upon the cross, so there is some likeness to this when a soul is converted: the heart is offered to God slain and broken.

§ From "Christians a Chosen Generation, a Royal Priesthood, a Holy Nation, a Peculiar People," pp. 942–43

THE ATTRIBUTES OF GOD

Thine, O LORD is the greatness, and the power, and the glory, and the victory, and the majesty: for all that is in the heaven and in the earth is thine; thine is the kingdom, O LORD, and thou art exalted as head above all.

—1 CHRONICLES 29:11

It is the will of God that the discoveries of His terrible majesty, awful holiness, and justice should accompany the discoveries of His grace and love, in order that He may give to His creatures worthy and just apprehensions of Himself. It is the glory of God that these attributes are united in the divine nature, that as He is a being of infinite mercy and love and grace, so He is a being of infinite and tremendous majesty and awful holiness and justice. The perfect and harmonious union of these attributes in the divine nature is what constitutes the chief part of their glory. God's awful and terrible attributes and His mild and gentle attributes reflect glory one on the other; and the exercise of the one is in perfect consistency and harmony with the exercise of the other. If there were the exercise of the mild and gentle attributes without the other, and if there were love and mercy and grace in inconsistency with God's authority and justice and infinite hatred of sin, it would be no glory. If God's love and grace did not harmonize with His justice and the honor of His majesty, far from being an honor, they would be a dishonor to God. Therefore, as God designs to glorify Himself when He makes discoveries of the one, He will also make discoveries of the other. When He makes discoveries of His love and grace, it shall appear that they harmonize with those other attributes; otherwise His true glory would not be discovered.

§ From "God Makes Men Sensible of Their Misery before He Reveals His Mercy and Love," p. 835

GOD HATES SIN

Thou art of purer eyes than to behold evil, and canst not look on iniquity.
—HABAKKUK 1:13

God is an infinitely holy being. The heavens are not pure in His sight. He is of purer eyes than to behold evil and cannot look on iniquity. If God should in any way countenance sin and should not give proper testimonies of His hatred of it and displeasure at it, it would be a prejudice to the honor of His holiness. But God can save the greatest sinner without giving the least countenance to sin. If He saves one who, for a long time, has stood out under the calls of the gospel and has sinned under dreadful aggravations; and if He saves one who, against light, has been a blasphemer, He may do it without giving any countenance to their wickedness because His abhorrence of it and displeasure against it have been already sufficiently manifested in the sufferings of Christ. It was a sufficient testimony of God's abhorrence against even the greatest wickedness that Christ, the eternal Son of God, died for it. Nothing can show God's infinite abhorrence of any wickedness more than this. If the wicked man himself should be thrust into hell and should endure the most extreme torments that are ever suffered there, it would not be a greater manifestation of God's abhorrence of it than the sufferings of the Son of God for it. God may save any of the children of men without prejudice to the honor of His majesty. Let the contempt be ever so great, yet if so honorable a person as Christ undertakes to be a mediator for the offender, and in the mediation suffer in his stead, it fully repairs the injury done to the majesty of heaven by the greatest sinner.

❧ From "God's Sovereignty in the Salvation of Men," pp. 850–51

CHRIST IS A FIT PERSON

To the praise of the glory of his grace, wherein he hath made us accepted in the beloved.
— EPHESIANS 1:6

When God designed the redemption of mankind, His great wisdom appears in that He chose His only begotten Son to be the person to perform the work. He was a redeemer of God's own choosing, and therefore He is called in Scripture, "[God's] elect" (Isa. 42:1). The wisdom of choosing this person to be the redeemer appears in His being every way a fit person for this undertaking. It was necessary that the person that is the redeemer should be a divine person. None but a divine person was sufficient for this great work. The work is infinitely unequal to any creature. It was requisite that the redeemer of sinners should be Himself infinitely holy. None could take away the infinite evil of sin but one that was infinitely far from and contrary to sin Himself. Christ is a fit person upon this account. It was requisite that the person, in order to be sufficient for this undertaking, should be one of infinite dignity and worthiness, that He might be capable of meriting infinite blessings. The Son of God is a fit person on this account. It was necessary that He should be a person of infinite power and wisdom. For this work is so difficult that it requires such a one. Christ is a fit person also upon this account. It was requisite that He should be a person infinitely dear to God the Father, in order to give an infinite value to His transactions in the Father's esteem and that the Father's love to Him might balance the offense and provocation by our sins. Christ is a fit person upon this account. Therefore called the beloved, He has made us accepted in the beloved (see Eph. 1:6).

꙳ From "The Wisdom of God, Displayed in the Way of Salvation," p. 142

BREAK FROM THE WORLD

They that are Christ's have crucified the flesh with the affections and lusts.
— GALATIANS 5:24

Let seeking the kingdom of God be so much your bent, and what you are so resolved in, that you will make everything give place to it. Let nothing stand before your resolution of seeking the kingdom of God. Whatever it be that you used to look upon as a convenience, or comfort, or ease, or thing desirable on any account, if it stands in the way of this great concern, let it be dismissed without hesitation; and if it be of that nature that it is likely always to be a hindrance, then wholly have done with it and never entertain any expectation from it more. If in time past you have, for the sake of worldly gain, involved yourself in more care and business than you find to be consistent with your being so thorough in the business of religion as you ought to be, then get into some other way, though you suffer in your worldly interest by it. Or if you have heretofore been conversant with company that you have reason to think have been and will be a snare to you and a hindrance to this great design in any wise, break off from their society, however it may expose you to reproach from your old companions or let what will be the effect of it. Whatever it be that stands in the way of your most advantageously seeking salvation—whether it be some dear sinful pleasure, or strong carnal appetite, or credit and honor, or the goodwill of some persons whose friendship you desire, and whose esteem and liking you have highly valued, and though there be danger, if you do as you ought, that you shall be looked upon by them as odd and ridiculous and become contemptible in their eyes, or if it be your ease and indolence and aversion to continual labor; or your outward convenience in any respect, whereby you might avoid difficulties of one kind or other—let all go; offer up all such things together, as it were, in one sacrifice, to the interest of your soul. Let nothing stand in competition with this, but make everything to fall before it. Have no dependence on any worldly enjoyment whatsoever. Let salvation be the one thing with you.

§ From "Pressing into the Kingdom of God," p. 658

RUTH'S RESOLUTION

And Ruth said, "Entreat me not to leave thee, or to return from following after thee: for whither thou goest, I will go; and where thou lodgest, I will lodge: thy people shall be my people, and thy God my God."

—RUTH 1:16

When those that we have formerly been conversant with are turning to God, and joining themselves to His people, it ought to be our firm resolution that we will not leave them, but that their people shall be our people, and their God our God. It sometimes happens that of those who have been conversant one with another, who have dwelt together as neighbors, and have been often together as companions or united in their relation, and have been together in darkness, bondage, and misery, in the service of Satan—some are enlightened, and have their minds changed, are made to see the great evil of sin, and have their hearts turned to God. They are influenced by the Holy Spirit of God to leave their company that are on Satan's side, and to join themselves with that blessed company that are with Jesus Christ. They are made willing to forsake the tents of wickedness, to dwell in the land of uprightness with the people of God. Sometimes this proves a final parting or separation between them and those with whom they have been formerly conversant. Though it may be no parting in outward respects, they may still dwell, and converse one with another. Yet in other respects, it sets them at a great distance. One is a child of God, and the other his enemy. One is in a miserable, and the other in a happy, condition. They are no longer together in those respects wherein they used to be together. It is doleful, when of those who have formerly been together in sin, some turn to God, and join themselves with His people, that it should prove a parting between them and their former companions and acquaintance. It should be our firm and inflexible resolution in such a case, that it shall be no parting, but that we will follow them, that their people shall be our people, and their God our God.

§ From "Ruth's Resolution," p. 665

THE JUSTICE OF THE LAW

*Therefore by the deeds of the law there shall no flesh be justi-
fied in his sight: for by the law is the knowledge of sin.*

— ROMANS 3:20

If we are in Christ Jesus, justice and the law have its course with respect to our sins, without our hurt. The foundation of the sinner's fear and distress is the justice and the law of God; they are against Him and they are unalterable, they must have their course. Every jot and tittle of the law must be fulfilled, heaven and earth shall be destroyed rather than justice should not take place; there is no possibility of sin's escaping justice. But yet if the distressed trembling soul, who is afraid of justice, would fly to Christ, He would be a safe hiding place. Justice and the threatening of the law will have their course as fully, while he is safe and untouched, as if he were to be eternally destroyed. Christ bears the stroke of justice, and the curse of the law falls fully upon Him; Christ bears all that vengeance that belongs to the sin that has been committed by him, and there is no need of its being borne twice over. His temporal sufferings, by reason of the infinite dignity of His person, are fully equivalent to the eternal sufferings of a mere creature. And then His sufferings answer for him who flees to Him as well as if they were his own, for indeed they are his own by virtue of the union between Christ and him. Christ has made Himself one with them; He is the head, and they are the members. Therefore, if Christ suffers for the believer, there is no need of his suffering; and what needs he to be afraid? His safety is not only consistent with absolute justice, but it is consistent with the tenor of the law. The law leaves fair room for such a thing as the answering of a surety.

§ From "Safety, Fullness, and Sweet Refreshment, to Be Found in Christ," p. 930

BRINGING FORTH FRUIT TO GOD

And now, Israel, what doth the LORD *thy God require of thee, but to fear the* LORD *thy God, to walk in all his ways, and to love him, and to serve the* LORD *thy God with all thy heart and with all thy soul?*

— DEUTERONOMY 10:12

Man cannot be useful actively any otherwise than in bringing forth fruit to God; serving God and living to His glory. This is the only way wherein he can be useful in doing; and that for this reason: that the glory of God is the very thing for which man was made, and to which all other ends are subordinate. Man is not an independent being, but he derives his being from another; and therefore hath his end assigned him by that other; and He who gave him his being made him for the end now mentioned. This was the very design and aim of the Author of man, this was the work for which He made him: to serve and glorify his Maker. Other creatures that are inferior were made for inferior purposes. But man is the highest, and nearest to God, of any in this lower world; therefore his business is with God, although other creatures are made for lower ends. There may be observed a kind of gradual ascent, in the order of different creatures, from the meanest clod of earth to man, who hath a rational and immortal soul. A plant—an herb or tree—is superior in nature to a stone or clod, because it hath a vegetable life. The brute creatures are a degree higher still, for they have sensitive life. But man, having a rational soul, is the highest of this lower creation, and is next to God; therefore his business is with God.

§ From "Wicked Men Useful in Their Destruction Only," p. 125

THE UNCHANGING CHRIST

Jesus Christ the same yesterday, and to day, and forever.
— HEBREWS 13:8

As Christ is one of the persons of the Trinity, He is God, and so hath the divine nature, or the Godhead, dwelling in Him, and all the divine attributes belong to Him, of which immutability or unchangeableness is one. Christ in His human nature was not absolutely unchangeable, though His human nature, by reason of its union with the divine, was not liable to those changes to which it was liable as a mere creature; as for instance, it was indestructible and imperishable. Having the divine nature to uphold it, it was not liable to fall and commit sin, as Adam and the fallen angels did; but yet the human nature of Christ, when He was upon earth, was subject to many changes. It had a beginning: it was conceived in the womb of the Virgin; it was in a state of infancy, and afterward changed from that state to a state of manhood. This was attended not only with a change on His body, by His increasing in stature, but also on His mind; for we read that He not only increased in stature but also in wisdom (see Luke 2:52). The human nature of Christ was subject to sorrowful changes, though not to sinful ones. He suffered hunger and thirst and cold; and at last He suffered dreadful changes by having His body tortured and destroyed and His soul poured out unto death; and afterward His body became subject to a glorious change at His resurrection and ascension. And that His human nature was not liable to sinful changes, as Adam's or the angels' was not owing to anything in His human nature, but to its relation to the divine nature that upheld it. But the divine nature of Christ is absolutely unchangeable, and not liable to the least alteration or variation in any respect. It is the same now as it was before the world was created.

§ From "Jesus Christ, the Same Yesterday, Today, and Forever," p. 949

GOSPEL TRUTH REVEALED

O Jerusalem, Jerusalem, thou that killest the prophets, and stonest them which are sent unto thee, how often would I have gathered thy children together, even as a hen gathereth her chickens under her wings, and ye would not!

— MATTHEW 23:37

When we read how the children of Israel conducted themselves in the wilderness, how often they murmured and offended, we are ready to wonder at the hardness of their hearts. And when we read the history of Christ, and how the Jews hated and rejected Him notwithstanding His many miracles, we are ready to wonder how they could be so hard-hearted. But we have as much reason to wonder at ourselves, for we have naturally the same sort of hearts that they had; and sinners in these days manifest a hardness of heart as much to be wondered at, in that they are not influenced by the word of God; for they who will not hear Moses and the prophets, Jesus Christ and His apostles, neither would be persuaded if one should rise from the dead, or if an angel should come from heaven. The best means of awakening and conversion are plentifully enjoyed by us, much more plentifully in several respects, than they were by those who had only Moses and the prophets. We have divine truth more fully revealed in the Bible than they had then. Light now shines abundantly clear. Gospel-truth is revealed, not in types and shadows, but plainly. Heaven and hell are much more clearly and expressly made known. We are told that the glory of that revelation was no glory in comparison with the revelation of the gospel.

§ From "The Warnings of Scripture Are in the Best Manner Adapted to the Awakening and Conversion of Sinners," p. 71

GOD'S GREATEST GLORY

But as truly as I live, all the earth shall be filled with the glory of the LORD.
— NUMBERS 14:21

God's greatest dishonor is made an occasion of His greatest glory. Sin is a thing by which God is greatly dishonored; the nature of its principle is enmity against God and contempt of Him. And man, by his rebellion, has greatly dishonored God. But this dishonor, by the contrivance of our redemption, is made an occasion of the greatest manifestation of God's glory that ever was. Sin, the greatest evil, is made an occasion of the greatest good. It is the nature of a principle of sin that it seeks to dethrone God, but this is hereby made an occasion of the greatest manifestation of God's royal majesty and glory that ever was. By sin, man has slighted and despised God, but this is made an occasion of His appearing the more greatly honorable. Sin casts contempt upon the authority and law of God, but this, by the contrivance of our redemption, is made the occasion of the greatest honor done to that same authority, and to that very law. It was a greater honor to the law of God that Christ was subject to it, and obeyed it, than if all mankind had obeyed it. It was a greater honor to God's authority that Christ showed such great respect, and such entire subjection to it, than the perfect obedience of all the angels in heaven. Man by his sin showed his enmity against the holiness of God, but this is made an occasion of the greatest manifestation of God's holiness. The holiness of God never appeared to so great a degree as when God executed vengeance upon His own dear Son.

§ From "The Wisdom of God, Displayed in the Way of Salvation," p. 148

THE CALLING OF THE SAINTS

And God shall wipe away all tears from their eyes; and there
shall be no more death, neither sorrow, nor crying, neither shall
there be any more pain: for the former things are passed away.
— REVELATION 21:4

Here much of the work to which the saints are called consists in laboring, in fighting, in toilsome traveling in a waste-howling wilderness, in mourning and suffering, and in offering up strong crying and tears. But there in heaven their work continually is to lift up their joyful songs of praise. This world is a valley of tears, a world filled with sighs and groans: one is groaning under some bodily pain; another is mourning and lamenting over a dear departed friend; another is crying out by reason of the arm of the oppressor. But in heaven there is no mixture of such sounds as these; there is nothing to be heard among them but the sweet and glorious melody of God's praises. There is a holy cheerfulness to be seen throughout that blessed society: "And God shall wipe away all tears from their eyes; and there shall be no more death, neither sorrow, nor crying" (Rev. 21:4). They shall never have anything more to do with sighing and crying; but their eternal work henceforward shall be praise. This should make us long for heaven, where they spend their time so joyfully and gloriously. The saints especially have reason to be earnestly breathing after that happy state, where they may in so joyful a manner praise God.

§ From "Praise, One of the Chief Employments of Heaven," p. 915

ACTS OF MERCY

Charity suffereth long, and is kind; charity envieth not; charity vaunteth not itself, is not puffed up.

— 1 CORINTHIANS 13:4

Love will dispose men to all acts of mercy toward their neighbors when they are under any affliction or calamity, for we are naturally disposed to pity those that we love, when they are afflicted. It will dispose men to give to the poor, to bear one another's burdens, and to weep with those that weep, as well as to rejoice with those that do rejoice. It will dispose men to the duties they owe to one another in their several places and relations. It will dispose a people to all the duties they owe to their rulers, and to give them all that honor and subjection that are their due. And it will dispose rulers to rule the people over whom they are set—justly, seriously, and faithfully—seeking their good, and not any by-ends of their own. It will dispose a people to all proper duty to their ministers, to hearken to their counsels and instructions and to submit to them in the house of God, and to support and sympathize with and pray for them, as those that watch for their souls; and it will dispose ministers faithfully and ceaselessly to seek the good of the souls of their people, watching for them as those that must give account. Love will dispose to suitable carriage between superiors and inferiors: it will dispose children to honor their parents, and servants to be obedient to their masters, not with eye service, but in singleness of heart; and it will dispose masters to exercise gentleness and goodness toward their servants. Thus love would dispose to all duties, both toward God and toward man. And if it will thus dispose to all duties, then it follows that it is the root, and spring, and, as it were, a comprehension of all virtues. It is a principle that, if it be implanted in the heart, is alone sufficient to produce all good practice; and every right disposition toward God and man is summed up in it, and comes from it, as the fruit from the tree, or the stream from the fountain.

§ From "Charity, or Love the Sum of All Virtue," pp. 8–9

CARRIED BY GOD TO JOY AND REST

Whoso putteth his trust in the LORD shall be safe.
— PROVERBS 29:25

Consider to what great blessedness God will carry you. He will not only keep you safe from enemies, but will bring you to Himself. And how much better is this for you. You shall not only go through the world in safety from your enemies, but when you have gotten through, then you shall enter into a state of eternal rest and joy, into a world where there are no more enemies who seek your hurt and ruin, where your peace nevermore shall be disturbed nor your joy interrupted. How happy it is when you have gotten through the world to be received up with songs into immortal glory. How much better this is than to be swallowed up by your enemies, to be a prey to the roaring lion, to be fixed by devils, to be hurried down to hell, there to dwell, to be tormented by him and to be tormented with him to all eternity. Why, how good will it be, after you have gotten through all the harms and tempests in your voyage, to enter with full sails into a fair, calm, and serene heaven, and to land on the heavenly shore. How much better this is than to sink and be swallowed up in the whirlpools of the bottomless gulf of woe and misery. Consider how happy and great a privilege it is to be in such a state as to have an infallible security of eternal glory, to be so carried along through the world toward glory that nothing can in any way reach you to hinder your going there. The godly have this glorious end to think of: God is carrying them to glory, their eternal blessedness, though they cannot see how. And 'tis your duty to rejoice in all things.

---

§ From "God Carries His People Along through the World toward Glory Far Above the Reach of All Their Enemies, or Anything That Might Hinder Their Blessedness," pp. 49–50

LOVING THROUGH DEED

*My little children, let us not love in word, neither in tongue;
but in deed and in truth. And hereby we know that we are of
the truth, and shall assure our hearts before him.*

— 1 JOHN 3:18–19

The main thing in that love that is the sum of the Christian spirit is benevolence, or goodwill to others. Christian love is variously denominated according to its various objects and exercises. Particularly, how, as it respects the good enjoyed or to be enjoyed by the beloved object, it is called the love of benevolence, and, as it respects the good to be enjoyed in the beloved object, it is called the love of complacence. Love of benevolence is that disposition that leads us to have a desire for, or delight in, the good of another. That is the main thing in Christian love, yea, the most essential thing in it, and that whereby our love is most of an imitation of the eternal love and grace of God, and of the dying love of Christ, which consists in benevolence or goodwill to men, as was sung by the angels at His birth (see Luke 2:13–14). So that the main thing in Christian love is goodwill, or a spirit to delight in and seek the good of those who are the objects of that love. The most proper and conclusive evidence that such a principle is real and sincere is its being effectual. The proper and conclusive evidence of our wishing or willing to do good to another is to do it. In every case nothing can be plainer than that the proper and conclusive evidence of the will is the act, and the act always follows the will where there is power to act. The proper and conclusive evidence of a man's sincerely desiring the good of another is his seeking it in his practice, for whatever we truly desire we do thus seek. The Scriptures therefore speak of doing good as the proper and full evidence of love. They often speak of loving in the deed or practice as being the same thing as loving in truth and reality. Sincerity of desire would lead not merely to words, but to the deeds of benevolence.

§ From "Charity Disposes Us to Do Good," pp. 103–4

A HEART GIVEN TO GOD

My son, give me thine heart.
— PROVERBS 23:26

Godliness consists not in a heart whose purpose is to do the will of God, but in a heart to do it. True godliness is a thing that has its seat originally in the heart. The word for "heart" oftentimes used in Scripture means the same as man's soul or his inward part, in opposition to what is external. But more commonly and more particularly by "heart" is meant the soul, with a more special relation to the faculty of the will, or with regard to its dispositions, affections, inclinations, and choices. And thus godliness is a thing that has its seat originally in the heart, and not in any outward profession, show, or external behavior. There is a great proneness in mankind to place religion in those things that are external. But God is a Spirit, and they who worship Him must worship Him in spirit and in truth. Man looks on the outward appearance, but God looks on the heart. God says, in Proverbs 23:26, "My son, give me thine heart." It is said in Psalm 51:6, "Thou desirest truth in the inward parts." God regards the truth in the inward parts. We find some condemned and rejected in Scripture though they are found to have done that which was right, because it was not done with a perfect heart. But God ponders the heart and weighs the spirit. And when God gives a man grace He is said to write His law on their hearts. Godliness has its origin in the heart rather than in speculation. As the heart is, so the man is. I say, godliness has its seat originally in the heart. It is not true that all that pertains to godliness has its seat there, but all true godliness has its seat originally in the heart, that is, it begins there; there must be the origin of all godly action.

❧ From "A Heart to Do the Will of God," pp. 116–17

THE KINDNESS OF GOD TOWARD THE EVIL

The hearts of the sons of men is full of evil.
— ECCLESIASTES 9:3

God's holiness is such as will not and cannot endure the least impurity or filthiness. God is so holy that it is utterly impossible that He should will the least evil; it is infinitely contradictory to His nature to do so. But man is a creature who comes into the world full of this filthiness that is so odious to God. Man is defiled all over with it from the crown of his head to the bottom of his feet. There is no place clean. Every disposition and principle has become corrupt and is polluted. His understanding is darkened with sin; his will is perverted with sin and every affection is debased and polluted with sin. Sin is the principal that has the dominion over man; it is absolute lord in his heart and governs all his powers and faculties: "The hearts of the sons of men is full of evil" (Eccl. 9:3); "God saw…that every imagination of the thoughts of [man's] heart was only evil continually" (Gen. 6:5); "The imagination of man's heart is evil from his youth" (Gen. 8:21). But, notwithstanding this, God's goodness is very great to mankind. The world of mankind is exceedingly full of actual sin and wickedness against God, and yet God is abundant in His goodness to the world. There is not one person who has come to be an adult but who has been guilty of an abundance of natural sin. The corruptions and perverse dispositions of the heart begin to show themselves while we are little children as reason and the natural faculties begin to bud forth and to exert themselves a little. And yet God is very good and kind to such from day to day. They live upon God's goodness, notwithstanding. He keeps them and has His bountiful hands open, and supplies and maintains them continually.

§ From "God Is Kind to the Unthankful and the Evil," pp. 72–73

HE GIVES WITH AN OPEN HAND

Every good gift and every perfect gift is from above, and cometh down from the Father of lights, with whom is no variableness, neither shadow of turning.
—JAMES 1:17

It is well for us that God's bounty and kindness are not so scanty as ours is to our fellow creatures. In our communication one with another, we soon think we have done enough, that we have done our share; we are ready to be careful not to do too much. We are ready to excuse ourselves from giving and doing for one another. When we give something liberally, or do any considerable matter for another person, it looks big in our eyes and we are ready to think that our kindness has proceeded to a great extent. We are ready to soon be weary of liberality to others. How well it is for us that it is not so with God, who is never weary nor wanting in doing us good. He gives us richly all things to enjoy. His bounty to us is like a river that is full of water: always flowing and never weary of flowing, often overflowing its banks. Every day He gives to us with an open hand, and bestows blessings upon us of an innumerable kind and in a vast variety. He thinks nothing is too much for us, who has given us more than if He had given us all the world, in that He has given us His own Son, a person of infinite glory, a Person infinitely dear to Him, who is infinitely His delight and is of the same nature as Himself. In His Son, He gives us His grace and Holy Spirit. He gives us Himself and makes us to inherit a kingdom. He gives us the possession of all things. He gives us infinite riches and eternal glory and blessedness. He gives us as much riches and blessedness as our appetites can have, let us extend our desires as far as we will. And He gives us as much as we can enjoy, and that to all eternity. God sets no bounds to His bounty, and nothing is too much to bestow.

§ From "It Is Well for Us That God Is Not as We Are," p. 18

GOD NEVER CHANGES HIS MIND

God is not a man, that he should lie; neither the son of man, that he should repent.
— NUMBERS 23:19

God never changes His mind. He never repents of anything that He has done. We are forced to distinguish understanding and will in God in one way of conceiving of Him (although they are indeed one in a manner that we cannot conceive of Him). So to speak of Him according to our way of conceiving, His will is always influenced and governed by His understanding or judgment. When God does anything, He does it because His understanding determines it to be the wisest and most fitting to be done. All His acts are influenced by His wisdom, and He never, upon reflection of what He has done, changes His mind or thinks that what He has done would have been better omitted, or that anything that He has omitted would have been better done. God is in Himself but one simple and pure act. But as we are forced to conceive of Him and speak of Him, His acts are innumerable. God's acts of creation are to be conceived of as innumerable as the things created. And His acts of providence are as manifold as the events of providence, which are immensely numerous every day. And yet God never repented of any one thing that ever He did since the beginning. He did not repent of His making or not making anything that He did in creation: "God saw everything that he had made, and, behold, it was very good" (Gen. 1:31). He never repented of any one act of providence relating to either angels or men, or any being whatsoever. He never repented either of the act or the manner of the act. He never sees, upon reflection, any excess or defect, any error or manner of wrong, in the motion of any one wheel of this vast machine that is the world. So, if He were to do it over again, He would not, in any kind of respect, do otherwise. Though God's works are so many, yet He has made them all in perfect wisdom: "O LORD, how manifold are thy works! in wisdom hast thou made them all" (Ps. 104:24).

᛬ From "God Never Changes His Mind," pp. 2–3

A WAY OF SALVATION

Herein is love, not that we loved God, but that he loved us, and sent his Son to be the propitiation for our sins.

—1 JOHN 4:10

Christ is a glorious person and every way fit to be a Savior of sinners; a person who has power sufficient, wisdom sufficient, merit sufficient, and love sufficient for perfecting this work. And He is the only fit person; but you have no right in Him; you can lay claim to no benefit by His power, wisdom, love, or merits. This wisdom of God hath found out a way whereby this Savior might satisfy justice and fulfill the law for us; a way whereby He might be capable or suffering for us, but you have no lot in the incarnation, death, and sufferings of Jesus Christ. The wisdom of God hath contrived a way of salvation, that there should be procured for us perfect and everlasting happiness. Here is that happiness procured that is most suitable to our nature and answerable to the salvation of our souls. Here is a most glorious portion, the Divine Being Himself, with His glorious perfections. Here it is purchased, that we should see God face to face; that we should converse and dwell with God in His own glorious habitation; that we should be the children of God, and be conformed to Him. Here are the highest honors, the most abundant riches, the most substantial satisfying pleasures for evermore. Here we have prepared all needed good, both for the souls and bodies of sinners: all needed earthly good things, while here; and glory, for both body and soul hereafter, forever.

֍ From "The Wisdom of God, Displayed in the Way of Salvation," p. 155

ALWAYS READY TO MEET GOD

A time to be born, and a time to die; a time to plant, and a time to pluck up that which is planted.

— ECCLESIASTES 3:2

God hath concealed from us the day of our death, without doubt, partly for this end: that we might be excited to be always ready, and might live as those that are always waiting for the coming of their Lord, agreeably to the counsel that Christ gives us. That watchman is not faithful who, being set to defend a house from thieves, or a city from an enemy at hand, will at any hour venture to sleep, trusting that the thief or the enemy will not come. Therefore it is expected of the watchman that he behave himself every hour of the night, as one who doth not depend upon it that the enemy will tarry until the next hour. Now therefore let me, in Christ's name, renew the call and counsel of Jesus Christ to you: to watch as those that know not what hour your Lord will come. Let me call upon you who are hitherto in an unrenewed condition. Depend not upon it, that you will not be in hell before tomorrow morning. You have no reason for any such dependence; God hath not promised to keep you from it, or to withhold His wrath so long. How can you reasonably be easy or quiet for one day, or one night, in such a condition, when you know not but your Lord will come this night? And if you should then be found, as you now are, unregenerate, how unprepared would you be for His coming, and how fearful would be the consequence! Be exhorted therefore, for your own sakes, immediately to awake from the sleep of sin, out of sleep, and sleep no more, as not depending on any other day.

§ From "Procrastination, or the Sin and Folly of Depending on Future Time," p. 242

CAST YOURSELF UPON CHRIST

Casting all your care upon him; for he careth for you.

— 1 PETER 5:7

When sinners come to Christ, He takes away that which was their burden, or their sin and guilt, that which was so heavy upon their hearts, that so distressed their minds. He takes away the guilt of sin, from which the soul before saw no way how it was possible to be freed, and that, if it was not removed, led to eternal destruction. When the sinner comes to Christ, it is all at once taken away, and the soul is left free: it is lightened of its burden, it is delivered from its bondage, and it is like a bird escaped from the snare of the fouler. The soul sees in Christ a way to peace with God, and a way by which the law may be answered and justice satisfied and yet he may escape; a wonderful way indeed, but yet a certain and a glorious one. And what rest does it give to the weary soul to see itself thus delivered, that the foundation of its anxieties and fears is wholly removed, and that God's wrath ceases, that it is brought into a state of peace with God, and that there is no more occasion to fear hell, but that it is forever safe! How refreshing is it to the soul to be at once thus delivered of that which was so much its trouble and terror, and to be eased of that which was so much its burden! This is like coming to a cool shade after one has been traveling in a dry and hot wilderness and almost fainting under the scorching heat.

✺ From "Safety, Fullness, and Sweet Refreshment, to Be Found in Christ," p. 934

SORROWS TURNED TO JOY

Come unto me, all ye that labor and are heavy laden, and I will give you rest.
— MATTHEW 11:28

Christ has purchased all that persons need under bereavement. He has purchased all that miserable men stand in need of under all their calamities, and comfort under every sort of affliction. And therefore that His invitation to those that "labor and are heavy laden" to come to Him for rest may be understood on the most extensive sense to extend to those that are heavy laden with either natural or moral evil: He has purchased divine cordials and supports for those hearts that are ready to sink; He has purchased all needed comfort and help for the widow and the fatherless; He has purchased a sanctified improvement and fruit of affliction for all such as come to Him and spread their sorrows before Him. He has purchased those things that are sufficient to make up their loss, that are bereaved of a great blessing in an eminent minister of the gospel. It is He that has purchased those divine blessings, those influences and fruits of the Spirit of God, that the work of the ministry is appointed to be the means of. Christ is able to afford all that help that is needed in such a case. His power and His wisdom are as sufficient as His purpose, and answerable to His compassions. By the bowels of His mercies, the love and tenderness of His heart, He is disposed to help those that are in affliction; and His ability is answerable to His disposition. He is able to support the heart under the heaviest sorrows, and to give light in the darkness. He can divide the thickest cloud with beams of heavenly light and comfort. He is one who gives songs in the night, and turns the shadow of death into the morning. Persons under sorrowful bereavements are ready to go and lay open their sorrows to them that they think will be ready to pity them, though they know they can but pity them and cannot help them. How much more is here in such a case to induce us to go to Jesus, who is not only so ready to pity, but so able to help, able abundantly more than to fill up the breach, and able to turn all our sorrows into joy!

§ From "The Sorrows of the Bereaved Spread before Jesus," pp. 968–69

THE GLORY OF ELECTION

*So then it is not of him that willeth, nor of him that runneth,
but of God that sheweth mercy.*
—ROMANS 9:16

It is a manifestation of God's glory that He has elected a certain and definite number from among fallen men from all eternity. It shows the glory of His divine sovereignty. By eternally choosing some and passing by others, He shows us how far His sovereignty and dominion extend. In this divine act, God appears in a majesty that is unparalleled. Those who can see no glory of dominion in this act have not attained to right thoughts of God and never have been sensible of His glorious greatness. God's having chosen His people to blessedness and glory long before they were born is evidence of the glory of divine grace: in His love to them being prior to all that they have or do, being uninfluenced by any excellency of theirs, by the light of any labors or endeavors of theirs, or any respect of theirs toward Him. The doctrine of election shows that it was the grace and mercy of God that caused them earnestly to seek conversion that they might obtain it. It shows also that faith itself is the gift of God, and that the saints persevering in a way of holiness unto glory is also the fruit of electing love. Believers' love to God is the fruit of God's love to them, and the giving of Christ, the preaching of the gospel, and the appointing of ordinances, are all fruits of the grace of election. All the grace that is shown to any of mankind, either in this world, or in the world to come is comprised in the electing love of God.

§ From "Christians a Chosen Generation, a Royal Priesthood, a Holy Nation,
a Peculiar People," p. 939

REDEEMING GRACE

For all have sinned, and come short of the glory of God; being justified freely by his grace through the redemption that is in Christ Jesus.
— ROMANS 3:23–24

When God reveals His redeeming grace to men, and makes them truly sensible of it, He would make them sensible of it as it is. God's grace and love toward sinners is in itself very wonderful, as it redeems from dreadful wrath. But men cannot be sensible of this until they perceive in some adequate degree how dreadful the wrath of God is. God's redeeming grace and love in Christ is free and sovereign, as it is altogether without any worthiness in those who are the objects of it. But men cannot be sensible of this until they are sensible of their own unworthiness. The grace of God in Christ is glorious and wonderful, as it is not only as the objects of it are without worthiness, but as they deserve the everlasting wrath and displeasure of God. But they cannot be sensible of this until they are made sensible that they deserve God's eternal wrath. The grace of God in Christ is wonderful, as it saves and redeems from so many and so great sins and from the punishment they have deserved. But sinners cannot be sensible of this until they are in some measure sensible of their sinfulness, and brought to reflect upon the sins of their lives, and to see the wickedness of their hearts. It is the glory of God's grace in Christ that it is so free and sovereign. When men see the glory of God's grace aright, they see it as free and unmerited, and contrary to the demerit of their sins. All who have a spiritual understanding of the grace of God in Christ have a perception of the glory of that grace.

§ From "God Makes Men Sensible of Their Misery before He Reveals His Mercy and Love," p. 835

THE LORD'S DAY

And let us consider one another to provoke unto love and to good works: not forsaking the assembling of ourselves together, as the manner of some is; but exhorting one another: and so much the more, as ye see the day approaching.

— HEBREWS 10:24–25

From the consideration of the nature and state of mankind in this world, it is most consonant to human reason that certain fixed parts of time should be set apart, to be spent by the church wholly in religious exercises and in the duties of divine worship. It is a duty incumbent on all mankind, in all ages alike, to worship and serve God. His service should be our great business. It becomes us to worship Him with the greatest devotion and engagedness of mind; and therefore to put ourselves, at proper times, in such circumstances as will most contribute to render our minds entirely devoted to this work, without being diverted or interrupted by other things. The state of mankind in this world is such that we are called to concern ourselves in secular business and affairs which will necessarily, in a considerable degree, take up the thoughts and engage the attention of the mind. However, some particular persons may be in circumstances more free and disengaged; yet the state of mankind is such that the bulk of them, in all ages and nations, are called ordinarily to exercise their thoughts about secular affairs, and to follow worldly business, which, in its own nature, is remote from the solemn duties of religion. It is therefore most meet and suitable that certain times should be set apart upon which men should be required to throw by all other concerns, that their minds may be the more freely and entirely engaged in spiritual exercises, in the duties of religion, and in the immediate worship of God; and that their minds being disengaged from common concerns, their religion may not be mixed with them.

§ From "The Perpetuity and Change of the Sabbath," p. 94

WATCH OVER YOUR LIFE

Therefore let us not sleep, as do others; but let us watch and be sober.
— 1 THESSALONIANS 5:6

If we live in any way of sin, we live in a way whereby God is dishonored; but the honor of God ought to be supremely regarded by all. If everyone would make it his great care in all things to obey God, to live justly and holily, to walk in everything according to Christian rules; would maintain a strict, watchful, and scrutinous eye over himself, to see if there were no wicked way in him; would give diligence to amend whatsoever is amiss; would avoid every unholy, unchristian, and sinful way; and if the practice of all were universally as becometh Christians; how greatly would this be to the glory of God, and of Jesus Christ! How greatly would it be to the credit and honor of religion! How would it tend to excite a high esteem of religion in spectators, and to recommend a holy life! How would it stop the mouths of objectors and opposers! How beautiful and amiable would religion then appear, when exemplified in the lives of Christians, not maimed and mutilated, but whole and entire, as it were in its true shape, having all its parts and its proper beauty! Religion would then appear to be an amiable thing indeed. If those who call themselves Christians thus walked in all the paths of virtue and holiness, it would tend more to the advancement of the kingdom of Christ in the world, the conviction of sinners, and the propagation of religion among unbelievers, than all the sermons in the world, so long as the lives of those who are called Christians continue as they are now.

§ From "Christian Cautions, or the Necessity of Self-Examination," pp. 174–75

THE SUPREME TREASURE

He that overcometh shall inherit all things; and I will be his God, and he shall be my son.
— REVELATION 21:7

The main reason why the godly man hath his heart thus to heaven is because God is there; that is the palace of the Most High. It is the place where God is gloriously present, where His love is gloriously manifested, where the godly may be with Him, see Him as He is, and love, serve, praise, and enjoy Him perfectly. If God and Christ were not in heaven, he would not be so earnest in seeking it, nor would he take so much pains in a laborious travel through this wilderness, nor would the consideration that he is going to heaven when he dies be such a comfort to him under toils and afflictions. The martyrs would not undergo cruel sufferings from their persecutors with a cheerful prospect of going to heaven, did they not expect to be with Christ and to enjoy God there. They would not with that cheerfulness forsake all their earthly possessions and all their earthly friends, as many thousands of them have done, and wander about in poverty and banishment, being destitute, afflicted, tormented, in hopes of exchanging their earthly for a heavenly inheritance, were it not that they hope to be with their glorious Redeemer and heavenly Father. The believer's heart is in heaven, because his treasure is there.

§ From "God the Best Portion of the Christian," pp. 104–5

THE PORTION OF THE GODLY

The LORD is my portion, saith my soul; therefore will I hope in him.
— LAMENTATIONS 3:24

A godly man prefers God before anything else that might be in heaven. Not only is there nothing actually in heaven that is in his esteem equal with God, but neither is there any of which he can conceive as possible to be there that by him is esteemed and desired equally with God. Some suppose quite different enjoyments to be in heaven from those that the Scriptures teach us. There he shall have all sin taken away, and shall be perfectly conformed to God, and shall spend an eternity in exalted exercises of love to Him, and in the enjoyment of His love. If God were not to be enjoyed in heaven, but only vast wealth, immense treasures of silver and gold, great honor of such kind as men obtain in this world, and a fullness of the greatest sensual delights and pleasures, all these things would not make up for the want of God and Christ and the enjoyment of them there. If it were empty of God, it would indeed be an empty melancholy place. The godly have been made sensible as to all creature enjoyments, that they cannot satisfy the soul, and therefore nothing will content them but God. Offer a saint what you will; if you deny him God he will esteem himself miserable. God is the center of his desires; and as long as you keep his soul from its proper center, it will not be at rest.

§ From "God the Best Portion of the Christian," p. 105

RECONCILED TO GOD

For if, when we were enemies, we were reconciled to God by the death of his Son, much more, being reconciled, we shall be saved by his life.

—ROMANS 5:10

Christ never did anything whereby His love to the Father was so eminently manifested as in His laying down His life, under such inexpressible sufferings, in obedience to His command, and for the vindication of the honor of His authority and majesty; nor did ever any mere creature give such a testimony of love to God as that was. And yet, this was the greatest expression of His love to sinful men who were enemies to God: "When we were enemies, we were reconciled to God by the death of his Son" (Rom. 5:10). The greatness of Christ's love to such appears in nothing so much as in its being dying love. That blood of Christ that fell in great drops to the ground, in His agony, was shed from love to God's enemies and His own. That shame and spitting, that torment of body, and that exceeding sorrow, even unto death, which He endured in His soul, was what He underwent from love to rebels against God, to save them from hell, and to purchase for them eternal glory. Never did Christ so eminently show His regard to God's honor as in offering up Himself a victim to justice. And yet in this above all, He manifested His love to them who dishonored God, so as to bring such guilt on themselves that nothing less than His blood could atone for it.

๑ From "The Excellency of Jesus Christ," p. 684

HE FIRST LOVED US

Herein is love, not that we loved God, but that he loved us,
and sent his Son to be the propitiation for our sins.

—1 JOHN 4:10

God does not choose men and set His care upon them because they love Him, for He has first loved us. It is not from any foresight of good works that men do before or after conversion that causes God to set His love upon them. On the contrary, men do good works because God has chosen them. Jesus said, "Ye have not chosen me, but I have chosen you, and ordained you, that ye should go and bring forth fruit, and that your fruit should remain: that whatsoever ye shall ask of the Father in my name, he may give it you" (John 15:16). Nor did God choose men because He foresaw that they would believe and come to Christ. Faith is the consequence of election, and not the cause of it. Acts 13:48 says, "And when the Gentiles heard this, they were glad, and glorified the word of the Lord: and as many as were ordained to eternal life believed." It is because God has chosen men that He calls them to Christ and causes them to come to Him. True Christians are chosen of God from all eternity, not only before they were born, but before the world was created. A God of infinite goodness and benevolence loves those that have no excellency to move or attract it. Believers were from all eternity beloved both by the Father and the Son. The eternal love of the Father appears in that He, from all eternity, contrived a way for their salvation, and chose Jesus Christ to be their Redeemer. It is a fruit of this electing love that God sent His Son into the world to die, it was to redeem those whom He so loved.

§ From "Christians a Chosen Generation, a Royal Priesthood, a Holy Nation, a Peculiar People," pp. 937–38

GOD SAVES SINNERS

Therefore hath he mercy on whom he will have mercy, and whom he will he hardeneth.
— ROMANS 9:18

God, in the gospel, has revealed that nothing is too hard for Him to do, nothing beyond the reach of His power, and wisdom, and sufficiency. Since Christ has wrought out the work of redemption, and fulfilled the law by obeying, there is none of mankind whom He may not save. There is no sinner, let him be ever so great, but God can save him without prejudice to any attribute; if he has been a murderer, or adulterer, or perjurer, or idolater, or blasphemer, God may save him if He pleases, and in no respect injure His glory. Though persons have sinned long, have been obstinate, have committed heinous sins a thousand times, even until they have grown old in sin, and have sinned under great aggravations—let the aggravations be what they may—if they have sinned under ever so great light; if they have been backsliders, and have sinned against ever so numerous and solemn warnings and strivings of the Spirit, and mercies of His common providence; though the danger of such is much greater than of other sinners, yet God can save them if He pleases, for the sake of Christ, without any prejudice to any of His attributes. He may have mercy on whom He will have mercy. He may have mercy on the greatest of sinners, if He pleases, and the glory of none of His attributes will be in the least stained. Such is the sufficiency of the satisfaction and righteousness of Christ, that none of the divine attributes stand in the way of the salvation of any of them. The glory of any attribute did not at all suffer by Christ's saving some of His crucifiers.

૭ From "God's Sovereignty in the Salvation of Men," p. 850

FAITH ALONE

Therefore as by the offence of one judgment came upon all men to condemnation; even so by the righteousness of one the free gift came upon all men unto justification of life. For as by one man's disobedience many were made sinners, so by the obedience of one shall many be made righteous.
—ROMANS 5:18–19

The thing that the Scripture guards and militates against is our imagining that it is our own goodness, virtue, or excellency that instates us in God's acceptance and favor. But, to suppose that God gives us an interest in Christ in reward for our virtue is as great an argument that it instates us in God's favor, as if He bestowed a title to eternal life as its direct reward. If God gives us an interest in Christ as a reward of our obedience, it will then follow that we are instated in God's acceptance and favor by our own obedience, antecedent to our having an interest in Christ; for rewarding anyone's excellency evermore supposes favor and acceptance on the account of that excellency. It is the very notion of a reward that it is a good thing, bestowed in testimony of respect and favor for the virtue or excellency rewarded. So it is not by virtue of our interest in Christ and His merits that we first come into favor with God, according to this scheme; for we are in God's favor before we have any interest in those merits; we have an interest in those merits as a fruit of God's favor for our own virtue. If our interest in Christ be the fruit of God's favor, then it cannot be the ground of it. If God did not accept us, and had no favor for us for our own excellency, He never would bestow so great a reward upon us as a right in Christ's satisfaction and righteousness. So such a scheme destroys itself, for it supposes that Christ's satisfaction and righteousness are necessary for us to recommend us to the favor of God, and yet supposes that we have God's favor and acceptance before we have Christ's satisfaction and righteousness, and have these given as a fruit of God's favor. Indeed, neither salvation itself, nor Christ the Savior, is given as a reward of anything in man. They are not given as a reward of faith, nor of anything else of ours. We are not united to Christ as a reward of our faith, but have union with Him by faith.

§ From "Justification by Faith Alone," p. 640

PRESSING INTO THE KINGDOM

The law and the prophets were until John: since that time the
kingdom of God is preached, and every man presseth into it.
—LUKE 16:16

This expression denotes strength of desire. Men, in general, who live under the light of the gospel and are not atheists, desire the kingdom of God; that is, they desire to go to heaven rather than to hell. Most of them indeed are not much concerned about it, but on the contrary, live a secure and careless life. And some, who are many degrees above these, being under some degrees of the awakenings of God's Spirit, are not yet pressing into the kingdom of God. But they that may be said to be truly so, have strong desires to get out of a natural condition, and to get an interest in Christ. They have such a conviction of the misery of their present state, and of the extreme necessity of obtaining a better, that their minds are, as it were, possessed with and wrapped up in concern about it. To obtain salvation is desired by them above all things in the world. This concern is so great that it very much shuts out other concerns. They used before to have the stream of their desires after other things, or, it may be, had their concern divided between this and them; but when they come to answer the expression of the text, of "pressing into the kingdom of God," this concern prevails above all others; it lays other things low, and does in a manner engross the care of the mind. This seeking eternal life should not only be one concern that our souls are taken up about with other things, but salvation should be sought as the one thing needful and as the one thing that is desired. Besides desires after salvation, there should be an earnest resolution in persons to pursue this good as much as lies in their power, to do all that in the use of their utmost strength they are able to do, in an attendance on every duty, and resisting and militating against all manner of sin, and to continue in such a pursuit.

§ From "Pressing into the Kingdom of God," p. 655

LION AND LAMB

And one of the elders saith unto me, Weep not: behold, the Lion of the tribe of Judah, the Root of David, hath prevailed to open the book, and to loose the seven seals thereof. And I beheld, and, lo, in the midst of the throne and of the four beasts, and in the midst of the elders, stood a Lamb as it had been slain.

— REVELATION 5:5–6

Many things might be observed in the words of the text, but it is to my present purpose only to take notice of the two distinct designations here given to Christ. He is called a Lion, "Behold, the Lion of the tribe of Judah." He seems to be called the Lion of the tribe of Judah in allusion to what Jacob said in his blessing of the tribe on his deathbed, who when he came to bless Judah, compares Him to a lion—"Judah is a lion's whelp: from the prey, my son, thou art gone up: he stooped down, he couched as a lion, and as an old lion; who shall rouse him up?" (Gen. 49:9)—and also in allusion to the standard of the camp of Judah in the wilderness, upon which was displayed a lion, according to the ancient tradition of the Jews. It is much on account of the valiant acts of David that the tribe of Judah, of which David was, is in Jacob's prophetical blessing compared to a lion, but more especially with an eye to Jesus Christ, who also was of that tribe, and was descended of David, and is in our text called "the Root of David." Therefore Christ is here called "the Lion of the tribe of Judah." He is also called a Lamb. John was told of a Lion that had prevailed to open the book, and probably expected to see a lion in his vision. But while he is expecting, behold, a Lamb appears to open the book, an exceeding diverse kind of creature from a lion. A lion is a devourer, one that is wont to make terrible slaughter of others, and no creature more easily falls a prey to him than a lamb. Christ is here represented not only as a Lamb, a creature very liable to be slain, but a "Lamb as it had been slain," that is, with the marks of its deadly wounds appearing on it. There is an admirable conjunction of diverse excellencies in Jesus Christ.

⏀ From "The Excellency of Jesus Christ," p. 680

SINNERS ARE BLIND

Draw nigh to God, and he will draw nigh to you. Cleanse your hands, ye sinners; and purify your hearts, ye double minded.
— JAMES 4:8

The heart of man is full of sin and corruption, and that corruption is of an exceedingly darkening, blinding nature. Sin always carries a degree of darkness with it; and the more it prevails, the more it darkens and deludes the mind. It is from hence that the knowing whether there is any wicked way in us is a difficult thing. The difficulty is not at all for want of light without us, not at all because the word of God is not plain, or the rules not clear; but it is because of the darkness within us. The light shines clear enough around us, but the fault is in our eyes; they are darkened and blinded by a pernicious distemper. Sin is of a deceitful nature, because, so far as it prevails, so far it gains the inclination and will, and that sways and biases the judgment. So far as any lust prevails, so far it biases the mind to approve of it. So far as any sin sways the inclination or will, so far that sin seems pleasing and good to the man; and that which is pleasing, the mind is prejudiced to think is right. Hence, when any lust hath so gained upon a man as to get him into a sinful way or practice, it, having gained his will, also prejudices his understanding. And the more irregular a man walks, the more will his mind probably be darkened and blinded; because by so much the more doth sin prevail.

§ From "Christian Cautions, or the Necessity of Self-Examination," p. 175

GAZING INTO OUR HEARTS

When he is come, he will reprove the world of sin, and of righteousness, and of judgment.

—JOHN 16:8

God sometimes, by a particular assistance of the understanding, enables men to see so much of their own hearts as at once causes them to despair of helping themselves. He sometimes convinces them by their own trials, suffering them to try a long time to effect their own salvation until they are discouraged. But God, if He pleases, can convince men without such endeavors of their own; and sometimes He does so; as must be the case in many sudden conversions, of which the instances are not infrequent. By revealing to them their own hearts, sometimes enables them to perceive that they are so remote from the exercise of love to God, of faith, and of every other Christian grace, as well as from the possession of the least degree of spiritual light, that they despair of ever bringing themselves to it. They perceive that within their souls all is darkness as darkness itself, and as the shadow of death, and that it is too much for them to cause light. They find themselves dead to anything good, and therefore despair of bringing themselves to the performance of gracious acts. Thus we have shown that it is God's ordinary manner, before He reveals His redeeming mercy to the souls of men, to make them sensible of their sinfulness and danger, of their desert of the divine wrath, and of their utter helplessness in themselves. This we have shown to be most accordant with the Holy Scriptures, as well as with God's method of dealing with mankind in other things. And we have shown in an imperfect manner how, and by what means it is that God thus convinces men. This work is what Christ speaks of, as one part of the work of the Holy Ghost.

෯ From "God Makes Men Sensible of Their Misery before He Reveals His Mercy and Love," pp. 834–35

A PRINCIPLE OF NEW LIFE

But when Jesus heard that, he said unto them, "They that be whole need not a physician, but they that are sick."

— MATTHEW 9:12

Christ puts strength and a principle of new life into the weary soul that comes to Him. The sinner, before he comes to Christ, is as a sick man that is weakened and brought low, and whose nature is consumed by some strong distemper: he is full of pain, and so weak that he cannot walk nor stand. Therefore, Christ is compared to a physician: "But when Jesus heard that, he saith unto them, They that be whole need not a physician, but they that are sick" (Matt. 9:12). When He comes and speaks the word, He puts a principle of life into him that was before as dead: He gives a principle of spiritual life and the beginning of eternal life; He invigorates the mind with a communication of His own life and strength, and renews the nature and creates it again, and makes the man to be a new creature. The fainting, sinking spirits are now revived, and this principle of spiritual life is a continual spring of refreshment, like a well of living water: "Whosoever drinketh of the water that I shall give him shall never thirst; but the water that I shall give him shall be in him a well of water springing up into everlasting life" (John 4:14). Christ gives His Spirit, which calms the mind and is like a refreshing breeze of wind. He gives that strength whereby He lifts up the hands that hang down, and strengthens the feeble knees.

§ From "Safety, Fullness, and Sweet Refreshment, to Be Found in Christ," p. 934

ENGAGED IN SECRET PRAYER

Continue in prayer, and watch in the same with thanksgiving.
— COLOSSIANS 4:2

We are often taught that the seeming goodness and piety of hypocrites is not of a lasting and persevering nature. It is so with respect to their practice of the duty of prayer in particular, and especially of secret prayer. They can omit this duty, and their omission of it not be taken notice of by others who know what profession they have made, so that a regard to their own reputation doth not oblige them still to practice it. If others saw how they neglect it, it would exceedingly shock their charity toward them. But their neglect doth not fall under their observation; at least not under the observation of many. Therefore they may omit this duty, and still have the credit of being converted persons. Men of this character can come to a neglect of secret prayer by degrees without shocking their peace. For though indeed for a converted person to live in a great measure without secret prayer is very wide of the notion they once had of a true convert, yet they find means by degrees to alter their notions, and to bring their principles to suit with their inclinations; and at length they come to a notion that a man may be a convert, and yet live very much in neglect of this duty. In time, they can bring all things to suit well together: a hope of heaven, an indulgence of sloth, gratifying carnal appetites, and living in a great measure a prayerless life. They cannot indeed suddenly make these things agree; it must be a work of time; and length of time will effect it. By degrees they find out ways to guard and defend their consciences against those powerful enemies; so that those enemies, and a quiet, secure conscience, can at length dwell together.

§ From "Hypocrites Deficient in the Duty of Prayer," p. 72

PURE IN HEART

What if God, willing to shew his wrath, and to make his power known, endured with much longsuffering the vessels of wrath fitted to destruction: and that he might make known the riches of his glory on the vessels of mercy, which he had afore prepared unto glory.

— ROMANS 9:22–23

To be pure in heart is the sure way to obtain the blessedness of seeing God. This is the divine road to the blissful and glorious presence of God, which, if we take it, will infallibly lead us thither. God is the giver of the pure heart, and He gives it for this very end: that it may be prepared for the blessedness of seeing Him. Thus we are taught in the Scriptures. The people of God are sanctified, and their hearts are made pure, that they may be prepared for glory, as vessels are prepared by the potter for the use He designs. They are elected from all eternity to eternal life, and have purity of heart given them, on purpose to fit them for that to which they are chosen: "And that he might make known the riches of his glory on the vessels of mercy, which he had afore prepared to glory" (Rom. 9:23). We read of the church being arrayed in fine linen, clean and white, by which is signified the church's purity; and it was to fit it for the enjoyment of Christ: "Let us be glad and rejoice, and give honor to him: for the marriage of the Lamb is come, and his wife hath made herself ready. And to her was granted that she should be arrayed in fine linen, clean and white: for the fine linen is the righteousness of the saints" (Rev. 19:7–8).

֍ From "The Pure in Heart Blessed," p. 911

EMPLOYMENT IN HEAVEN

Therefore are they before the throne of God, and serve him day and night in his temple: and he that sitteth on the throne shall dwell among them.
— REVELATION 7:15

The saints in heaven are employed; they are not idle; they have there much to do: they have a work before them that will fill up eternity. We are not to suppose, when the saints have finished their course and done the works appointed them here in this world, and are got to their journey's end, to their Father's house, that they will have nothing to do. It is true, the saints, when they get to heaven, rest from their labors and their works follow them. Heaven is not a place of labor and travail, but a place of rest (see Heb. 4:9). There remaineth a rest for the people of God. And it is a place of the reward of labor. But yet the rest of heaven does not consist in idleness, and a cessation of all action, but only a cessation from all the trouble and toil and tediousness of action. The most perfect rest is consistent with being continually employed. So it is in heaven. Though the saints are exceedingly full of action, yet their activity is perfectly free from all labor, or weariness, or unpleasantness. They shall rest from their work, that is, from all work of labor and self-denial, and grief, care, and watchfulness, but they will not cease from action. The saints in glory are represented as employed in serving God, as well as the saints on earth, though it be without any difficulty or opposition: "And there shall be no more curse: but the throne of God and of the Lamb shall be in it; and his servants shall serve him" (Rev. 22:3).

🔖 From "Praise, One of the Chief Employments of Heaven," p. 913

WALKING CONTRARY TO GOD

If ye will…walk contrary unto me; then will I walk contrary unto you also in fury.
— LEVITICUS 26:27–28

They who walk contrary to God's revealed will shall find that God will walk contrary to their will; and, inversely, they who comply with His will shall find that God will comply with their desires. Wicked men set themselves in a way that is cross to the holy commands of God; they will not yield obedience to His revealed will. God will therefore act contrary to their inclinations. He will cross them in His providential dealings. They desire happiness, but they shall have misery; they desire ease and pleasure, but they shall have pains; they desire honor, but they shall have shame. They who are obstinate in a way of obedience, God will set Himself against them as they do against Him. As they are stiff-necked and forward in a way of disobedience, so God will set Himself to cross the inclinations and appetites of their nature: "If ye…will walk contrary unto me; then will I walk contrary unto you also in fury" (Lev. 26:27–28). But they who heartily comply with God's commands and walk with Him, He will walk with them. He will order things so as shall be agreeable to them. God will perfectly and in everything comply with their desires; they shall have all the good, all the pleasure and happiness that their hearts can wish; yea, their desires shall be fully satisfied. They who seek the advancement of God's kingdom in the world, God will seek the advancement of their interest and welfare. And while they seek a kingdom for them in another world, God will seek a kingdom for them in another world: "Fear not, little flock; for it is your Father's good pleasure to give you the kingdom" (Luke 12:32).

---

§ From "God Will Deal with Men According to Their Own Temper and Practice," pp. 131–32

PROPER RESPECT TO GOD

And thou shalt love the LORD *thy God with all thine heart, and with all thy soul, and with all thy might.*
— DEUTERONOMY 6:5

Religion is nothing without proper respect to God. The very notion of religion among mankind is that it is the creature's exercise and expression of such respect toward the Creator. But if there be no true respect or love, then all that is called religion is but a seeing show, and there is no real religion in it, but it is unreal and vain. Thus, if a man's faith be of such a sort that there is no true respect to God in it, reason teaches that it must be in vain; for if there be no love to God in it, there can be no true respect to Him. From this it appears: that love is always contained in a true and living faith; and that it is its true and proper life and soul, without which, faith is as dead as the body is without its soul; and that it is that which especially distinguishes a living faith from every other, but of this more particularly hereafter. Without love to God, again, there can be no true honor to Him. A man is never hearty in the honor he seems to render to another whom he does not love; so that all the seeming honor or worship that is ever paid, without love, is but hypocritical. And so reason teaches that there is no sincerity in the obedience that is performed without love; for if there be no love, nothing that is done can be spontaneous and free, but all must be forced. So, without love there can be no hearty submission to the will of God, and there can be no real and cordial trust and confidence in Him. He that does not love God will not trust Him: he never will, with true acquiescence of soul, cast himself into the hands of God, or into the arms of His mercy.

§ From "Charity, or Love the Sum of All Virtue," p. 10

SUFFERING WITHOUT LOVE IS NOTHING

And though I bestow all my goods to feed the poor, and though I give my body to be burned, and have not charity, it profiteth me nothing.
— 1 CORINTHIANS 13:3

All that men can do, and all that they can suffer, can never make up for the want of sincere Christian love in the heart. There may be great performance, and so there may be great sufferings, without sincere Christian love in the heart. And, there may be great performances without it. The apostle Paul, in the third chapter of the epistle to the Philippians, tells us what things he did before his conversion, and while he remained a Pharisee. In the fourth verse, he says, "If any other man thinketh that he hath whereof he might trust in the flesh, I more." Many of the Pharisees did great things, and abounded in religions performances. The Pharisee mentioned in Luke 18:11–12 boasted of the great things that he had done, both toward God and men, and thanked God that he so exceeded other men in his doings. And many of the heathen have been eminent for their great performances: some for their integrity, or for their justice, and others for their great deeds done for the public good. Many men, without any sincerity of love in their hearts, have been exceeding magnificent in their gifts for pious and charitable uses, and have thus gotten to themselves great fame, and had their names handed down in history to posterity with great glory. Many have done great things from fear of hell, hoping thereby to appease the Deity and make atonement for their sins, and many have done great things from pride, and from a desire for reputation and honor among men. And though these motives are not wont to influence men to a constant and universal observance of God's commands, and to go on with a course of Christian performances, and with the practice of all duties toward God and man through life, yet it is hard to say how far such natural principles may carry men in particular duties and performances.

❧ From "The Greatest Performances or Sufferings in Vain without Charity," pp. 53–54

FULLNESS OF THE LOVE OF CHRIST

Herein is love, not that we loved God, but that he loved us,
and sent his Son to be the propitiation for our sins.

— 1 JOHN 4:10

Christ thus loved us: without any expectation of ever being requited by us for His love. He did not stand in need of anything we could do for Him and well knew that we should never be able to requite Him for His kindness to us, or even to do anything toward it. He knew that we were poor, miserable, and empty-handed outcasts, who might receive from Him but could render nothing to Him in return. He knew that we had no money or price with which to purchase anything and that He must freely give us all things that we needed, or else we should be eternally without them. And shall not we be far from a selfish spirit, and utterly contrary to it, if we love one another after such a manner as this or if we have the same spirit of love toward others that was in Christ toward ourselves? If this is our spirit, our love to others will not depend on their love to us, but we shall do as Christ did to us: love them, even though they are enemies. We shall not only seek our own things, but we shall in our hearts be so united to others that we shall look on their things as our own. We shall endeavor to be interested in their good, as Christ was in ours; and shall be ready to forego and part with our own things, in many cases, for the things of others, as Christ did toward us. And these things we shall be willing and ready to do for others, without any expectation of being repaid by them, as Christ did such great things for us without any expectation of requital or return. If such be our spirit, we shall not be under the influence of a selfish spirit, but shall be unselfish in principle, and heart, and life.

᭺ From "The Spirit of Charity, the Opposite of a Selfish Spirit," pp. 179–80

LOVE ONE ANOTHER

But as touching brotherly love ye need not that I write unto you: for ye yourselves are taught of God to love one another.
— 1 THESSALONIANS 4:9

If you would be in the way to the world of love, which is heaven, see that you live a life of love—of love to God, and love to men. All of us hope to have part in the world of love hereafter; therefore we should cherish the spirit of love and live a life of holy love here on earth. This is the way to be like the inhabitants of heaven who are now confirmed in love forever. Only in this way can you be like them in excellence and loveliness, and like them, too, in happiness, and rest, and joy. By living in love in this world you may be like them, too, in sweet and holy peace, and thus have, on earth, the foretastes of heavenly pleasures and delights. Thus, also, you may have a sense of the glory of heavenly things, as of God, and Christ, and holiness; and your heart may be disposed and opened by holy love to God, and by the spirit of peace and love to men, to a sense of the excellence and sweetness of all that is to be found in heaven. Thus shall the windows of heaven be as it were opened, so that its glorious light shall shine in upon your soul. Thus you may have the evidence of your fitness for that blessed world, and that you are actually on the way to its possession. And being thus made meet, through grace, for the inheritance of the saints in light, when a few more days shall have passed away you shall be with them in their blessedness forever. Happy, thrice happy, those who shall thus be found faithful to the end, and then shall be welcomed to the joy of their Lord! There, "they shall hunger no more, neither thirst any more; neither shall the sun light on them, nor any heat. For the Lamb which is in the midst of the throne shall feed them, and shall lead them unto living fountains of waters, and God shall wipe away all tears from their eyes" (Rev. 7:16–17).

§ From "Heaven, a World of Charity, or Love," pp. 367–68

GOD IS NOT AS WE ARE

I am God, and not man.

—HOSEA 11:9

It is well for us that God is not toward us as we are toward one another. If God had no more love and goodness in His heart than we do; if His goodness was confined to as narrow limits, and He were so straightened in His bowels as we are; our case would be very wretched. If the love of God was confined to as few objects as ours is, it would be ill for us. Human love and goodness is ordinarily a very narrow thing, with respect to both the objects and exercises and expressions of it. It is confined to a few objects. There are but few of their fellow creatures that they ever feel the exercise of love or benevolence to, or upon whom they stand ready to bestow their liberality. It is well for us that God is not so, whose love and goodness is infinitely diffusive; whose goodness is like the light of the sun that shines upon all the universe around. God's bounty extends to every one of mankind. There are none but who partake of the streams of His goodness and live upon it. He maintains all mankind. He gives them all life and breath and preserves their lives and provides all with food and raiment. He causes the sun to shine on them and His rain to descend on them. He causes the earth from year to year to bring forth substance to them. The angels in heaven all live upon His goodness. His goodness extends to the brute creatures. He provides for them. He hears "the young ravens which cry" (Ps. 147:9). "These wait all upon thee; that thou mayest give them their meat in due season" (Ps. 104:27). Yea, the goodness of God extends to the whole universe. They all do or have partaken of His bounty: "The LORD is good to all: and his tender mercies are over all his works" (Ps. 145:9).

❧ From "It Is Well for Us That God Is Not as We Are," pp. 16–17

DOING WHAT IS COMMANDED

Doth he thank that servant because he did the things that were commanded him? I trow not.

—LUKE 17:9

Let the godly beware that they do not imagine that what they do in religion deserves thanks from God. They also need to take care that they do not make a righteousness of what they do, for there are remains of self-righteousness in them as well as remains of other corruption. They should beware, therefore, that they do not sometimes imagine that there is some desert in their exercises of grace. When they seek the exercises of love for God, and when they are thankful for mercies and are enabled to rejoice in Christ Jesus, when they exercise acts of love and charity toward men, they must take great care that their hearts are not exalted by spiritual discoveries and by reflecting upon their good deeds. We must not think after we have been in lively, vigorous frames that we have now done that which is worthy that God should love and delight in us on account of it. Good works, though they are done in sincerity and from true love to God, and though they are real exercises of grace, do not in themselves deserve anything from God. When the saints do duties from love to God, and with a gracious respect to Him, they do no more than is commanded of them. And does God thank His servants for doing those things that He has commanded them? Surely not. The best of saints in this world do not do near all that is commanded of them, and what they do is with great imperfection and a mixture of corruption. It is God's mere grace to you that you are able to do anything at all in sincerity; and it is this for which you should bless and praise Him while you have a being, not for which God should thank you.

⏳ From "God Doesn't Thank Men for Doing Those Things He Commands," pp. 53–54

UNTHANKFUL FOR HIS KINDNESS

The God in whose hand thy breath is, and whose are all thy ways.
— DANIEL 5:23

God is kind to the unthankful in the temporal mercies He bestows on men. Men live wholly on the fruits of God's bounty. God maintains them out of His stores, and the men absolutely depend on Him a great deal more for their support and all good things than a little child does on its parents; for it is God's goodness that keeps their breath in their nostrils. He preserves the frame of nature. He keeps alive the vital flame, and He supplies it and nourishes it. He provides amendment with their food, and He, of His bounty, takes care to provide them with clothing and habitations lest they perish through cold and the injuries of the weather. He has created for men that wonderful element of fire for their use and supplies them with fuel. God provides for men in a vast variety of temporal good things. The earth yields her fullness into their bosom. If God had made for men only one sort of food for them to live upon, if only bread and water, they would have had great cause of thankfulness. But, instead of that, quite a vast variety God has provided for them! How many sorts of food He has provided to feast and entertain them with. How many things God causes the earth to bring forth for them. How many kinds of beasts, birds, and fishes He has made for their food. But how unthankful men are under the receipt of all this kindness. Those who have the most thankfulness have but very little in proportion to the kindness they receive.

꙳ From "God Is Kind to the Unthankful and the Evil," pp. 84–85

GOD DOES WHAT HE PLEASES

And all the inhabitants of the earth are reputed as nothing: and he doeth according to his will in the army of heaven, and among the inhabitants of the earth: and none can stay his hand, or say unto him, What doest thou?
— DANIEL 4:35

God is able to do whatever He pleases. God's infinite power implies two things: First, He is able to do everything that does not apply a contradiction to itself or to His own holy nature. Second, He is able to do whatever He pleases without any difficulty or pain; for if it were painful for Him to do anything, that would argue that He lacked strength and that, if He had more strength, it would be less painful. But that God is thus able to do what He pleases is very evident from these two arguments: First, He is an independent being, for He, being the first being and an eternal being, must be an independent being; that is, He cannot depend upon any other being for anything in Himself. Therefore He does not depend on any other being for power or assistance, and if no other being can help Him, so neither can any other being hinder Him from doing anything. For if they could hinder Him, then He would be so far dependent upon them that He could not do anything if they obstructed it. And if no other being can hinder Him, then nothing can resist Him; and if nothing can resist Him, it follows that He can do quite as He will, that He can do everything. Second, it appears that He can do whatever He pleases among all creatures because He has given them their beings and all their powers, and therefore they must be dependent upon Him, since He must have them in His hands. That which God has made, given being to, and upheld in being must necessarily be absolutely in His hands to convert to nothing again or to dispose of as He pleases, which He can do with perfect ease and in a moment's time.

᪥ From "God Does What He Pleases," pp. 150–51

PROOF OF RELIGION

Lord, I will follow thee whithersoever thou goest.
— LUKE 9:57

How does your religion prove itself? You look back and you can remember the time when you had what you call a great discovery, a great sense, a time when you had great affections. But that was not the chief time of trial. We read of some who hear the Word and receive it with joy, but in the time of trial following fall away. We read of some who believed on Christ, but Christ would not commit Himself to them (see John 2:24). The reason was that He knew they did not have a heart to actually do the will of God. So inquire whether or not, after all your affections and good intentions, you are like the man of whom Christ speaks in Matthew 21:30, who said, "I go, sir," and went not. The grand characteristic of counterfeit grace is that it is ineffectual; it doesn't bring anything to pass, and so it appears to be void of the power of godliness. It is like a picture or image of a man. False religion may have an effect in these two ways: first, to make men purpose to do the will of God; and second, to make them sorrowful in not actually complying. But it is not effectual to bring men to actually do what they purpose. Counterfeit grace is not effectual because it is not substantial. These experiences of hypocrites are not substantial. There is a certain solidity in the experiences and affections of the true saints, wherein they become effectual and are sufficient to carry them through trials. There is a solidity and weight whereby they have power with the man and govern him. They reach the bottom of the heart and have hold of his very nature; they influence all his faculties whereby he is fixed in the way of duty. There is something in the experiences and affections of true saints that render them of a practical nature.

§ From "A Heart to Do the Will of God," pp. 122–23

BE WARNED

Behold, ye have sinned against the LORD: and be sure your sin will find you out.

—NUMBERS 32:23

To those who are going on in sin, be warned. If you dare to go on in sin, you do not know how soon God may swear in His wrath concerning you. Do not presume, you who have gone on in ways of wickedness hitherto; take heed that you proceed no further. You who have been addicted to any particular way of wickedness, who have gone on in a way of indulgence of any particular lust, take heed that you are guilty of that wicked practice no more. You do not know but that the next time you are guilty of that wickedness will be the last time that God will bear with it before He will take up such a resolution that you will never be saved. Do not venture for ten thousand worlds to indulge that lust again; if you do, you may, for all you know, do that which never can be undone again. It may, for all you know, prove to be the irreparable ruin of your soul. If you should venture to commit the sin again, consider how many sins you have committed already and what aggravations with which they are attended; what warnings you have had, what light you have gone against, and how dreadfully you have provoked the infinite Majesty of heaven! Consider how much you have provoked Him in that particular practice in which you have gone on. And, if you should, it is just if His practice is at an end. Would it be a strange thing if God's patience should be quite at an end if you are guilty but once more? If you should yet run the venture and commit the sin again, and the effect of it is that God should resolve that you should never obtain salvation, how doleful a thing would it be? You will, as it were, be as dreadful as if you then should sink down into hell.

❧ From "Some Men Shall Never Be Saved," pp. 108–9

THE HUMBLE EXAMPLE OF CHRIST

For I have given you an example, that ye should do as I have done to you. Verily, verily, I say unto you, The servant is not greater than his lord, neither he that is sent greater than he that sent him.
— JOHN 13:15–16

The spiritual washing and cleansing of believers was the end for which Christ so abased Himself for them. Christ's washing His disciples' feet signified this spiritual washing of the soul. Christ, in being obedient unto death, even the death of the cross, not only did the part of a servant unto God, but in some respects also of a servant unto us. And this is not the only place where His so abasing Himself for our sakes is compared to the doing of the part of a servant to guests. We have the like representation made in Luke 22:27: "For whether is greater, he that sitteth at meat, or he that serveth? Is not he that sitteth at meat? But I am among you as he that serveth." And, wherein Christ was among the disciples as He that did serve is explained in Matthew 20:28; namely, in His giving His life a ransom for them. When Christ had finished washing His disciples' feet, He solemnly requires their attention to what He had done, and commands them to follow His example therein. When our Savior calls on His disciples to imitate the example He had given them in what He had done, we are to understand Him, not merely by the example He gave in the emblematical action in washing His disciples' feet, in itself considered, but more especially of that much greater act of His that was signified by it, in abasing Himself so low and suffering so much for the spiritual cleansing and salvation of His people. This is what is chiefly insisted on as the great example Christ has given us to follow. So it is once and again afterward, in the discourse Christ had with His disciples this same night, in John 13:34 wherein is the text, "A new commandment I give unto you, that ye love one another; as I have loved you, that ye also love one another."

⚜ From "Christ the Example of Ministers," p. 961

CHRIST STANDS FOR US

Stand fast therefore in the liberty wherewith Christ hath made
us free, and be not entangled again with the yoke of bondage.
— GALATIANS 5:1

When Christ had once undertaken with God to stand for us and put Himself under our law, by that law He was obliged to suffer and by the same law He was obliged to obey; by the same law, after He had taken man's guilt upon Him, He Himself, being our surety, could not be acquitted until He had suffered, nor rewarded until He had obeyed; but He was not acquitted as a private person, but as our head, and believers are acquitted in His acquittance; nor was He accepted to a reward for His obedience, as a private person, but as our head, and we are accepted to a reward in His acceptance. The Scripture teaches us that when Christ was raised from the dead, He was justified; which justification implies both His acquittance from our guilt and His acceptance to the exaltation and glory that was the reward of His obedience; but believers, as soon as they believe, are admitted to partake with Christ in this His justification; hence we are told, that He was "raised again for our justification" (Rom. 4:25), which is true, not only of that part of His justification that consists in His acquittance, but also His acceptance to His reward. The Scripture teaches us that He is exalted and gone to heaven to take possession of our glory in our name, as our forerunner (see Heb. 6:20). We are, as it were, both raised up together with Christ and also made to sit together with Christ in heavenly places and in Him (see Eph. 2:6).

§ From "Justification by Faith Alone," p. 637

LOVE TO ENEMIES

For if, when we were enemies, we were reconciled to God by the death of his Son, much more, being reconciled, we shall be saved by his life.

— ROMANS 5:10

How wonderful is the love that is manifested in giving Christ to die for us. For this is love to enemies. "When we were enemies, we were reconciled to God by the death of his Son" (Rom. 5:10). How wonderful was the love of God the Father in giving such a gift to those who not only could not be profitable to Him but were His enemies, and to so great a degree! They had great enmity against Him; yet so did He love them, that He gave His own Son to lay down His life, in order to save their lives. Though they had enmity that sought to pull God down from His throne, yet He so loved them that He sent down Christ from heaven, from His throne there, to be in the form of a servant; and, instead of a throne of glory, He gave Him to be nailed to the cross and to be laid in the grave, that so we might be brought to a throne of glory. How wonderful was the love of Christ in thus exercising dying love toward His enemies! He loved those that hated Him with hatred that sought to take away His life, so as voluntarily to lay down His life that they might have life through Him. "Herein is love, not that we loved God, but that he loved us, and sent his Son to be the propitiation for our sins" (1 John 4:10). If we are all naturally God's enemies, hence we may learn what a spirit it becomes us as Christians to possess toward our enemies. Though we are enemies to God, yet we hope that God has loved us, that Christ has died for us, that God has forgiven or will forgive us and will do us good and bestow infinite mercies and blessings upon us, so as to make us happy forever. All this mercy we hope has been, or will be, exercised toward us.

⚘ From "Men Naturally Are God's Enemies," p. 141

TIME IN IDLENESS

*Let him that stole steal no more: but rather let him labor,
working with his hands the thing which is good, that he may
have to give to him that needeth.*
— EPHESIANS 4:28

Those who are chiefly deserving of reproof from the subject of the preciousness of time: those who spend a great part of their time in idleness, or in
doing nothing that turns to any account, either for the good of their souls or
bodies; nothing either for their own benefit or for the benefit of their neighbor, either of the family or of the body-politic to which they belong. There
are some persons upon whose hands time seems to lie heavy, who, instead
of being concerned to improve it as it passes and taking care that it pass not
without making it their own, act as if it were rather their concern to contrive
ways how to waste and consume it—as though time, instead of being precious, were rather a mere encumbrance to them. Their hands refuse to labor,
and rather than put themselves to it, they will let their families suffer and will
suffer themselves: "An idle soul shall suffer hunger" (Prov. 19:15); "Drowsi-
ness shall clothe a man with rags" (Prov. 23:21). Some spend much of their
time at the tavern, over their cups, and in wandering about from house to
house, wasting away their hours in idle and unprofitable talk that will turn
to no good account: "In all labor there is profit: but the talk of the lips ten-
deth only to penury" (Prov. 14:23). The direction of the apostle Paul is that
we should "labor, working with [our] hands the thing that is good, that [we]
may have to give to him that needeth" (Eph. 4:28). But indolent men, instead
of gaining anything to give to him that needeth, do but waste what they have
already: "He also that is slothful in his work is brother to him that is a great
waster" (Prov. 18:9).

 From "The Preciousness of Time and the Importance of Redeeming It," pp. 234–35

GOD'S PARTICULAR TREASURE

But ye are a chosen generation, a royal priesthood, an holy nation, a peculiar people; that ye should shew forth the praises of him who hath called you out of darkness into his marvelous light.
— 1 PETER 2:9

How wonderful that God should take such thought of a poor worm from all eternity! God might have left you as well as many others, but it pleased the Lord to set His love upon you. What cause have you for love and thankfulness, that God should make choice of you, and set you apart for Himself, rather than so many thousands of others! God has chosen you not merely to be His subjects and servants, but to be His children, to be His particular treasure. He has chosen you to be blessed forever in the enjoyment of Himself, and to dwell with Him in His glory. He has given you from all eternity to His Son, to be united unto Him, to become the spouse of Christ. He has chosen you that you might be holy and without blame, that you might have your filth taken away, and that you might have the image of God put upon you, and that your soul might be adorned, to be the bride of His glorious and dear Son. What cause for love is here! If believers are a chosen generation, let all labor earnestly to make their election sure. If true Christians are chosen of God, this should induce all earnestly to inquire whether they are true Christians. The apostle Peter says, in 2 Peter 1:5–7, "And besides this, giving all diligence, add to your faith, virtue; and to virtue, knowledge; and to knowledge, temperance; and to temperance, patience; and to patience, godliness; and to godliness, brotherly kindness; and to brotherly kindness, charity."

§ From "Christians a Chosen Generation, a Royal Priesthood, a Holy Nation, a Peculiar People," pp. 938–39

CHRIST SUFFERED FOR SINS

For Christ also hath once suffered for sins, the just for the unjust, that he might bring us to God, being put to death in the flesh, but quickened by the Spirit.
— 1 PETER 3:18

The justice of God requires the punishment of sin. God is the Supreme Judge of the world, and He is to judge the world according to the rules of justice. It is not the part of a judge to show favor to the person judged; but he is to determine according to a rule of justice without departing to the right hand or left. God does not show mercy as a judge, but as a sovereign. Therefore, when mercy sought the salvation of sinners, the inquiry was how to make the exercise of the mercy of God as a sovereign, and of His strict justice as a judge, agree together. And this is done by the sufferings of Christ, in which sin is punished fully and justice answered. Christ suffered enough for the punishment of the sins of the greatest sinner that ever lived. So that God, when He judges, may act according to a rule of strict justice, and yet acquit the sinner, if he be in Christ. Justice cannot require any more for any man's sins, than those sufferings of one of the persons in the Trinity that Christ suffered. God can save any sinner whatsoever, without any prejudice to the honor of His truth. God passed His word, that sin should be punished with death, which is to be understood not only of the first, but of the second death. God can save the greatest sinner consistently with His truth in this threatening. For sin is punished in the sufferings of Christ, inasmuch as He is our surety.

§ From "God's Sovereignty in the Salvation of Men," p. 851

A HOLY PRIESTHOOD

Ye also, as lively stones, are built up a spiritual house, an holy priesthood, to offer up spiritual sacrifices, acceptable to God by Jesus Christ.
— 1 PETER 2:5

Let all who profess themselves Christians take heed that they do not defile themselves and profane their sacred character. There was great strictness required of old of the priests, lest they should defile themselves and profane their office, and it was regarded as a dreadful thing to profane it. So holy a God hath threatened in the New Testament, that "if any man defile the temple of God, him shall God destroy" (1 Cor. 3:17). As Christians are here called the temple of God, so it is said, in 1 Peter 2:5, "Ye…are a spiritual house, an holy priesthood." Avoid the commission of all immoralities, or things that have a horrid filthiness in them, things that will dreadfully profane the sacred name by which you are called and the sacred station wherein you are set. Take heed especially of lascivious impurities. Such things were looked upon as defiling the holy office of the priesthood of old, insomuch, that if but a daughter of a priest was guilty of whoredom, she was to be burned. Remember Hophni and Phinehas, how sorely God dealt with them for profaning their office by their impurities; and with good Eli, that He was no more thorough to restrain them. God brought a curse upon the whole family that never was removed. God took away the priesthood from him and took away the ark of the covenant from him and from Israel and delivered it into captivity and fulfilled his threatening, that there should not be an old man of his house forever. Take heed of every sin, and allowing any sin whatever is a dreadful presumption of your holy character.

§ From "Christians a Chosen Generation, a Royal Priesthood, a Holy Nation, a Peculiar People," p. 944

THE EXALTATION OF CHRIST

And God shall wipe away all tears from their eyes; and there shall be no more death, neither sorrow, nor crying, neither shall there be any more pain: for the former things are passed away.
— REVELATION 21:4

Christ will appear gloriously above all evil in the consummation of the redemption of His elect church at the end of the world. Then will be completed the whole work of redemption with respect to all that Christ died for, both in its impetration and its application—and not until then. And then will Christ's exaltation above all evil be most perfectly and fully manifest. Then shall the conquest and triumph be completed with respect to all of them. Then shall all the devils and all their instruments be brought before Christ to be judged and condemned. And then shall be completed their destruction in their consummate and everlasting misery: they shall be all cast into the lake of fire, no more to range and usurp dominion in the world or have liberty to make opposition against God and Christ; they shall forever be shut up, thenceforward only to suffer. Then shall death be totally destroyed. All the saints shall be delivered everlastingly from it. Even their bodies shall be taken from the power of death by a glorious resurrection. Then shall all guilt, and all sin and corruption, and all affliction, all sighs and tears, be utterly and eternally abolished, concerning every one of the elect; they being all brought to one complete body, to their consummate and immutable glory. And all this as the fruit of Christ's blood, and as an accomplishment of His redemption. Then all that evil, which has so prevailed and so exalted itself and usurped and raged and reigned, shall be perfectly and forever thrust down and destroyed, with respect to all the elect; and all will be exalted to a state wherein they will be forever immensely above all these things.

§ From "Christ Exalted," p. 216

GOOD WORKS

Not by works of righteousness which we have done, but according to his mercy he saved us, by the washing of regeneration, and renewing of the Holy Ghost.
— TITUS 3:5

Men are not saved on the account of any work of theirs, and yet they are not saved without works. If we merely consider what it is for which, or on the account of which, men are saved, no work at all in men is necessary to their salvation. In this respect they are saved wholly without any work of theirs, "Not by works of righteousness which we have done, but according to his mercy he saved us, by the washing of regeneration, and renewing of the Holy Ghost" (Titus 3:5). We must indeed be saved on the account of works, but not our own. It is on account of the works that Christ hath done for us. Works are the fixed price of eternal life; it is fixed by an eternal, unalterable rule of righteousness. But, since the fall, there is no hope of our doing these works without salvation offered freely without money and without price. But, though it is not needful that we do anything to merit salvation, which Christ hath fully merited for all who believe in Him, yet God, for wise and holy ends, hath appointed that we should come to final salvation in no other way but that of good works done by us.

🜚 From "The Manner in Which the Salvation of the Soul is to Be Sought," p. 53

PEACE AND PLEASURE

For I am persuaded, that neither death, nor life, nor angels, nor principalities, nor powers, nor things present, nor things to come, nor height, nor depth, nor any other creature, shall be able to separate us from the love of God, which is in Christ Jesus our Lord.

— ROMANS 8:38–39

Peace and pleasure are the portion of Christians in this world. Their peace and joy in God begin in the present life, and are no less excellent than the glory with which He invests them, and the honor to which He advances them. They have ground for peace because of their safety. They are safe in Jesus Christ from the wrath of God and from the power of Satan. They that are in Christ shall never perish, for none shall pluck them out of His hand. They are delivered from all their dreadful misery, that indignation and wrath, tribulation and anguish, which shall come on ungodly men. They were naturally exposed to it, but they are delivered from it; their sins are all forgiven them. The handwriting is eternally blotted out. Their sins are all done away; God has cast them behind His back and buried their sorrows in the depths of the sea, and they shall no more come into remembrance. They are most safe from misery, for they are built on Christ their everlasting rock. Who is he that condemns? It is Christ that died, yea, rather is risen again, who is even at the right hand of God. They have the faithful promise of God for their security, which is established as a sure witness in heaven. They have an interest in that covenant, which is well ordered in all things and sure.

๑ From "The Portion of the Righteous," p. 889

GOD REQUIRES PRAYER

After this manner therefore pray ye: Our Father which art in heaven, Hallowed be thy name. Thy kingdom come, Thy will be done in earth, as it is in heaven.
—MATTHEW 6:9–10

Why doth God require prayer in order to the bestowment of mercies? It is not in order that God may be informed of our wants or desires. He is omniscient, and, with respect to his knowledge, unchangeable. God never gains any knowledge by information. He knows what we want, a thousand times more perfectly than we do ourselves, before we ask Him. For though, speaking after the manner of men, God is sometimes represented as if He were moved and persuaded by the prayers of His people, yet it is not to be thought that God is properly moved or made willing by our prayers; for it is no more possible that there should be any new inclination or will in God than new knowledge. The mercy of God is not moved or drawn by anything in the creature, but the spring of God's beneficence is within Himself only. He is self-moved; and whatsoever mercy He bestows, the reason and ground of it is not to be sought for in the creature, but in God's own good pleasure. It is the will of God to bestow mercy in this way, namely in answer to prayer, when He designs beforehand to bestow mercy, yea, when He has promised it: "I the Lord have spoken it, and I will do it. Thus saith the Lord GOD, I will yet for this be enquired of by the house of Israel, to do it for them" (Ezek. 36:36–37). God has been pleased to constitute prayer to be antecedent to the bestowment of mercy; and He is pleased to bestow mercy in consequence of prayer, as though He were prevailed on by prayer. When the people of God are stirred up to prayer, it is the effect of His intention to show mercy; therefore He pours out the spirit of grace and supplication.

RELATIVE HOLINESS

Before I formed thee in the belly I knew thee; and before thou camest forth out of the womb I sanctified thee, and I ordained thee a prophet unto the nations.
— JEREMIAH 1:5

Christians are a holy nation by a relative holiness, as they are set apart by God for a divine and holy use. So things are often called holy in Scripture. The utensils of the tabernacle and temple are in this sense called holy; the priests' garments are called holy, the places of worship appointed of God in the Old Testament are called holy, because they were set apart by Him for a holy use and service. Things thus set apart are said to be sanctified. Thus Jeremiah is said to have been sanctified before he came forth out of the womb: "Before I formed thee in the belly, I knew thee; and before thou camest forth out of the womb I sanctified thee, and I ordained thee a prophet unto the nations" (Jer. 1:5). God sanctified, that is, God set him apart for this holy use and service, to be a prophet to the nations, as Paul says of himself: "But when it pleased God, who separated me from my mother's womb, and called me by his grace" (Gal. 1:15). So the people of Israel of old seem to be called a holy nation: "For thou art an holy people unto the LORD thy God: the LORD thy God hath chosen thee to be a special people unto himself, above all people that are upon me face of the earth" (Deut. 7:6). Not that they were a holy people by inherent holiness, for God often tells them that they are a stiff-necked people, but God had called and separated them from other nations to be the keepers of the sacred oracles, and for other purposes.

❦ From "Christians a Chosen Generation, a Royal Priesthood, a Holy Nation, a Peculiar People," p. 946

THE FUTURE STATE

Fear God, and give glory to him; for the hour of his judgment is come.
—REVELATION 14:7

The state of unconverted men is very dreadful, if we consider its relation to the future world. Our state here is not lasting, but temporary. The redeemed are pilgrims and strangers here, and are principally designed for a future world. We continue in this present state but a short time; we are to be in that future state for all eternity. Therefore, men are to be either happy or miserable, in regard to that future state. In comparison it matters very little what our state is here, because it will continue but a short time; it is nothing to eternity. But that man is a happy man who is entitled to happiness, and he is miserable who is in danger of misery, in his eternal state. Prosperity or adversity in the present state alters them but very little, because this state is so short. Those who are in a natural condition have no title to any inheritance in another world. There are glorious things in another world; there are unsearchable riches, an unspeakable and inconceivable abundance; but they have nothing to do with it. Heaven is a world of glory and blessedness; but they have no right to the least portion of those blessings. If they should die and go out of the world as they are, they would go destitute, having no inheritance, no friend, and no enjoyments to go to. They will have no God to whom they may go; no Redeemer to receive their departing souls; no angel to be a ministering spirit to them, to take care of them, to guard or defend them; no interest in that Redeemer, who has purchased those blessings.

⟡ From "Natural Men in a Dreadful Condition," p. 820

GIVING WITH LOVE

Whosoever shall give to drink unto one of these little ones a cup of cold water only in the name of a disciple, verily I say unto you, he shall in no wise lose his reward.

— MATTHEW 10:42

If you give with a spirit of true love, you will be rewarded in what is infinitely more valuable than what you give; even eternal riches in heaven. Matthew 10:42 says, "Whosoever shall give to drink unto one of these little ones a cup of cold water only in the name of a disciple, verily I say unto you, he shall in no wise lose his reward." Giving to our needy brothers and sisters is, in Scripture, called laying up treasures in heaven, in bags that do not grow old: "Sell that ye have, and give alms; provide yourselves bags which wax not old, a treasure in the heavens that faileth not, where no thief approacheth, neither moth corrupteth" (Luke 12:33). Men, when they have laid up their money in their chests, do not suppose that they have thrown it away; but, on the contrary, that it is laid up safe. Treasure that is laid up in heaven is much safer than what is laid up in chests or cabinets. You cannot lay up treasure on earth, but that it is liable to be stolen, or otherwise fail. But in heaven no thief will come near it, nor moth corrupt. It is committed to God's care, and He will keep it safely for you; and when you die, you will receive it with infinite increase. Instead of a part of your earthly substance given to you, you will receive heavenly riches on which you may live in the greatest fullness, honor, and happiness, to all eternity; and you shall never be in want of anything. After feeding with bread those who cannot repay you, you will be rewarded at the resurrection, and eat bread in the kingdom of God.

§ From "Christian Charity," p. 167

SEPARATED FROM GOD

*They are terrible and dreadful: their judgment and their dig-
nity shall proceed of themselves.*
— HABAKKUK 1:7

How can a creature be more miserable than to be separated from the Creator, and to have no god whom he can call his own god? He is wretched indeed, who goes up and down in the world without a god to take care of him, to be his guide and protector, and to bless him. The very light of nature teaches that a man's god is his all. There is but one God, and in Him they have no right. They are without that God whose will must determine their whole well being, both here and forever. Unconverted men who are without God are liable to all manner of evil. They are liable to the power of the devil, to the power of all manner of temptation, for they are without God to protect them. They are liable to be deceived and seduced into erroneous opinions and to embrace damnable doctrine. It is not possible to deceive the saints in this way. But the unconverted may be deceived. They may become papists, heathens, or even atheists. They have nothing to secure them from it. They are liable to be given up of God to judicial hardness of heart. They deserve it and since God is not their god they have no certainty that God will not inflict this awful judgment upon them. As they are without God in the world, they are liable to commit all manner of sin, and even the unpardonable sin itself. They cannot be sure they shall commit that sin. They are liable to build up a false hope of heaven, and so go hoping to hell. As many have already died they are liable to die senseless and stupid. They are not safe one moment.

§ From "Natural Men in a Dreadful Condition," p. 819

ENGAGED IN PRAISE

I will give thanks unto thee, O LORD, among the heathen, and I will sing praises unto thy name.
— 2 SAMUEL 22:50

The mercy and grace of God for which the saints in heaven will chiefly praise Him is the mercy exercised in the work of redemption. The chief object of the saints' admiration, contemplation, and that which employs their most ardent praises is the love of God. The grace of Christ, about which their praises will be principally employed, is that He should so love sinful man as to undertake for him, to take upon Him man's nature, and to lay down His life for him. We find that is the subject of their praises in Revelation 5:8–9: "And when he had taken the book, the four beasts and four and twenty elders fell down before the Lamb, having every one of them harps, and golden vials full of odours, which are the prayers of saints. And they sung a new song, saying, Thou art worthy to take the book, and to open the seals thereof: for thou wast slain, and hast redeemed us to God by thy blood out of every kindred, and tongue, and people, and nation." They will chiefly praise God for these fruits of His mercy, because these are the greatest fruits of it that ever have been. The saints in heaven will praise God for bestowing glory upon them, but the actual bestowing of glory upon them, after it has been purchased by the blood of Christ, is in no measure so great as the purchasing of it by His blood. For Christ, the eternal Son of God, to become man and lay down His life was a far greater thing than the glorifying of all the saints that ever have been or ever will be glorified, from the beginning of the world to the end of it. The giving of Christ to die comprehends all other mercies, for all other mercies are given through the death of Christ.

꙳ From "Praise, One of the Chief Employments of Heaven," p. 916

FLEE TEMPTATION

And [Joseph] left his garment in [his master's wife's] hand, and fled, and got him out.

—GENESIS 39:12

Joseph not only refused actually to commit uncleanness with his master's wife, who enticed him, but he refused to be there, where he should be in the way of temptation. He refused to lie by her or be with her. And in the text we are told, he "fled, and got him out"; he would by no means be in her company. Though it was no sin in itself, for Joseph to be in the house where his master's wife was, under these circumstances it would expose him to sin. Joseph was sensible that he had naturally a corrupt heart that tended to betray him to sin. And therefore he would by no means be in the way of temptation, but with haste he fled; he ran from the dangerous place. Inasmuch as he was exposed to sin in that house, he fled out of it with as much haste as if it had been on fire or full of enemies who stood ready with drawn swords to stab him to the very heart. When she took him by the garment, he left his garment in her hands. He had rather lose his garment than stay a moment there where he was in such danger of losing his chastity. Persons should avoid things that expose to sin, as far as may be; because it is possible that persons may be called to expose themselves to temptation; and, when it is so, they may hope for divine strength and protection under temptation. It may be a man's indispensable duty to undertake an office, or a work, attended with a great deal of temptation. Christ thus directs His disciples, "When they persecute you in this city, flee ye into another" (Matt. 10:23). Yet, the case may be so, that a man may be called not to flee from persecution, but to run the venture of such a trial, trusting in God to uphold him under it. We ought to avoid not only those things that are in themselves sinful, but also those things that lead and expose to sin.

§ From "Temptation and Deliverance," p. 228

GREAT AND PRECIOUS PROMISES

Whereby are given unto us exceeding great and precious promises: that by these ye might be partakers of the divine nature, having escaped the corruption that is in the world through lust.

— 2 PETER 1:4

God loves His people to the end; He will never leave them or forsake them. He will be their God and they will be His people. He will deliver them from all evil. He is their refuge, their most high habitation; He is their defense. They shall dwell under secret places; therefore they shall never fall. Their place of defense shall be their munitions. He will subdue Satan under foot; He will tread on the lion and the adder. He will destroy the great leviathan, and give him to be meat to them. He will be to them a Father, and they will be His children. He will pity them all and will be ready to help when they cry. He will hear their prayers. He will be a God close at hand and not a God afar off. He will provide for them. He will be with them when passing through the valley of the shadow of death; the second death shall have no power. He will raise them up at the last day. Christ will confess their names; their life shall be hidden with Christ. They shall see length of days forever and ever. They shall see God. Christ has promised them mansions of glory in His Father's house; He has gone to prepare a place for them and will come again for them. They shall see Him face to face; they shall be like Him and see Him as He is. They shall sit with Him on His throne; He will give them a crown of life, and they shall be made most blessed forever. They will drink of the rivers of pleasure, enter in through the gates into the city, and have a right to the tree of life. Such promises as these, and many others of the like nature, God has made. Well might it therefore be said, as in 2 Peter 1:4, that God has given them exceedingly great and precious promises. How blessed then are they who have believed, for there shall be a performance of all those things that have been told them by the Lord.

⸕ From "The Covenant of Grace, Firm and Sure," pp. 96–97

BOASTING ABOUT TOMORROW

Boast not thyself of tomorrow; for thou knowest not what a day may bring forth.
— PROVERBS 27:1

"Boast not thyself of tomorrow." In this precept two things seem to be forbidden. First, boasting ourselves of what shall be on the morrow, or behaving ourselves as though we depended on particular things to come to pass in this world, in some future time. As when men behave themselves, as though they depended on being rich, or promoted to honor hereafter; or as though they were sure of accomplishing any particular design another day, so did the rich man in the gospel, when he did not only promise himself that he should live many years, but promised himself also that he should be rich many years. Hence he said to his soul that he had much goods laid up for many years. And if men act as though they depended upon it, that they should another day accomplish such and such things for their souls, then may they be said to boast themselves of tomorrow, and not to behave themselves as though they depended on no other day. As when they behave themselves as though they depended upon it; that they should at another day have such and such advantages for the good of their souls; that they should at another day have the strivings of God's Spirit; that they should at another day find themselves disposed to be thorough in seeking their salvation; that they should at another day have a more convenient season; and that God at another day would stand ready to hear their prayers, and show them mercy. Or if they act as though they depended upon it that they should have considerable opportunity on a deathbed to seek mercy; or whatever they promise themselves should come to pass respecting them in this world, if they act as depending on it, they boast themselves of tomorrow. Second, another thing implied is our boasting of future time itself, or acting as though we depended on it, that we should have our lives continued to us another day. Not only is the command of God delivered in the text transgressed by those who behave themselves as depending upon it that they shall see and obtain such and such things tomorrow; but by those who act as depending upon it that they shall remain in being in this world tomorrow.

§ From "Procrastination, or The Sin and Folly of Depending on Future Time," pp. 237–38

ROOM ENOUGH FOR ALL

In my Father's house are many mansions.
—JOHN 14:2

There are many mansions in the house of God. By many mansions is meant many seats or places of abode. As it is a king's palace, there are many mansions. Kings' houses are wont to be built very large, with many stately rooms and apartments. So there are many mansions in God's house. When this is spoken of heaven, it is chiefly to be understood in a figurative sense, and the following things seem to be taught us in it. First, there is room in this house of God for great numbers. There is room in heaven for a vast multitude, yea, room enough for all mankind that are or ever shall be. This is partly what Christ intended in the words of the text, as is evident from the occasion of His speaking them. The disciples manifested a great desire to be where Christ was, and Christ, therefore, to encourage them that it should be as they desired, tells them that in His Father's house where He was going were many mansions; room enough for them. There is mercy enough in God to admit an innumerable multitude into heaven. There is mercy enough for all, and there is merit enough in Christ to purchase heavenly happiness for millions of millions, for all men that ever were, are, or shall be. There is a sufficiency in the fountain of heaven's happiness to supply and fill and satisfy all; and there is in all respects enough for the happiness of all. Second, there are sufficient and suitable accommodations for all the different sorts of persons that are in the world: for great and small, for high and low, rich and poor, wise and unwise, bond and free, persons of all nations and all conditions and circumstances, for those that have been great sinners as well as for moral livers; for weak saints and those that are babes in Christ as well as for those that are stronger and more grown in grace. There is in heaven a sufficiency for the happiness of every sort; there is a convenient accommodation for every creature that will hearken to the calls of the gospel.

⚓ From "The Many Mansions," pp. 67–68

A LADDER TO HEAVEN

And he dreamed, and behold a ladder set up on the earth, and the top of it reached to heaven.
— GENESIS 28:12

Upon whom do you depend for happiness? Do you depend on the Lord Jesus Christ alone? Jacob had heaven opened to him; he had a ladder set down before him from heaven to earth while he rested on the stone of Bethel that was a type of Christ. If ever you find this ladder, if you are ascending to heavenly happiness, you have been brought to rest on Jesus, that stone that God has laid in Zion. This ladder is the way of salvation by Jesus Christ in the covenant of grace that God has established in Him. None, therefore, are in this way but those who have their dependence on Him. What is the foundation of your trust and hope? On what basis do you take encouragement that God will have mercy on you and that you shall be happy? Is not the thought of what you have done and the lovely qualifications that you have obtained, your own goodness or loveliness of heart or life, the thing that is the secret ground of your encouragement and comfort? Or do you see that this is nothing, and that there is no dependence to be had on it? Is the consideration of the greatness and sovereignty of mercy through a Savior the only ground of your encouragement? Does your heart and soul seem to close with this way of salvation as a far more excellent way than by your own righteousness? Is that way of being saved through the merits of Christ and sovereign grace through Him only, making no account of your righteousness, sweet to your soul and a thousand times sweeter than being saved by your own righteousness? Jacob rested and had sweet repose on the stone of Bethel. Does your soul take rest and acquiesce in the way of sovereign grace revealed in the gospel, seeing that there is no need of any other way, and that there can be no better way?

❧ From "The Ladder That God Has Set on the Earth for Man to Ascend to Happiness Reaches Even unto Heaven," pp. 167–68

FOLLOW GOOD EXAMPLES

*Brethren, be followers of me, and mark them which walk so as
ye have us for an ensample.*
— PHILIPPIANS 3:17

We ought to follow the good examples of the apostle Paul. We are to consider that the apostle did not say this of himself from an ambitious spirit, from a desire of being set up as a pattern and eyed and imitated as an example to other Christians. His writings are not of any private interpretation, but he spoke as he was moved by the Holy Ghost. The Holy Ghost directed that the good examples of the apostle Paul should be noticed by other Christians and imitated. And we are also to consider that this is not a command to the Philippians only, to whom the epistle was more immediately directed, but to all those for whose use this epistle was written: for all Christians to the end of the world. The precepts that we find in those epistles are no more to be regarded as precepts intended only for those to whom the epistle was sent than the Ten Commandments that were spoken from Mount Sinai to the children of Israel are to be regarded as commands intended only for that people. When we are directed to follow the good examples of the apostle Paul by the Holy Ghost, it is not merely as we are to imitate whatever we see that is good in anyone, let him be how he may, but there are spiritual obligations that lie on Christians to follow the good examples of this great apostle. It has pleased the Holy Ghost in an especial manner to set up the apostle Paul, not only as a teacher of the Christian church, but as a pattern to other Christians. The greatest example of all, that is set before us in Scripture to imitate, is the example of Jesus Christ that He set us in His human nature, and when in His state of humiliation. This is presented to us not only as a great pattern, but as a perfect rule. And the example of no man is set forth, as our rule, but the example of Christ.

§ From "The Character of Paul an Example to Christians," p. 855

BY APPOINTED MEANS

And now, I pray you, beseech God that he will be gracious unto us: this hath been by your means: will he regard your persons? saith the LORD *of hosts.*
— MALACHI 1:9

It is God's manner to bestow His grace and blessing in a way of the use of appointed means. God is the sovereign disposer of His own favor and blessing. He may bestow it on whom He pleases and in what way He pleases. None of us can challenge any right to God's grace. We have, to a great degree, deserved the contrary from Him. He might, in our first state of innocence, bestow His favors and bounties in what way He pleased. Then, He might appoint what conditions He would, as He was absolute Lord over us. Much more now, since we have sinned and His justice has infinite demands upon us, it is wonderful, unspeakable grace that He is willing to be gracious to us in any way. But if He is, it is His prerogative to say in what way He will do so, whether in the use of means or without them. And it has pleased God to bestow His mercy by the use of certain means, and He has told us by what means. God has not only appointed a way of salvation for us by Jesus Christ, by what He has done and suffered, but He has also appointed something to be done by us as a way wherein we are to seek the benefit of what our Savior has done for us. God does not let mankind alone, everyone to go his own way, without any sort of directions from Him how to behave and act. He chooses not, in some extraordinary, miraculous way, to immediately snatch one and another out of their misery and bestow salvation upon them without any directions given by Him how to seek salvation, or anything at all done by them any way in order to obtain it. But God chooses to bestow His mercy in a way of appointed means.

❦ From "God's Wisdom in His Stated Method of Bestowing Grace," pp. 200–201

GOD IS WORTHY

Now I know that the LORD is greater than all gods: for in the
thing wherein they dealt proudly he was above them.
— EXODUS 18:11

God is worthy to be sovereign over all things. Sometimes men are the owners of more than they are worthy of. God is not only the owner of the whole world, as all is from and dependent on Him, but such is His perfection, the excellency and dignity of His nature, that He is worthy of sovereignty over all. No man ought in the temper of his mind to be opposite to God's exercising the sovereignty of the universe, as if He were not worthy of it; for to be the absolute sovereign of the universe is not a glory or dignity too great for Him. All things in heaven and earth, angels and men, are nothing in comparison with Him; all are as the drop of the bucket, and as the light dust of the balance. It is therefore fit that everything should be in His hands, to be disposed of according to His pleasure. His will and pleasure are of infinitely greater importance than the will of creatures. It is fit that His will should take place, though contrary to the will of all other beings; that He should make Himself His own end and order all things for Himself. God is possessed of such perfections and excellencies as to qualify Him to be the absolute sovereign of the world. Certainly it is more fit that all things be under the guidance of a perfect unerring wisdom, than that they should be left to themselves to fall in confusion, or be brought to pass by blind causes. Yea, it is not fit that any affairs within the government of God should be left without the direction of His wise providence—least of all, things of the greatest importance.

§ From "The Sole Consideration, That God Is God, Sufficient to Still All Objections to His Sovereignty," p. 108

REST AND REFRESHMENT IN CHRIST

For he that is entered into his rest, he also hath ceased from his own works, as God did from his.

— HEBREWS 4:10

There is in Christ quiet rest and sweet refreshment for God's people, when wearied with the buffetings of Satan. The devil, that malicious enemy of God and man, does whatever lies in his power to darken and hinder and tempt God's people and render their lives uncomfortable. Often he raises needless and groundless scruples and casts in doubts and fills the mind with such fear as is tormenting and tends to hinder them exceedingly in the Christian course; and he often raises mists and clouds of darkness and stirs up corruption and thereby fills the mind with concern and anguish and sometimes wearies out the soul. So that they may say as the psalmist: "Many bulls have compassed me: strong bulls of Bashan have beset me round. They gaped upon me with their mouths, as a ravening and a roaring lion" (Ps. 22:12–13). In such a case, if the soul flies to Jesus Christ they may find rest in Him, for He came into the world to destroy Satan, and to rescue souls out of his hands. And He has all things put under His feet, whether they are things in heaven, or things on earth, or things in hell, and therefore He can restrain Satan when He pleases. And that He is doubtless ready enough to pity us under such temptations, we may be assured, for He has been tempted and buffeted by Satan as well as we. He is able to succor those that are tempted, and He has promised that He will subdue Satan under His people's feet. Let God's people therefore, when they are exercised with any of those kinds of weariness, make their resort unto Jesus Christ for refuge and rest.

ﾉ From "Safety, Fullness, and Sweet Refreshment, to Be Found in Christ," p. 935

CONSIDER WHAT GOD HAS DONE

For ye know the grace of our Lord Jesus Christ, that, though he was rich, yet for your sakes he became poor, that ye through his poverty might be rich.
— 2 CORINTHIANS 8:9

Consider how much God hath done for us; how greatly He hath loved us; what He hath given us, when we were so unworthy and when He could have no addition to His happiness by us. Consider that silver and gold and earthly crowns were in His esteem but mean things to give us, and He hath therefore given us His own Son. Christ loved and pitied us when we were poor, and He laid out Himself to help and even did shed His own blood for us without grudging. He did not think much to deny Himself and to be at great cost for us vile wretches in order to make us rich and to clothe us with kingly robes when we were naked; to feast us at His own table with dainties infinitely costly when we were starving; to advance us from the dunghill and set us among princes and make us to inherit the throne of His glory, and so to give us the enjoyment of the greatest wealth and plenty to all eternity; agreeably to 2 Corinthians 8:9: "For ye know the grace of our Lord Jesus Christ, that, though he was rich, yet for your sakes he became poor, that ye through his poverty might be rich." Considering all these things, what a poor business will it be that those who hope to share these benefits yet cannot give something for the relief of a poor neighbor without grudging. That it should grieve them to part with a small matter, to help a fellow servant in calamity, when Christ did not grudge shedding His own blood for them!

§ From "Christian Charity," p. 165

EXPRESSING LOVE IN HEAVEN

And I heard a great voice out of heaven saying, Behold, the tabernacle of God is with men, and he will dwell with them, and they shall be his people, and God himself shall be with them, and be their God.
— REVELATION 21:3

There shall be nothing within themselves to clog or hinder the saints in heaven in the exercises and expressions of love. In this world the saints find much to hinder them in this respect. They have a great deal of dullness and heaviness. They carry about with them a heavy-molded body—a clod of earth, a mass of flesh and blood that is not fitted to be the organ for a soul inflamed with high exercises of divine love; but which is found a great clog and hindrance to the spirit—so that they cannot express their love to God as they would and cannot be so active and lively in it as they desire. Often they fain would fly, but they are held down as with a dead weight upon their wings. Fain would they be active, and mount up, as a flame of fire, but they find themselves, as it were, hampered and chained down, so that they cannot do as their love inclines them to do. But in heaven they shall have no such hindrance. There they will have no dullness and unwieldiness and no corruption of heart to war against divine love and hinder its expressions; and there no earthly body shall clog with its heaviness the heavenly flame. The saints in heaven shall have no difficulty in expressing all their love. Their souls being on fire with holy love shall not be like a fire pent up, but like a flame uncovered and at liberty. Their spirits, being winged with love, shall have no weight upon them to hinder their flight. There shall be no want of strength or activity or any want of words wherewith to praise the object of their affection. Nothing shall hinder them from communing with God and praising and serving Him just as their love inclines them to do. Love naturally desires to express itself; and in heaven the love of the saints shall be at full liberty to express itself as it desires, whether it be toward God or to created beings.

§ From "Heaven, a World of Charity, or Love," pp. 341–42

GOD NEVER CHANGES

For I am the LORD, I change not.
— MALACHI 3:6

God never changes His mind with respect to what He has purposed to do. God's purposes are eternal, all of them. He purposes nothing anew. He decreed, infinite ages back, every act and every event, little and great, that ever comes to pass. And these events do not grow out of conceit of any of His old purposes and by thinking more upon the matter. Nor does He ever add to His purposes. He purposes nothing anew. Men purpose and form resolutions as they find occasion; they mend their designs and form them more perfectly by thinking longer upon them. But it is not so with God. God never changes His mind with respect to the rules that He has fixed for Himself to act by. God is pleased to act by rules that He fixes. Thus the law of nature, the laws by which natural effects are produced (such as the motions of the heavenly bodies), these rules are not so properly laws by which the creature acts as fixed rules according to which God acts with respect to the creature. God's nature and disposition is never changed. It implies great absurdities to suppose that nature that is eternal and self-existent could be changeable. That being that is eternal and self-existent and wholly self-dependent depends on no cause in any respect. But if a being is changed in his nature, that will necessarily argue that that being depends on some cause; for if his nature is changed, there must be some cause of that change. He must be influenced in some way or another by something. He who is infinite in all perfection cannot be changed; for that which is already infinitely perfect, if He varies, cannot be so. If God varies from Himself, He has either fallen from infinite perfection or never was infinitely perfect.

❧ From "God Never Changes His Mind," pp. 4, 7–8

LEAVE THE DEVIL'S BAIT

As an ox goeth to the slaughter, or as a fool to the correction of the stocks; until a dart strike through his liver; as a bird hasteth to the snare, and knoweth not that it is for his life.

— PROVERBS 7:22–23

A person may insensibly fall into such a course and custom of sin as shall gain an entire assent over them. Persons come to this place before they are aware. They commit the sin once, it may be, without any great fault of danger; they venture upon it again, and so again, intending to leave it. But they go on until they are past recovery, until they are so entangled that they cannot cease. They go as the young men mentioned in Proverbs 7:22–23: "As an ox goeth to the slaughter, or as a fool to the correction of the stocks; until a dart strike through his liver; as a bird hasteth to the snare, and knoweth not that it is for his life." Let all, therefore, take heed that they do not thus entangle themselves; for if they do, it is a hundred to one whether they are ever recovered. When a man comes to that place, he has, as it were, one foot in the grave; and if he is delivered, it will be plucking a brand out of the burning hell. The devil has him in his snare, and it is rare that the snare is broken and the bird escapes. And if he does not escape he will not only perish, but he will be doubly miserable when he comes to be damned. He will have a life of the vice to answer for; he will suffer the damnation of one of the greatest of sinners. Therefore, if any of you who now hear me have begun a vicious practice, take heed that you proceed no further, but escape for your life. Leave the devil's bait before he has gotten fast hold of you with his hook.

✄ From "Men's Addiction to Sin Is No Excuse, but an Aggravation," pp. 66–67

ESTABLISHED DECREES

He hath also stablished them for ever and ever: he hath made
a decree which shall not pass.
— PSALM 148:6

If it is so that God does whatever He pleases, hence we learn that the doctrine of the decrees is certainly true; that is, that God did from all eternity absolutely appoint and determine everything that comes to pass. The truth of it appears from the doctrine thus: In the first place, none will deny that God knows all things and that He knew all things from eternity. They who deny the decrees do not pretend to deny that God knows all things; but if God foreknew everything that should come to pass, and did not Himself from all eternity determine that they should come to pass according to His own will, a great many things would fall out contrary to His will. And so, it would not be true that God does whatever He pleases; for all things must come to pass according as God from all eternity knew they would. And if He did not also from all eternity will that they should so come to pass, then a great many things would come to pass otherwise than He would have chosen they should. If God foreknew how things would be, and He could order and dispose them just as He pleased, there could be no lack of power. He had a right to ordain as He pleased, and therefore there could be no want of that. It necessarily follows, therefore, that He did actually determine that things should be according to His will. It is impossible that a being who knows all things and can do all things should not have all things done according to His will and should not fix and appoint how they should be done from all eternity. In God there is no change of will. That which He wills now He foresaw from all eternity that He would will; and therefore He actually willed and ordained that which would be.

🕯 From "God Does What He Pleases," p. 163

IN AND BY CHRIST

In the LORD *have I righteousness.*
—ISAIAH 45:24

The Christian is what he is as a Christian in no other way than as he is a member of Christ's body. He receives life and holiness from Him as his Head, and as he is a branch in the Vine. There is a vital union between Christ and the believer; the believer lives by His life. And therefore the apostle says in Galatians 2:20, "I live; yet not I, but Christ liveth in me." Christ is said to be the believer's life in Colossians 3:4: "When Christ, who is our life, shall appear, then shall ye also appear with him in glory." Thus all that the Christian is, he is in and by Christ. The Christian has all the righteousness by which he is accepted in Christ. He has his own inherent holiness in and by Christ, but this is not the righteousness by which he becomes accepted; that is yet more immediately in Christ. That righteousness is not so much inherent in the Christian, but is immediately in Christ Himself; it is the righteousness that He wrought: "In the LORD have I righteousness" (Isa. 45:24). This is one name that is given to Christ in the Scriptures: "the LORD our righteousness" (Jer. 23:6). He is said to be made sin for us that we might be the righteousness of God in Him. It is He only who has made atonement for our sins, and so it is by Him only that we have the pardon of sin. It is by His blood that we are cleansed from guilt, and so delivered from eternal punishment. It is by His obedience to God, His fulfillment of the law, that we are received as having a right to life. The soul of the Christian is clothed with His righteousness; for the sake of that only He is received into God's favor. The happiness with which the Christian is blessed, he has all in and by Christ and that in three respects: all is communicated by Him, all is enjoyed in fellowship with Him, and He Himself is the Christian's objective happiness.

ᔑ From "Christ Is the Christian's All," pp. 199–200

SATAN OPPOSES SALVATION

And no marvel; for Satan himself is transformed into an angel of light.
— 2 CORINTHIANS 11:14

We may learn one reason why the devil so exceedingly opposes the conversion of sinners. It is because if they are once converted, they are forever converted, and thus forever put beyond his reach, so that he can never overthrow and ruin them. If there was such a thing as falling from grace, doubtless the devil would even then oppose our having grace; but more especially does he oppose it since he knows that if, once we have it, he can never expect to overthrow it, but that we, by its very possession, are finally lost to him, and forever out of the reach of his destroying power. This may show us something of the reason of that violent opposition that persons who are under awakenings and convictions, and who are seeking conversion, meet with through the many and great temptations they are assailed with by the adversary. He is always active, and greatly bestirs himself for the overthrow of such, and heaps mountains in their way, if possible, to hinder the saving work of the Holy Spirit, and prevent their conversion. He labors to the utmost to quench convictions of sin, and, if possible, to head persons that are under them to return to the ways of heedlessness and sloth in transgression. Sometimes he endeavors to flatter, and at other times to discourage them, laboring to entangle and perplex their minds, and to his utmost stirring up exercises of corruption, suggesting blasphemous thoughts, and leading them to quarreling with God. By many subtle temptations he endeavors to make them think that it is in vain to seek salvation. In these, and innumerable other ways, Satan endeavors to hinder the conversion of men, for he knows the truth of the doctrine we have insisted on, that if ever grace be implanted in the soul, he can never overthrow it, and the gates of hell cannot prevail against it.

꙳ From "Charity, or True Grace, Not to Be Overthrown by Opposition," pp. 299–300

A GRACIOUS SPIRIT

Charity...beareth all things.
— 1 CORINTHIANS 13:4-7

They who have a truly gracious spirit are willing to undergo all sufferings that they may be exposed to in the way of their duty. If we have not such a spirit, it is an evidence that we have never given ourselves unreservedly to Christ. It is necessary to our being Christians, or followers of Christ, that we should give ourselves to Him unreservedly, to be His wholly, and His only, and His forever. And therefore the believer's closing with Christ is often, in the Scriptures, compared to the act of a bride in giving herself in marriage to her husband; as when God says to His people, "I will betroth thee unto me for ever; yea, I will betroth thee unto me in righteousness, and in judgment, and in lovingkindness, and in mercies" (Hos. 2:19). But a woman, in marriage, gives herself to her husband to be his, and his only. True believers are not their own, for they are bought with a price, and they consent to the full right that Christ has in them, and recognize it by their own act, giving themselves to Him as a voluntary and living sacrifice, wholly devoted to Him. To give ourselves wholly to Christ implies the sacrificing of our own temporal interest wholly to Him. But he that wholly sacrifices his temporal interest to Christ is ready to suffer all things in his worldly interests for Him. If God be truly loved, He is loved as God; and to love Him as God is to love Him as the supreme good. But he that loves God as the supreme good is ready to make all other good give place to that; or, which is the same thing, he is willing to suffer all for the sake of this good.

⸎ From "Charity or a Christian Spirit Willing to Undergo All Sufferings in the Way of Duty," pp. 256–57

PRACTICAL KNOWLEDGE

Have all the workers of iniquity no knowledge? who eat up my people as they eat bread, and call not upon the LORD.

— PSALM 14:4

A true knowledge of God and divine things is a practical knowledge. As to a mere speculative knowledge of the things of religion, many wicked men have attained to great measures of it. Men may possess vast learning, and their learning may consist very much of their knowledge in divinity, and of the Bible, and of the things pertaining to religion, and they may be able to reason very strongly about the attributes of God and the doctrines of Christianity, and yet herein their knowledge fails of being a saving knowledge, in that it is only speculative and not practical. He that has a right and saving acquaintance with divine things sees the excellency of holiness, and of all the ways of holiness, for he sees the beauty and excellency of God, which consist in his holiness; and, for the same reason, he sees the hatefulness of sin, and of all the ways of sin. And if a man knows the hatefulness of the ways of sin, certainly this tends to his avoiding these ways; and if he sees the loveliness of the ways of holiness, this tends to incline him to walk in them. He that knows God sees that He is worthy to be obeyed. Pharaoh did not see why he should obey God, because he did not know who He was, and therefore he says, "Who is the LORD, that I should obey his voice to let Israel go? I know not the LORD, neither will I let Israel go" (Ex. 5:2). This is signified to be the reason why wicked men work or practice iniquity, and carry themselves so wickedly, that they have no spiritual knowledge, as says the psalmist, "Have all the workers of iniquity no knowledge? who eat up my people as they eat bread, and call not upon the LORD" (Ps. 14:4).

֍ From "All True Grace in the Heart Tends to Holy Practice in the Life," pp. 226–27

GOD'S ENCOURAGEMENT

When they had read, they rejoiced for the consolation.
— ACTS 15:31

Consider the great encouragement that God gives you, earnestly to strive for the same blessing that others have obtained. There is great encouragement in the Word of God to sinners to seek salvation in the revelation we have of the abundant provision made for the salvation even of the chief of sinners and in the appointment of so many means to be used with and by sinners in order to their salvation, and by the blessing that God in His Word connects with the means of His appointment. There is hence great encouragement for all, at all times, that will be thorough in using of these means. But now God gives extraordinary encouragement in His providence, by pouring out His Spirit so remarkably among us and bringing savingly home to Himself all sorts, young and old, rich and poor, wise and unwise, sober and vicious, old self-righteous seekers and profligate livers: no sort are exempt. There is at this day among us the loudest call and the greatest encouragement and the widest door opened to sinners to escape out of a state of sin and condemnation that perhaps God ever granted in New England. Who is there that has an immortal soul, so sottish as not to improve such an opportunity and that will not bestir himself with all his might? How unreasonable is negligence and how exceeding unreasonable is discouragement at such a day as this! Will you be so foolish as to neglect your soul now? Will any mortal among us be so unreasonable as to lag behind or look back in discouragement when God opens such a door? Let every person be thoroughly awake! Let everyone encourage himself now to press forward and fly for his life!

§ From "Ruth's Resolution," p. 667

CASTING OFF PRAYER AND WORSHIP

Now when Daniel knew that the writing was signed, he went into his house; and his windows being open in his chamber toward Jerusalem, he kneeled upon his knees three times a day, and prayed, and gave thanks before his God, as he did aforetime.

—DANIEL 6:10

If you live in the neglect of secret prayer, you show your goodwill to neglect all the worship of God. He that prays only when he prays with others would not pray at all, were it not that the eyes of others are upon him. He that will not pray where none but God seeth him manifestly doth not pray at all out of respect to God or regard to His all-seeing eye and therefore doth, in effect, cast off all prayer. And he that casts off prayer in effect casts off all the worship of God, of which prayer is the principal duty. Now, what a miserable saint is he who is no worshiper of God! He that casts off the worship of God in effect casts off God Himself: he refuses to own Him or to be conversant with Him as his God. For the way in which men own God and are conversant with Him as their God is by worshiping Him. How can you expect to dwell with God forever if you so neglect and forsake Him here? This your practice shows, that you place not your happiness in God, in nearness to Him and communion with Him. He who refuses to visit and converse with a friend and who in a great measure forsakes him when he is abundantly invited and importuned to come, plainly shows that he places not his happiness in the company and conversation of that friend. Now, if this be the case with you respecting God, then how can you expect to have it for your happiness to all eternity, to be with God and to enjoy holy communion with Him?

From "Hypocrites Deficient in the Duty of Prayer," p. 75

OUR HIGHEST END

But lay up for yourselves treasures in heaven, where neither moth nor rust doth corrupt, and where thieves do not break through nor steal.
— MATTHEW 6:20

Heaven is that place alone where our highest end, and highest good, is to be obtained. God hath made us for Himself. "Of him, and through him, and to him, are all things" (Rom. 11:36). Therefore, then, do we attain to our highest end when we are brought to God: but that is by being brought to heaven; for that is God's throne, the place of His special presence. There is but a very imperfect union with God to be had in this world, a very imperfect knowledge of Him in the midst of much darkness; a very imperfect conformity to God, mingled with abundance of estrangement. Here we can serve and glorify God but in a very imperfect manner; our service being mingled with sin, which dishonors God. But, when we get to heaven (if ever that be), we shall be brought to a perfect union with God and have more clear views of Him. There we shall be fully conformed to God, without any remaining sin, for "we shall see him as he is" (1 John 3:2). There we shall serve God perfectly, and glorify Him in an exalted manner, even to the utmost of the powers and capacity of our nature. Then we shall perfectly give up ourselves to God; our hearts will be pure and holy offerings, presented in a flame of divine love. God is the highest good of the reasonable creature, and the enjoyment of Him is the only happiness with which our souls can be satisfied. To go to heaven, fully to enjoy God, is infinitely better than the most pleasant accommodations here. Fathers and mothers, husbands, wives, children, or the company of earthly friends are but shadows, but the enjoyment of God is the substance. These are but scattered beams, but God is the sun. These are but streams, but God is the fountain. These are but drops, but God is the ocean.

§ From "The Christian Pilgrim, or the True Christian's Life a Journey toward Heaven," p. 244

HUMILITY PRODUCES PRAISE

*Not unto us, O LORD, not unto us, but unto thy name give
glory, for thy mercy, and for thy truth's sake.*
— PSALM 115:1

In order to a person's being rightly disposed to the work of praise, he must
be an humble person. A proud person is for assuming all praise to himself
and is not disposed to ascribe it to God. It is humility only that will enable
us to say from the heart, "Not unto us, not unto us, O LORD, but unto thy
name give glory" (Ps. 115:1). The humble person admires the goodness and
grace of God to him. He sees more how wonderful it is that God should take
such notice of him and show such kindness to him who is so much below
His notice. Now the saints in heaven have this grace of humility perfected
in them. They do as much excel the saints on earth in humility as in other
graces. Though they are so much above the saints on earth in holiness and in
their exalted state, yet they are vastly more humble than the saints on earth
are. They are as much lower in humility as they are higher in honor and happiness. And the reason of it is that they know more of God. They see more
of His greatness and infinite highness and therefore are so much the more
sensible of their own comparative nothingness. They are the more sensible of
the infinite difference there is between God and them and therefore are more
sensible how wonderful it is that God should take so much notice of them,
to have such communion with them and give them such a full enjoyment of
Him. They are far more sensible what unworthy creatures they have been,
that God should bestow such mercies upon them than the saints on earth.
They have a greater sight of the evil of sin.

⚘ From "Praise, One of the Chief Employments of Heaven," p. 915

WITHOUT GOD

For when we were yet without strength, in due time Christ died for the ungodly.

— ROMANS 5:6

The relative state of those who are in an unconverted condition is dreadful. They are without God in the world. They have no interest or part in God: He is not their God. He hath declared He will not be their God (see Hos. 1:9). God and believers have a mutual covenant relation and right to each other. They are His people, and He is their God. But He is not the covenant God of those who are in an unconverted state. There is a great alienation and estrangement between God and the wicked: He is not their Father and portion. They have nothing to challenge of God; they have no right to any one of His attributes. The believer can challenge a right in the power of God, in His wisdom and holiness, His grace and love. All are made over to him to be for his benefit. But the unconverted can claim no right in any of God's perfections. They have no God to protect and defend them in this evil world, to defend them from sin or from Satan or any evil. They have no God to guide and direct them in any doubts or difficulties, to comfort and support their minds under afflictions. They are without God in all their affairs, in all the business they undertake, in their family affairs, and in their personal affairs, in their outward concerns, and in the concerns of their souls.

§ From "Natural Men in a Dreadful Condition," p. 819

LOVE ONE ANOTHER

Finally, be ye all of one mind, having compassion one of another;
love as brethren, be pitiful, be courteous.
— 1 PETER 3:8

Christians ought to bear with one another. They are the children of the same universal church of God; they are all the children of Abraham; they are the seed of Jesus Christ; they are the offspring of God. They are all of one family and should therefore love one another as family. It is very unbecoming those who are God's offspring to entertain a spirit of hatred and ill will toward one another. It is very unbecoming to be backward in helping and assisting one another and supplying each other's wants—much more, to contrive and seek one another's hurt, to be revengeful one toward another. Let Christians take heed so to walk that they may not dishonor their pedigree. You are of a very honorable race, more honorable by far than if you were the offspring of kings and had royal blood in your veins. You are a heavenly offspring, the seed of Jesus Christ, the children of God. They that are of noble race value themselves highly upon the honor of their families, to dwell on their titles, their coats of arms, and their ensigns of honor and to recount the exploits of their illustrious forefathers. How much more careful should you be of the honor of your descent: that you in nothing behave yourself unworthy of the great God, the eternal and omnipotent King of heaven and earth, whose offspring you are!

⬧ From "Christians a Chosen Generation, a Royal Priesthood, a Holy Nation, a Peculiar People," p. 940

MERCY IN A SAVIOR

For we ourselves also were sometimes foolish, disobedient, deceived, serving divers lusts and pleasures, living in malice and envy, hateful, and hating one another. But after that the kindness and love of God our Saviour toward man appeared.

— TITUS 3:3–4

Until the sinner is convinced of his sin and misery, he is not prepared to receive the redeeming mercy and grace of God. He does not see his need of a mediator to God until he sees his sin and misery. All God's mercy to sinners is through a Savior. The redeeming mercy and grace of God is mercy and grace in Christ. When God discovers His mercy to the soul, He will discover it as mercy in a Savior. It is His will that the mercy should be received as in and through a Savior, with a full consciousness of its being through His righteousness and satisfaction. It is the will of God that as all the spiritual comforts that His people receive are in and through Christ; so they should be sensible that they receive them through Christ and that they can receive them in no other way. It is the will of God that His people should have their eyes directed to Christ and should depend upon Him for mercy and favor. Since God glorified His Son as mediator, and as the glory of man's salvation belongs to Christ, so it is the will of God that all the people of Christ, all who are saved by Him, should receive their salvation as of Him and should attribute the glory of it to Him. None who will not give the glory of salvation to Christ should have the benefit of it. Upon this account God insists, and it is absolutely necessary, that a sinner's conviction of his sin, and misery, and helplessness in himself should precede or accompany the revelation of the redeeming love and grace of God.

§ From "God Makes Men Sensible of Their Misery before He Reveals His Mercy and Love," p. 836

THE GLORY OF GOD'S SOVEREIGNTY

I am the LORD: that is my name: and my glory will I not give to another, neither my praise to graven images. —ISAIAH 42:8

God's design in the creation was to glorify Himself, or to make a discovery of the essential glory of His nature. It was fit that infinite glory should shine forth, and it was God's original design to make a manifestation of His glory, as it is. It was His design to make a true manifestation of His glory, such as should represent every attribute. If God glorified one attribute and not another, such manifestation of His glory would be defective, and the representation would not be complete. If all God's attributes are not manifested, the glory of none of them is manifested as it is; for the divine attributes reflect glory on one another. The glory of God's mercy does not appear as it is unless it is manifested as a just mercy, or as a mercy consistent with justice. And so with respect to God's sovereignty, it reflects glory on all His other attributes. It is part of the glory of God's mercy that it is sovereign mercy. So all the attributes of God reflect glory on one another. The glory of God eminently appears in His absolute sovereignty over all creatures, great and small. If the glory of a prince be his power and dominion, then the glory of God is His absolute sovereignty. Herein appear God's infinite greatness and highness above all creatures. Therefore it is the will of God to manifest His sovereignty. And His sovereignty, like His other attributes, is manifested in the exercises of it. He glorifies His power in the exercise of power. He glorifies His mercy in the exercise of mercy. So He glorifies His sovereignty in the exercise of sovereignty.

⸹ From "God's Sovereignty in the Salvation of Men," p. 853

MAN IS MADE HOLY

For as by one man's disobedience many were made sinners, so by the obedience of one shall many be made righteous.

— ROMANS 5:19

Man hath now a greater dependence on the grace of God than he had before the fall. He depends on the free goodness of God for much more than he did then. Then, he depended on God's goodness for conferring the reward of perfect obedience; for God was not obliged to promise and bestow that reward. Now we are dependent on the grace of God for much more; we stand in need of grace, not only to bestow glory upon us but to deliver us from hell and eternal wrath. Under the first covenant we depended on God's goodness to give us the reward of righteousness, and so we do now. But we stand in need of God's free and sovereign grace to give us that righteousness, to pardon our sin, and release us from the guilt and infinite demerit of it. And as we are dependent on the goodness of God for more now than under the first covenant, so we are dependent on a much greater, more free and wonderful goodness. We are now more dependent on God's arbitrary and sovereign good pleasure. We were in our first estate dependent on God for holiness. We had our original righteousness from Him, but then holiness was not bestowed in such a way of sovereign good pleasure as it is now. Man was created holy. But now when fallen man is made holy, it is from mere and arbitrary grace. We are more apparently dependent on God for holiness, because we are first sinful and utterly polluted, and afterward holy.

§ From "God Glorified in Man's Dependence," p. 4

BREAKING THROUGH DIFFICULTIES

If by any means I might attain unto the resurrection of the dead.
— PHILIPPIANS 3:11

By pressing into the kingdom of God is denoted a breaking through of opposition and difficulties. There is in the expression a plain intimation of difficulty. If there were no opposition, but the way was all clear and open, there would be no need of pressing to get along. They, therefore, that are pressing into the kingdom of God, go on with such engagedness that they break through the difficulties that are in the way. They are so set for salvation that those things by which others are discouraged and stopped and turned back do not stop them. They press through them. Persons ought to be so resolved for heaven that, if by any means they can obtain, they will obtain. Whether those means are difficult or easy, cross or agreeable, if they are requisite means of salvation, they should be complied with. When anything is presented to be done, the question should not be, is it easy or hard? Is it agreeable to my carnal inclinations or interest, or against them? But is it a required means of my obtaining an interest in Jesus Christ and eternal salvation? Thus the apostle Paul says in Philippians 3:11, "If by any means I might attain unto the resurrection of the dead." He tells us there in the context what difficulties he broke through, that he suffered the loss of all things and was willingly made conformable even to Christ's death, though that was attended with such extreme torment and ignominy. He that is pressing into the kingdom of God commonly finds many things in the way that are against the grain, but he is not stopped by the cross that lies before him, but takes it up and carries it. Everything that is found to be a weight that hinders him in running this race he casts from him, though it be a weight of gold or pearls; yea, if it be a right hand or foot that offends him, he will cut them off and will not stick at plucking out a right eye with his own hands.

§ From "Pressing into the Kingdom of God," p. 656

THE CONDESCENSION OF CHRIST

Who hath ascended up into heaven, or descended? who hath
gathered the wind in his fists? who hath bound the waters in a
garment? who hath established all the ends of the earth? what
is his name, and what is his son's name, if thou canst tell?

— PROVERBS 30:4

There do meet in Jesus Christ infinite highness and infinite condescension. Christ, as He is God, is infinitely great and high above all. He is higher than the kings of the earth, for He is King of kings, and Lord of lords. He is higher than the heavens, and higher than the highest angels of heaven. So great is He, that all men, all kings and princes, are as worms of the dust before Him. All nations are as the drop of the bucket and as the light dust of the balance; yea, angels themselves are as nothing before Him. He is so high that He is infinitely above any need of us, above our reach that we cannot be profitable to Him, and above our conceptions that we cannot comprehend Him. Our understandings, if we stretch them never so far, cannot reach up to His divine glory. Christ is the creator and great possessor of heaven and earth. He is sovereign Lord of all. He rules over the whole universe and does whatsoever pleaseth Him. His knowledge is without bound. His wisdom is perfect, and what none can circumvent. His power is infinite, and none can resist Him. His riches are immense and inexhaustible. His majesty is infinitely awful. And yet He is one of infinite condescension. None are so low or inferior, but Christ's condescension is sufficient to take a gracious notice of them. He condescends not only to the angels, humbling Himself to behold the things that are done in heaven, but He also condescends to such poor creatures as men, and that not only so as to take notice of princes and great men, but of those that are of meanest rank and degree, "the poor of this world" (James 2:5). Such as are commonly despised by their fellow creatures, Christ does not despise. Christ condescends to take notice of beggars (see Luke 16:22) and people of the most despised nations.

ᛏ From "The Excellency of Jesus Christ," p. 680

LOOKING BACK

Remember Lot's wife.
—LUKE 17:32

There is nothing in Sodom that is worth looking back upon. All the enjoyments of Sodom will soon perish in the common destruction; all will be burnt up. Surely it is not worth the while to look back on things that are perishing and consuming in the flames, as it is with all the enjoyments of sin. They are all appointed to the fire. Therefore it is foolish for any who are fleeing out of Sodom to hanker any more after them. For when they are burnt up, what good can they do? And is it worth the while for us to return back for the sake of a moment's enjoyment of them, before they are burnt, and so expose ourselves to be burnt up with them? Lot's wife looked back because she remembered the pleasant things that she left in Sodom. She hankered after them. She could not help but look back with a wishful eye upon the city where she had lived in such ease and pleasure. Sodom was a place of great outward plenty. They ate the fat and drank the sweet. The soil about Sodom was exceedingly fruitful. Here Lot and his wife lived plentifully; and it was a place where the inhabitants wallowed in carnal pleasures and delights. But however much it abounded in these things, what were they worth now, when the city was burning? Lot's wife was very foolish in lingering in her escape for the sake of things that were all on fire. So the enjoyments, the profits and pleasures of sin, all have the wrath and curse of God on them. Brimstone is scattered on them. Hell-fire is ready to kindle on them. It is not therefore worthwhile for any person to look back after such things.

§ From "The Folly of Looking Back in Fleeing Out of Sodom," p. 65

CHRIST, OVER ALL

For he must reign, until he hath put all enemies under his feet.
The last enemy that shall be destroyed is death.

— 1 CORINTHIANS 15:25–26

Jesus Christ, in the work of redemption, appears gloriously above all evils. It was not the will of the infinitely wise and holy Governor of the world that things should remain in this confusion, this reign of evil, which had prevailed and exalted itself to such a height. But He had a design of subduing it, and delivering an elect part of the world from it, and exalting them to the possession of the greatest good and to reign in the highest glory, out of a state of subjection to all these evils. He chose His Son as the person most fit for an undertaking that was infinitely too great for any mere creature. And He has undertaken the work of our redemption. And though these evils are so many and so great and have prevailed to such a degree and have risen to such a height and have been, as it were, all combined together, yet wherein they have exalted themselves, Christ, in the work of redemption, appears above them. He has gloriously prevailed against them all, and brings them under His feet and rides forth, in the chariots of salvation, over their heads, or leading them in triumph at His chariot wheels. He appears in this work infinitely higher and mightier than they and sufficient to carry His people above them and utterly to destroy them all. Christ appears gloriously above all evil in what He did to procure redemption for us in His state of humiliation, by the righteousness He wrought out, and by the atonement He made for sin. The evils mentioned never seemed so much to prevail against Him as in His sufferings; but in them, the foundation was laid for their overthrow.

§ From "Christ Exalted," p. 215

PASTOR AND PEOPLE

Thy land shall be married. For as a young man marrieth a virgin, so shall thy sons marry thee: and as the bridegroom rejoiceth over the bride, so shall thy God rejoice over thee.

—ISAIAH 62:4–5

A faithful minister that is in a Christian manner united to a Christian people as their pastor has his heart united to them in the most ardent and tender affection. And they, on the other hand, have their hearts united to him, esteeming him very highly in love for his work's sake, and receiving him with honor and reverence, and willingly subjecting themselves to him and committing themselves to his care, as being under Christ their head and guide. Such a pastor and people are like a young man and virgin united in marriage, with respect to the purity of their regard one to another. The young man gives himself to his bride in purity, as undebauched by meretricious embraces. And she also presents herself to him a chaste virgin. So, in such a union of a minister and people as we are speaking of, the parties united are pure and holy in their affection and regard one to another. The minister's heart is united to the people, not for filthy lucre or any worldly advantage, but with a pure benevolence to them and desire of their spiritual welfare and prosperity and complacence in them as the children of God and followers of Christ Jesus. And, on the other hand, the people love and honor him with a holy affection and esteem. Not merely as having their admiration raised and their carnal affection moved by having their curiosity and other fleshly principles gratified by a florid eloquence and the excellency of speech and man's wisdom, but receiving him as the messenger of the Lord of Hosts, coming to them on a divine and infinitely important errand, and with those holy qualifications that resemble the virtues of the Lamb of God.

♭ From "The Church's Marriage to Her Sons, and to Her God," pp. 19–20

GROW IN KNOWLEDGE

*For when for the time ye ought to be teachers, ye have need
that one teach you again which be the first principles of the
oracles of God; and are become such as have need of milk, and
not of strong meat.*
— HEBREWS 5:12

Every Christian should make a business of endeavoring to grow in knowledge in divinity. This is indeed esteemed the business of divines and ministers; it is commonly thought to be their work, by the study of the Scriptures and other instructive books, to gain knowledge. Most seem to think that it may be left to them, as what belongs not to others. But if the apostle had entertained this notion, he would never have blamed the Christian Hebrews for not having acquired knowledge enough to be teachers. Or, if he had thought that this concerned Christians in general only as a thing by the by, and that their time should not in a considerable measure be taken up with this business, he never would have so much blamed them, that their proficiency in knowledge had not been answerable to the time that they had had to learn. There is no other way by which any means of grace whatsoever can be of any benefit but by knowledge. All teaching is in vain, without learning. Therefore, the preaching of the gospel would be wholly to no purpose if it conveyed no knowledge to the mind. There is an order of men that Christ has appointed on purpose to be teachers in His church; but they teach in vain if no knowledge in these things is gained by their teaching. It is impossible that their teaching and preaching should be a mean of grace, or of any good in the hearts of their hearers, any otherwise than by knowledge imparted to the understanding.

§ From "Christian Knowledge," p. 157

LOVE YOUR NEIGHBOR

Bear ye one another's burdens, and so fulfill the law of Christ.
— GALATIANS 6:2

How unsuitable is it for us, who live only by kindness, to be unkind! What would have become of us if Christ had been so saving of His blood, and loath to bestow it, as many men are of their money or goods? Or if He had been as ready to excuse Himself from dying for us, as men commonly are to excuse themselves from charity to their neighbor? If Christ would have made objections of such things, as men commonly object to performing deeds of charity to their neighbor, He would have found enough of them. Besides, Christ, by His redemption, has brought us into more near relations one to another, hath made us children of God, children in the same family. We are all brethren, having God for our common Father, which is much more than to be brethren in any other family. He hath made us all one body. Therefore we ought to be united, and subserve one another's good, and bear one another's burdens, as is the case with the members of the same natural body. If one of the members suffers, all the other members bear the burden with it. If one member be diseased or wounded, the other members of the body will minister to it and help it. So surely it should be in the body of Christ. Apply these things to yourselves, and inquire whether you do not lie under guilt on account of the neglect of this duty, in withholding that charity that God requires of you toward the needy. You have often been put upon examining yourselves to see whether you do not live in some way displeasing to God. Perhaps at such times it never came into your minds, to know whether you do not lie under guilt on this account. This neglect certainly brings guilt upon the soul in the sight of God.

§ From "Christian Charity," p. 165

GOD IS ALL

He is the Rock. His work is perfect: all his ways are judgment:
a God of truth and without iniquity, just and right is he.
— DEUTERONOMY 32:4 (SONG OF MOSES)

Moses begins this song by taking notice of the greatness and majesty of the God of Israel, which he had mentioned more generally in the foregoing verse, and describes, particularly in this, wherein he takes notice of the power, holiness, faithfulness, and justice of God. The expressions are such that several attributes are implied. First, God is a rock, which implies His power. A rock is a place of strength, a place of defense. He who dwells upon a high and steep rock is not easily come at by his enemy. Hereby also is signified the faithfulness of God, since one may safely trust in a strong rock, being able to defend and preserve him as a fortress that will not fail him. So we may safely trust in God. Second, Moses says that His work is perfect, which seems principally to respect the holiness of His works. The word "perfect" signifies "holy" oftentimes in Scripture, perfect so that it cannot be blamed. This seems more evident by the following words: "all his ways are judgment: a God of truth and without iniquity, just and right is he" (Deut. 32:4). These expressions are much of the same significance: the more strongly to signify the justice and righteousness of God. In ourselves we distinguish between ourselves and souls and the disposition or inclination of our souls; the one is a substance, the other a property of that substance. But there is no distinction in God of substance and property. This is opposite to the simplicity of God's nature; but all that is in God is God. God is all thought, and He is all love. God is all joy, justice, and mercy. He is an infinitely wise justice. He is all comprehensive, simple, and unchangeable.

᭥ From "God Is a Just and Righteous God," pp. 1–3

TWO OPINIONS

And Elijah came unto all the people, and said, How long halt ye between two opinions? If the LORD *be God, follow him: but if Baal, then follow him. And the people answered him not a word.*

— 1 KINGS 18:21

It is the manner of God, before He bestows any signal mercy on the people, first to prepare them for it. Before He removes any awful judgments that He hath brought upon them for their sins, first to cause them to forsake those sins that procured those judgments. We have an instance of this in the context. It was a time of sore famine in Israel. There had been neither rain nor dew for the space of three years and six months. This famine was brought upon the land for their idolatry, but God was now about to remove this judgment. Therefore, to prepare them for it, He sends Elijah to convince them of the folly of idolatry and to bring them to repentance for it. In order to do this, Elijah, by the command of the Lord, shows himself to Ahab and directs Ahab to send and gather all Israel, the prophets of Baal (450), and the prophets of the groves that ate at Jezebel's table (400) at Mount Carmel, that they might determine the matter and bring the controversy to an issue: whether Jehovah or Baal were God. To this end, Elijah proposes that each should take a bullock—that he should take one, and the prophets of Baal another—and each should cut his bullock to pieces, lay it on the wood, and put no fire under it: the God who should answer by fire should be concluded to be God. There were two opinions upon which the people wavered: God or Baal. Many who professed to believe in the true God were yet very cold and indifferent, and many were wavering and unsettled. They saw that the king and queen were for Baal, and Baal's party was the prevailing party. But their forefathers had been for the Lord, and they knew not which were right. Thus they halted between two opinions: "How long halt ye between two opinions? If the LORD be God, follow him; but if Baal, then follow him" (1 Kings 18:21), which implies that they ought to determine one way or the other.

§ From "The Unreasonableness of Indetermination in Religion," p. 57

HOPE AND COMFORT

And I will give her vineyards from thence, and the valley of Achor for a door of hope: and she shall sing there, as in the days of her youth, and as in the day when she came up out of the land of Egypt.

—HOSEA 2:15

Souls are wont to be brought into trouble before God bestows true hope and comfort. The corrupt hearts of men naturally incline to stupidity and senselessness before God comes with the awakening influences of His Spirit. They are quiet and secure. They have no true comfort and hope, and yet they are quiet; they are at ease. They are in miserable slavery and yet seek not a remedy. They say, as the children of Israel did in Egypt to Moses, "Let us alone, that we may serve the Egyptians" (Ex. 14:12). But if God has a design of mercy to them, it is His manner before He bestows true hope and comfort on them to bring them into trouble, to distress them and spoil their ease and false quietness and to rouse them out of their old resting and sleeping places and to bring them into a wilderness. They are brought into great trouble and distress so that they can take no comfort in those things in which they used to take comfort. Their hearts are pinched and stung, and they can find no ease in anything. They have, as it were, an arrow sticking fast in them that causes grievous and continual pain—an arrow they cannot shake off or pull out. The pain and anguish of it drinks up their spirit. Their worldly enjoyments were a sufficient good before, but they are not now. They wander about with wounded hearts, seeking rest and finding none, like one wandering in a dry and parched wilderness under the burning, scorching heat of the sun, seeking for some shadow where he may sit down and rest, but finding none. They are like the children of Israel while Achor troubled them; they go forth against their enemies, and they are smitten down and flee before them.

◈ From "Hope and Comfort Usually Follow Genuine Humiliation and Repentance," p. 839

THE HONOR OF GOD VINDICATED

*I say unto you, That every idle word that men shall speak, they
shall give account thereof in the day of judgment.*
— MATTHEW 12:36

Impenitent sinners, while in this world, hear how dreadful hell is, but they will not believe that it is as dreadful as ministers represent. They cannot think that they shall, to all eternity, suffer such exquisite and horrible torments. But they will be taught and convinced that the representations given of those torments, which are agreeable with the Word of God, are indeed as dreadful as declared. Since God has undertaken to deal with sinners and to rectify their judgments in these matters, He will do it thoroughly. For His work is perfect, and when He undertakes to do things, He does not do them half way. Therefore, before He is done with sinners, He will convince them effectually, so that they shall never be in danger of relapsing into their former errors. He will convince them of their folly and stupidity in entertaining such notions as they now entertain. God has undertaken to deal with obstinate unbelievers. They carry things on in great confusion, but we need not to be dismayed at it: let us wait, and we will see that God will rectify things. The honor of God will in due time be vindicated, and sinners will be subdued and convicted and shall give an account. There is no sin, not so much as an idle word that they shall speak, but they must give an account of it (see Matt. 12:36). Their sins must be fully balanced and recompensed, and satisfaction obtained. Because judgment against their evil works is not speedily executed, their hearts are fully set in them to do evil. Yet, God is a righteous judge, and He will see that judgment is executed in due time.

From "The Future Punishment of the Wicked Unavoidable and Intolerable," p. 79

THE FALL OF MAN

The publican, standing afar off, would not lift up so much as his eyes unto heaven, but smote upon his breast, saying, God be merciful to me a sinner.
— LUKE 18:13

God's sovereign power and right is such that He is under no obligation to keep men from sinning but may, in His providence, permit and leave them to sin. He is not obliged to keep either angels or men from falling. It is unreasonable to suppose that God should be obliged, if He makes a reasonable creature capable of knowing His will and receiving a law from Him and being subject to His moral government at the same time, to make it impossible for him to sin or break His law. For, if God be obliged to this, it destroys all use of any commands, laws, promises, or threatenings, and the very notion of any moral government of God over those reasonable creatures. To what purpose would it be for God to give such and such laws, and declare His holy will to a creature, and annex promises and threatenings to move him to his duty, and make him careful to perform it, if the creature at the same time has this to think of: that God is obliged to make it impossible for him to break His laws? How can God's threatenings move to care or watchfulness, when, at the same time, God is obliged to render it impossible that he should be exposed to the threatenings? Or, to what purpose is it for God to give a law at all? For, according to this supposition, it is God, and not the creature, that is under law. It is the lawgiver's care, and not the subject's, to see that His law is obeyed; and this care is what the lawgiver is absolutely obliged to! If God be obliged never to permit a creature to fall, there is an end of all divine laws, or government, or authority of God over the creature; there can be no manner of use of these things.

§ From "The Justice of God in the Damnation of Sinners," p. 670

OUR EXCEEDING SINFULNESS

When Simon Peter saw it, he fell down at Jesus' knees, saying,
Depart from me; for I am a sinful man, O Lord. —LUKE 5:8

Seek, that you may be brought to lie at God's feet in a sense of your own exceeding sinfulness. Seek earnestly, that you may have such a sight yourself: what an exceedingly sinful creature you are, what a wicked heart you have, and how dreadfully you have provoked God to anger; that you may see that God would be most just if He should never have any mercy upon you. Labor, that all quarreling about God's dispensations toward sinners may be wholly subdued; that your heart may be abased and brought down to the dust before God; that you may see yourself in the hands of God; and that you can challenge nothing of God, but that God and His throne are blameless in the eternal damnation of sinners and would be in your damnation. Seek, that you may be brought off from all high opinion of your own worth, all trust in your own righteousness, and to see that all you do in religion is so polluted and defiled that it is utterly unworthy of God's acceptance and that you commit sin enough in your best duties to condemn you forever. Seek, that you may come to see that God is sovereign, that He is the potter and you the clay, and that His grace is His own and He may bestow it on whom He will, and that He might justly refuse to show you mercy. Seek, that you may be sensible that God is sovereign as to the objects of His grace and also as to the time and manner of bestowing it. Seek to God and wait upon Him as a sovereign God.

⟋ From "Natural Men in a Dreadful Condition," p. 829

EXAMINE YOURSELVES

Examine yourselves, whether ye be in the faith; prove your own selves. Know ye not your own selves, how that Jesus Christ is in you, except ye be reprobates?
— 2 CORINTHIANS 13:5

We ought to be much concerned to know whether we do not live in a state of sin. All unregenerate men live in sin. We are born under the power and dominion of sin, are sold under sin; every unconverted sinner is a devoted servant to sin and Satan. We should look upon it as of the greatest importance to us to know in what state we are, whether we ever had any change made in our hearts from sin to holiness or whether we be not still in the gall of bitterness and bond of iniquity; whether ever sin were truly mortified in us; whether we do not live in the sin of unbelief, and in the rejection of the Savior. This is what the apostle insists upon with the Corinthians, "Examine yourselves, whether ye be in the faith; prove your own selves. Know ye not your own selves, how that Jesus Christ is in you, except ye be reprobates?" (2 Cor. 13:5). Those who entertain the opinion and hope of themselves, that they are godly, should take great care to see that their foundation be right. Those that are in doubt should not give themselves rest until the matter be resolved. Every unconverted person lives in a sinful way. He not only lives in a particular evil practice, but the whole course of his life is sinful. The imagination of the thoughts of his heart is only evil continually. He not only doth evil, but he doth no good: "They are altogether become filthy: there is none that doeth good, no, not one" (Ps. 14:3).

§ From "Christian Cautions, or the Necessity of Self-Examination," p. 174

THE THIRSTY SOUL

I stretch forth my hands unto thee: my soul thirsteth after thee, as a thirsty land.

— PSALM 143:6

There is provision in Christ for the satisfaction and full contentment of the needy and thirsty soul. This is the sense of those words in the text, "as rivers of water in a dry place" (Isa. 32:2), in a dry and parched wilderness, where there is a great want of water and where travelers are ready to be destroyed with thirst. Such was that wilderness in which the children of Israel wandered. This comparison is used elsewhere in the Scriptures: "O God, thou art my God; early will I seek thee: my soul thirsteth for thee, my flesh longeth for thee in a dry and thirsty land, where no water is" (Ps. 63:1); "I stretch forth my hands unto thee: my soul thirsteth after thee, as a thirsty land" (Ps. 143:6). Those who travel in such a land, who wander in such a wilderness, are in extreme need of water; they are ready to perish for the want of it; and thus they have a great thirst and longing for it. It is said that Christ is a river of water, because there is such a fullness in Him and so plentiful a provision for the satisfaction of the needy and longing soul. When one is extremely thirsty, though it is not a small draught of water that will satisfy him, yet, when he comes to a river he finds a fullness; there he may drink full draughts. Christ is like a river in that He has a sufficiency not just for one thirsty soul: by supplying him the fountain is not lessened; there is not the less afforded to those who come afterward. A thirsty man does not sensibly lessen a river by quenching his thirst.

§ From "Safety, Fullness, and Sweet Refreshment, to Be Found in Christ," pp. 931–32

DESIRE COMMUNION WITH CHRIST

*If any man love not the Lord Jesus Christ, let him be Anath-
ema Maranatha.*
— 1 CORINTHIANS 16:22

When one person has true love for another, he desires communion with him
for its own sake; to be with him, to see him, and to converse with him will
be desired and prized for the sake of the sweetness and pleasantness of their
conversation. Whether he expects any other benefit by it or not, whether he
thinks it is any honor to him or not, yet he will desire his company. So they
who truly love Christ will desire His company for its own sake, just to have
the communication of His Spirit. To see Him spiritually in this world, to see
Him face-to-face in the world to come and to be with Him and to dwell in
His presence forever, these things will appear in themselves as exceedingly
desirable. If a Christian were to live in this world always, he would desire
communion with Christ; if he were to live in great prosperity in this world,
he would desire the communion of Christ; if he were to live in a dungeon,
he would desire communion with Christ; and if he went to another world,
his desire there would be to enjoy Christ. Those who truly love Jesus Christ
love His glory; they seek and prize it; they are jealous over it. It rejoices their
hearts when any honor is done to the name of Christ, and they lay themselves
out so that He may be honored and glorified, whether the honor of Christ is
in any way to his advantage or not.

§ From "It Is Crime Enough to Render Any Man a Cursed Person
Not to Love Jesus Christ," p. 34

JUSTIFIED BY FAITH

Wherefore the law was our schoolmaster to bring us unto Christ, that we might be justified by faith.

—GALATIANS 3:24

God doth, in the sentence of justification, pronounce a man perfectly righteous, or else he would need a further justification after he is justified. His sins being removed by Christ's atonement is not sufficient for his justification; for justifying a man, as has been already shown, is not merely pronouncing him innocent or without guilt, but standing right with regard to the rule that he is under and righteous unto life. But this, according to the established rule of nature, reason, and divine appointment, is a positive, perfect righteousness. As there is the same need that Christ's obedience should be reckoned to our account as that His atonement should, so there is the same reason why it should. As, if Adam had persevered, and finished his course of obedience, we should have received the benefit of his obedience, so now we have the mischief of his disobedience. In like manner there is reason that we should receive the benefit of the second Adam's obedience, as of His atonement of our disobedience. Believers are represented in Scripture as being so in Christ that they are legally one, or accepted as one, by the Supreme Judge: Christ has assumed our nature and has so assumed all in that nature that belongs to Him into such a union with Himself that He is become our head and has taken us to be His members. Therefore, what Christ has done in our nature, whereby He did honor to the law and authority of God by His acts as well as the reparation to the honor of the law by His sufferings, is reckoned to the believer's account, so the believer should be made happy, because it was so well and worthily done by his Head, as well as freed from being miserable, because He has suffered for our ill and unworthy doing.

§ From "Justification by Faith Alone," p. 637

DIFFERENCE FROM OTHER MEN

And if ye salute your brethren only, what do ye more than others? do not even the publicans so?
— MATTHEW 5:47

Consider what a vast difference has God made between you and other men, how vastly different your relative state is from theirs, how much more has God done for you than for them. Seek therefore those things that are above, where God is. Will it not be a shame if one who is entitled to such glory conducts no better than a child of the devil? Consider it seriously; and let it not be asked with reference to you (see Matt. 5:47). What do you more than others? Other men love those that love them; other men do good to those that do good to them. Walk worthy of the vocation wherewith ye are called, and let it appear that you are of a spirit more excellent than your neighbor; manifest more love, and more meekness, and more humility, with all lowliness and meekness, with longsuffering, forbearing one another in love. Walk worthy of the Lord to all pleasing, strengthened with all might according to His glorious power unto all patience and longsuffering. Put ye on as the elect of God, holy and beloved, bowels of mercies, kindness, gentleness of mind, meekness, longsuffering, forbearing one another, forgiving one another; and let your light so shine before men, that they, seeing your good works, may glorify your Father who is in heaven. Seeing God has given you so much, God and men may well expect of you that you should be greatly distinguished in your life from other men.

§ From "The Portion of the Righteous," pp. 904–5

INFINITE WORTHINESS

But unto them which are called, both Jews and Greeks, Christ the power of God, and the wisdom of God.

—1 CORINTHIANS 1:24

Christ is a great and glorious person, a person of infinite worthiness. On this account He is infinitely esteemed and loved of the Father and is continually adored by the angels. But unbelievers have no esteem at all for Him on that account. They have no value for Him on account of His being the Son of God. He is not set the higher in their esteem on the account of His standing in so near and honorable a relation to God the Father. He is not valued at all the more for His being a divine person. By His having the divine nature, He is infinitely exalted above all created beings, but He is not at all exalted by it in their esteem. They set nothing by His infinite majesty; His glorious brightness and greatness excite not any true respect or reverence in them. Christ is the Holy One of God: He is so holy that the heavens are not pure in His sight. He is possessed of all that holiness that is the infinite beauty and loveliness of the divine nature; but an unbeliever sets nothing by the holiness of Christ. Christ is the wisdom of God and the power of God (see 1 Cor. 1:24); but an unbeliever sets nothing by His power and wisdom. The Lord Jesus Christ is full of grace and mercy: the mercy and love of God appear nowhere else so brightly and gloriously as they do in the face of Jesus Christ.

§ From "Unbelievers Condemn the Glory and Excellency of Christ," p. 61

THE PLEASURE OF THE SOUL

O the depth of the riches both of the wisdom and knowledge of God! how unsearchable are his judgments, and his ways past finding out!
— ROMANS 11:33

The pleasure that the soul has in seeing God is not only its delight, but it is, at the same time, its highest perfection and excellency. Man's true happiness is his perfection and true excellency. When any reasonable creature finds that his excellency and his joy are the same thing, then he is come to right and real happiness, and not before. If a man enjoys any kind of pleasure and lives in it—however much he may be taken with what he enjoys—yet if he be not the more excellent for his pleasures, it is a certain sign that he is not a truly happy man. There are many pleasures that men are wont violently to pursue, which are no part of their dignity or perfection, but that, on the contrary, debase the man and make him vile. Instead of rendering the mind beautiful and lovely, they only serve to pollute it; instead of exalting its nature, they make it more akin to that of beasts. But it is quite the contrary with the pleasure that is to be enjoyed in seeing God. To see God is the highest honor and dignity that the human nature can attain; that intellectual beholding of Him is itself the highest excellency of the understanding. The great cart of the excellency of man is his knowledge and understanding, but the knowledge of God is the most excellent and noble kind of knowledge.

⸋ From "The Pure in Heart Blessed," p. 907

EVERY DAY IS PRECIOUS

Walk in wisdom toward them that are without, redeeming the time.

— COLOSSIANS 4:5

Every day that you have enjoyed has been precious; yea, your moments have been precious. But have you not wasted your precious moments, your precious days, yea, your precious years? If you should reckon up how many days you have lived, what a sum would there be! And how precious hath every one of those days been! Consider, therefore: What have you done with them? What is become of them all? What can you show of any improvement made, or good done, or benefit obtained, answerable to all this time that you have lived? When you look back and search, do you not find this past time of your lives in a great measure empty, having not been filled up with any good improvement? And if God, who hath given you your time, should now call you to an account, what account could you give to Him? How much may be done in a year! How much good is there opportunity to do in such a space of time! How much service may persons do for God, and how much for their own souls, if to their utmost they improve it! How much may be done in a day! But what have you done in so many days and years that you have lived? What have you done with the whole time of your youth, you that are past your youth? What is become of all that precious season of life? Hath it not all been in vain to you? Would it not have been as well or better for you if, all that time, you had been asleep or in a state of nonexistence? Consider those things seriously, and let your own consciences make answer.

🕭 From "The Preciousness of Time and the Importance of Redeeming It," p. 234

MAKE RESTITUTION WITH YOUR NEIGHBOR

Thou shalt not steal.
—EXODUS 20:15

I exhort those who are conscious in themselves that they have heretofore wronged their neighbor to make restitution. This is a duty the obligation to which is exceedingly plain. If a person was wronged in taking away anything that was his, certainly he is wronged also in detaining it. And all the while that a person, who has been guilty of wronging his neighbor, neglects to make restitution, he lives in that wrong. He not only lives impenitent as to that first wrong of which he was guilty, but he continually wrongs his neighbor. A man who hath gotten anything from another wrongfully, goes on to wrong him every day that he neglects to restore it, particularly when he has opportunity to do it. The person injured did not only suffer wrong from the other when his goods were first taken from him, but also he suffers new injustice from him all the while his goods are unjustly kept from him. Therefore, I counsel you who are conscious that you have heretofore wronged your neighbor, either by fraud, or oppression, or unfaithfulness, or stealing—whether lately or formerly, though it may have been a great while ago—speedily to go and make restitution for all the wrong your neighbor has suffered at your hands. That it was done long ago, doth not quit you from obligation to restore. This is a duty with which you must comply; you cannot be acquitted without it. As long as you neglect it, it will be unreasonable in you to expect any forgiveness of God. For what ground can you have to think that God will pardon you, as long as you willfully continue in the same wrong and wrong the same man every day, by detaining from him that which is his? You, in your prayers, ask of God that He would forgive all your sins; but your very prayers are mockery if you still willfully continue in those sins. Indeed, if you go and confess your faults to your neighbor, and He freely acquits you from making restitution, you are acquitted from the obligation.

⟡ From "The Sin of Theft and of Injustice," p. 226

A TRUE SPIRIT OF PRAYER

For we are the circumcision, which worship God in the spirit,
and rejoice in Christ Jesus, and have no confidence in the flesh.
— PHILIPPIANS 3:3

Hypocrites never had the spirit of prayer. They may have been stirred up to the external performance of this duty, and that with a great deal of earnestness and affection, and yet always they have been destitute of the true spirit of prayer. The spirit of prayer is a holy spirit, a gracious spirit. We read of the spirit of grace and supplication: "I will pour out upon the house of David and upon the inhabitants of Jerusalem, the spirit of grace and supplications" (Zech. 12:10). Wherever there is a true spirit of supplication, there is the spirit of grace. The true spirit of prayer is none other than God's own spirit dwelling in the hearts of the saints. And, as this spirit comes from God, so doth it naturally tend to God in holy breathings and pantings. It naturally leads to God to converse with Him by prayer. Therefore, the Spirit is said to make intercession for the saints with groanings that cannot be uttered (see Rom. 8:26). The Spirit of God makes intercession for them, as it is that Spirit that in some respect indites their prayers and leads them to pour out their souls before God. Therefore the saints are said to worship God in the spirit: "We are the circumcision, which worship God in the spirit" (Phil. 3:3); and "The true worshipers shall worship the Father in spirit and in truth" (John 4:23). The truly godly have the spirit of adoption, the spirit of a child, and so it is natural to go to God and call upon Him, crying to Him as to a father.

⚓ From "Hypocrites Deficient in the Duty of Prayer," p. 72

MEEKNESS

Charity suffereth long, and is kind.
— 1 CORINTHIANS 13:4

The apostle Paul, in the previous verses of 1 Corinthians 13, sets forth how great and essential a thing charity, or a spirit of Christian love, is in Christianity. It is far more necessary and excellent than any of the extraordinary gifts of the Spirit; it far exceeds all external performances and sufferings, and, in short, it is the sum of all that is distinguishing and saving in Christianity and the very life and soul of all religion; without charity, though we give all our goods to feed the poor and our bodies to be burned, we are nothing. And now he proceeds, as his subject naturally leads him, to show the excellent nature of charity, by describing its several amiable and excellent fruits. In the text, two of these fruits are mentioned: suffering long, which has respect to the evil or injury received from others, and being kind, which has respect to the good to be done to others. Meekness is a great part of the Christian spirit. Christ, in that earnest and touching call and invitation of His that we have in the eleventh chapter of Matthew, in which He invites all that labor and are heavy laden to come to Himself for rest, particularly mentions that He would have them come to learn of Him, for, He adds, "I am meek and lowly in heart" (Matt. 11:29). And meekness, as it respects injuries received from men, is called longsuffering in the Scriptures and is often mentioned as an exercise, or fruit of, the Christian spirit: "The fruit of the Spirit is love, joy, peace, longsuffering" (Gal. 5:22); "I therefore, the prisoner of the Lord, beseech you that ye walk worthy of the vocation wherewith ye are called, with all lowliness and meekness, with longsuffering," (Eph. 4:1–2); and "Put on therefore, as the elect of God, holy and beloved, bowels of mercy, kindness, humbleness of mind, meekness, longsuffering; forbearing one another, and forgiving one another, if any man have a quarrel against any: even as Christ forgave you, so also do ye" (Col. 3:12–13).

⸙ From "Charity Disposes Us Meekly to Bear the Injuries Received from Others," pp. 66–67

PERFECT LOVE IN HEAVEN

An inheritance incorruptible, and undefiled, and that fadeth not away, [is] reserved in heaven for you. — 1 PETER 1:4

In heaven there shall be no remaining enmity, or distaste, or coldness, or deadness of heart toward God and Christ. Not the least remainder of any principle of envy shall exist to be exercised toward angels or other beings who are superior in glory, nor shall there be aught like contempt or slighting of those who are inferiors. Those that have a lower station in glory than others suffer no diminution of their own happiness by seeing others above them in glory. On the contrary, all the members of that blessed society rejoice in each other's happiness, for the love of benevolence is perfect in them all. Everyone has a sincere and perfect goodwill to every other. Sincere and strong love is greatly gratified and delighted in the prosperity of the beloved object; and if the love be perfect, the greater the prosperity of the beloved is, the more is the lover pleased and delighted; for the prosperity of the beloved is, as it were, the food of love, and therefore the greater that prosperity, the more richly is love feasted. The love of benevolence is delighted in beholding the prosperity of another, as the love of complacence is, in beholding the beauty or perfection of another. So, the superior prosperity of those that are higher in glory is so far from being a hindrance to the degree of love felt toward them, that it is an addition to it, or a part of it.

🔥 From "Heaven, a World of Charity, or Love," pp. 335–36

KINDNESS GIVEN TO DEBASED CREATURES

The LORD looked down from heaven upon the children of men, to see if there were any that did understand, and seek God. They are all gone aside, they are all together become filthy: there is none that doeth good, no, not one. — PSALM 14:2–3

God beholds nothing lovely in us to draw His good will or to move His kindness to us. When we first came out of the hands of our Creator in our primitive state, we were lovely. We were lovely in the sight of God. He saw His own lovely image upon our souls; though then, when we had loveliness, it could not be supposed that that loveliness could draw God's goodwill, for it was what God gave us. It was of His imparting; it was the fruit of His goodness and goodwill, and it therefore could not be the cause of them. But since man has fallen from that state, none of mankind has any loveliness, anything that is or justly may be lovely in the sight of God. Man is left without so much as one desirable disposition or qualification. He is born without any inclination to any good and is without anything but deformity and filthiness in his mind. A creature that is born without so much as one good or amiable thing or qualification must indeed be an ill creature. But upon such a one does God bestow all the bounties and blessings of His good providence in this world. There is not one of mankind who, as he is by nature, has anything at all in him that is good to move God to be, in any respect, gracious to him. The first spring of God's bounty and goodness toward men is within Himself; there is nothing in man that can give rise to it.

⟆ From "God Is Kind to the Unthankful and the Evil," pp. 70–71

PERFECT RIGHTEOUSNESS

Thou lovest righteousness, and hatest wickedness.
— PSALM 45:7

We cannot be accepted of God without righteousness. If God is a just and righteous God, He loves righteousness and hates wickedness. He can never be a friend to unrighteousness. Unrighteousness is a thing to which God never can be reconciled; and therefore, if ever we are accepted, it must be for the sake of some righteousness or other to which we are entitled. God will never take pleasure in us without a righteousness; and it must not only be some righteousness, but it must be a perfect righteousness. God will never accept any person unless it is for a perfect righteousness. It is the eternal rule that God proceeds by, with both men and angels, that the condition of their being accepted with Him should be that they have a perfect righteousness. He has not departed, nor ever will He depart, from this rule. The guilt of one sin is sufficient to effectually block the way of God's favor and acceptance; for every sin is infinitely odious to God, and if there is the guilt of it yet upon the soul it is enough to render that soul odious in God's sight. Let no person, therefore, ever hope to be saved and go to heaven without a perfect righteousness. 'Tis folly for any to have dependence upon a righteousness that is imperfect, that comes short of full perfection, and that is mixed with sin; for God will have no regard at all to it, but will reject it and cast it as dung in our faces if we pretend to bring it and offer it to Him. He is so righteous and holy a being that He will not accept such an offering.

§ From "God Is a Just and Righteous God," pp. 13–15

SHINING LIGHT

And they that be wise shall shine as the brightness of the firmament; and they that turn many to righteousness as the stars for ever and ever.
— DANIEL 12:3

Our office and work is most honorable, in that we are set by Christ to be lights or luminaries in the spiritual world. Light is the most glorious thing in the material world, and there are, it may be, no parts of the natural world that have so great an image of the goodness of God as the lights or luminaries of heaven, especially the sun, who is constantly communicating his benign influence to enlighten, quicken, and refresh the world by his beams, which is probably the reason that the worship of the sun was (as is supposed) the first idolatry that mankind fell into. But so are ministers honored by their great Lord and Master, that they are set to be to men's souls what the lights of heaven are to their bodies, and that they might be the instruments and vehicles of God's greatest goodness and the most precious fruits of His eternal love to them, and means of that life, and refreshment, and joy that are spiritual and eternal, and infinitely more precious than any benefit received by the benign beams of the sun in the firmament. Herein our glory will answer the honorable station Christ has set us in, and hereby our ministry will be likely to be as beneficial as our office is honorable. We shall be like Christ, and shall shine with His beams. Christ will live in us and be seen in His life and beauty in our ministry and in our conversation. We shall be most likely to be the means of bringing others to Him and of their receiving of His light and being made partakers of His life, and having His joy fulfilled in them. And this will be the way for us hereafter, to be as much advanced and distinguished in our reward as we are honored in the office and business we are called to here. In this way, those whom Christ has set to be lights in His church and to be stars in the spiritual world here shall be lights also in the church triumphant, and shine as stars forever in heaven.

§ From "The True Excellency of a Gospel Minister," p. 959

EXAMINE YOUR WORSHIP

For when they had slain their children to their idols, then they came the same day into my sanctuary to profane it; and, lo, thus have they done in the midst of mine house.

— EZEKIEL 23:39

You are such as do enjoy the ordinances of divine worship. You come into the holy presence of God, attending on those ordinances that God, by sacred authority, has hallowed and set apart, that in them we might have immediate intercourse with Himself, that we might worship and adore Him and express to Him a humble, holy, supreme respect, and that in them we might receive immediate communications from Him. Here you come and speak to God, pretending to express your sense of how glorious He is, and how worthy that you should fear and love Him, humble yourselves before Him, devote your-selves to Him, obey Him, and have a greater respect to His commands and to His honor than to any temporal interest, ease, or pleasure of your own. Here you pretend before God that you are sensible of how unworthily you have done by sins committed in times past, and that you have a great desire not to do the like in time to come. You pretend to confess your sins, and to humble yourselves for them. Here you pray that God would give you His Spirit to assist you against sin, to keep you from the commission of it, to enable you to overcome temptations, and to help you to walk holy in all your conversation, as though you really had a great desire to avoid such sins as you have been guilty of in time past. For all your pretenses of respect to God, of humiliation for sin and desires to avoid it, have you not come directly from the allowed practice of known sin to God's ordinances, and did not at all repent of what you had done, nor at all sorry for it at the very time when you stood before God, making these pretenses, and even had no design of reformation, but intended to return to the same practice again after your departure from the presence of God? Examine yourselves, how it has been with you.

⟡ From "A Warning to Professors," p. 188

THE LEGACY OF CHRIST TO HIS FOLLOWERS

Whoever drinketh of the water that I shall give him shall never thirst.

— JOHN 4:14

The legacy of Christ to His true disciples is very diverse from all that the men of this world ever leave to their children when they die. The men of this world, many of them, when they come to die, have great estates to bequeath to their children, an abundance of the good things of this world, large tracts of ground, perhaps in a fruitful soil, covered with flocks and herds. They sometimes leave to their children stately mansions and vast treasures of silver, gold, jewels, and precious things, fetched from both the Indies and from every side of the globe of the earth. They leave them the wherewithal to live in much state and magnificence, to make a great show among men, to fare very sumptuously, and to swim in worldly pleasures. Some have crowns, scepters, and palaces, and great monarchies to leave to their heirs. But none of these things are to be compared to that blessed peace of Christ that He has bequeathed to His true followers. These things are such as God commonly, in His providence, gives His worst enemies—those whom He hates and despises most. But Christ's peace is a precious benefit that He reserves for His peculiar favorites. These worldly things, even the best of them, which the men and princes of the world leave for their children, are things that God in His providence throws out to those whom He looks upon as dogs. But Christ's peace is the bread of His children. All these earthly things are but empty shadows, which, however men set their hearts upon them, are not bread and can never satisfy their souls. But this peace of Christ is a truly substantial, satisfying food. None of those things, if men have them to the best advantage and in ever so great abundance, can give true peace and rest to the soul. This is abundantly manifest not only in reason, but experience: it being found in all ages, that those who have the most of them have commonly the least quietness of mind. But Christ's peace, which He gives to His true disciples, vastly differs from this peace that men may have in the enjoyments of the world.

§ From "The Peace Which Christ Gives His True Followers," p. 91

A PRACTICE OF GOD'S WILL

Herein is my Father glorified, that ye bear much fruit; so shall ye be my disciples.

— JOHN 15:8

Godliness has relation to godly practice. It is a conformity of heart to God's will that translates into a practice of God's will. It is not an inactive thing; nothing in heaven or on earth is of a more active nature. It is life itself: spiritual life. The divine nature is pure act, not an unfruitful thing. Nothing in the universe has a greater tendency to bear fruit. Godliness in the heart has a relationship to practice as much as a fountain has a relationship to the stream, a root to the fruit, a foundation to the superstructure, or a luminary to the light—as life has to breathing or the beating of the pulse, or any other vital acts. A habit has a relationship to acts; it consists of thinking and hearing. A habit of being anything has to the doing of it. Conversion, which is the work by which God's grace is infused into the heart, has a relationship to act in practice. That is the end of conversion. It is related to it in God's purpose: "we are…created in Christ Jesus unto good works" (Eph. 2:10); "I have chosen you, and ordained you, that ye should go and bring forth fruit" (John 15:16). It is related in its nature. The nature of true godliness of heart is not to rest in itself. Sincerity is not locked up in the heart, anymore than it is the nature of a spring to produce stagnating dead water. If there is a fruitful principle in a good tree, it doesn't rest in the principle, but produces fruit. Hence, all godliness is in Scripture oftentimes expressed by doing the will of God, in obeying God, and in keeping His commandments. There is not one gracious and holy principle but what has a great relationship to holy practice, whether it is repentance, faith, or the like. Those principles that have no relationship to practice are as much in vain as a vine, apple tree, or fig tree is in vain without fruit.

ᔈ From "A Heart to Do the Will of God," pp. 117–18

KEEPING GOD'S COMMANDS

What doth the LORD *thy God require of thee, but to keep the commandments of the* LORD, *and his statutes, which I command thee this day for thy good?*

—DEUTERONOMY 10:12–13

The goodness and mercy of God is manifested in His giving us such commands as He has, that He requires of us such duties as He does, that He has given us commands that are in their own nature so excellent, that are so holy and righteous. God herein has not only manifested His holiness, but also His goodness. His commands are not only holy and just, but good (see Rom. 7:12), and they are therefore good as expressions of divine goodness because they are holy and just. 'Tis spoken of as an instance of the great and distinguishing favor that God had shown to the people of Israel that He had given them such a just and righteous law: "And what nation is there so great, that hath statutes and judgments so righteous as all this law, which I set before you this day?" (Deut. 4:8). So God has shown us great mercy in giving us such commands as He has, and that for this general reason: God's commands are such as in their own nature they tend to our good. They do not only tend to our benefit by divine constitution or because He has been pleased to annex a glorious reward to obedience, but they are such as in their own nature tend to our good, and would do so if God had promised no reward at all. There is a great reward in keeping God's commands (see Ps. 19:11). God, in giving us such commands, has consulted the good and happiness of our souls. Keeping these commands tends, on their own nature, to prevent the soul's misery and renders it happy. These commands tend to prevent the soul's misery since they restrain it from those things that in their own nature tend to make a soul miserable. In the commands that God gives, God consults our good; for He only commands us to be excellent creatures.

---

§ From "There Is Much of the Goodness and Mercy of God Appearing in the Commands He Has Given Us," pp. 240–41

THE PLEASURES OF SPIRITUAL LIFE

[Wisdom's] ways are ways of pleasantness, and all her paths are peace.
— PROVERBS 3:17

Religion is not a sour thing that is contrived for nothing but to cross our inclinations and to cut us short of the delights of life. No, it is quite of another nature; it abridges us of no pleasures but only such as of their own nature (however pleasing for the present) lay a foundation for woe and misery. They are in their own nature a poison that, though sweet in the mouth, really does, as it were, destroy the constitution of the soul: "At last it biteth like a serpent and stingeth like an adder" (Prov. 23:32). But as for those delights that better the soul and have a tendency to the future, as well as the present well being of it, they are allowed fully and are promoted by religion; yea, true religion is the only source from whence they flow. How much happier therefore is the man who chooses a holy and a spiritual religious life than he who chooses a carnal, sensual life. Sensual men may be ready to think they would be happy men if there were nothing to restrain their enjoyment of their appetites, if they might at all times satisfy their appetites and have their full swing at their pleasures and impunity, and without any danger of any succeeding inconvenience; but if it were so, they would be but miserable men in comparison to the godly man who enjoys the pleasures of acquaintance with the glorious God and His Son Jesus Christ, a communion of the holy and blessed Spirit of God and Christ, a true peace of conscience and inward testimonies of the favor and acceptance of God and Christ, and has liberty without restraint to indulge himself in the enjoyment of those pleasures. "[Wisdom's] ways are ways of pleasantness, and all her paths are peace" (Prov. 3:17).

From "Spiritual Appetites Need No Bounds," pp. 232–33

CHRIST IS ALL

Christ is all, and in all.
—COLOSSIANS 3:11

Christ is the author of all that Christians are as Christians. It is not only He who procures, but it is He who also produces and causes it in the soul. It is He who converts men and brings them home to Himself. Christ turns men's darkness to light. He calls men out of darkness into marvelous light. He causes the light to shine into the dark heart. He says, "Let there be light" (Gen. 1:3), and there is light. He gives grace and holiness. He is the author of the new creature. It is He who is the creator of it. He does it all by His Spirit. The Spirit of God, in producing these things in the hearts of men, acts under Christ as His messenger. It is the will of God to transact with fallen men only by Christ. He leaves the whole affair of the redemption and salvation of mankind in His hands. He not only procures holiness by His purchase, but it is He who produces it by His power. It is God's will that the same person who procures it by His blood should produce it by His Spirit. The new creature is the beautiful workmanship of Jesus Christ. The image of God is an image of His drawing by His Spirit; the Spirit of God in it acts as His Spirit. All the strength that a believer has to perform any gracious or holy act is from Christ; it is His strength that enables a believer to put forth acts of grace, to resist and overcome temptation, to bring forth fruit: "I can do all things through Christ which strengtheneth me" (Phil. 4:13). Though means are made use of, yet those means are in no way effectual but by the strength of Christ; and Christ is the author of those means. The Word and ordinances are of His appointing, and ministers are of His sending. It is He who furnishes, helps, and succeeds them, and without this they are nothing.

⏁ From "Christ Is the Christian's All," pp. 198–99

LONGING FOR HEAVEN

In my Father's house are many mansions.

—JOHN 14:2

A godly man prefers God above anything else in heaven. Every godly man has his heart in heaven. His affections are mainly set on heaven and what is to be had there. Heaven is his chosen country and inheritance. He prefers heaven to this world, but not as a natural man does, who will, it may be, eternally own that heaven is a better place than this world. They are taught from infancy what a glorious place heaven is, and they give a kind of assent to it; they do not dispute it, but are yet to do what will get them past this world to heaven. But the godly have a sense and an essential conviction of the preferableness of heaven to this world. For the present they live in this world; their hearts are not mainly here, but are in another country. A godly man has respect to heaven as a traveler, who is occasionally abroad in a distant land, has to his own country. He can content himself to be in a strange land for a while until his present business is over, but he prefers his own native land to all others: "These all died in faith, not having received the promises, but…were persuaded of them, and embraced them, and confessed that they were strangers and pilgrims on the earth…but now they desire a better country, that is, an heavenly" (Heb. 11:13, 16). So also the respect that a godly person has to heaven may be compared to the respect a child, when he is abroad, has for his father's house. He can be content a little while when abroad, but he desires to remain and to dwell in his own home at his father's house. Heaven is the true saint's Father's house. Now the main reason the godly man has his heart there in heaven is because God is there. It is the palace of the Most High God; it is the place where God is gloriously present; it is the place where God is to be seen, where He is to be enjoyed, where His love is graciously manifested, where he may be with Him and see Him as He is, where he may love, praise, and enjoy Him perfectly.

☙ From "'Tis the Spirit of a Truly Godly Man to Prefer God before All Other Things Either in Heaven or on Earth," pp. 178–79

COMPARED WITH HOLY LIGHT

God is light, and in him is no darkness at all.
— 1 JOHN 1:5

He who knows what God is has the infinite holiness and purity of God with which to compare himself. We may easily conceive how there could be nothing that would give the man such a sense of his own deformity as to compare himself with the bright, pure, and spotless holiness of God. By comparing those things together, the infinite difference may be seen. They who do not know God cannot compare themselves with His holy nature, for His holy nature is what they do not see. He who knows what God is sees Him to be a being of transcendently glorious holiness. The sight of this glory fills him with admiration. But when from seeing this sight he comes to turn his eye inward upon himself, how filthy he appears to himself, how all over polluted and deformed! There is in God an infinite luster and brightness by reason of His holiness whereby, if we behold the moon, it does not shine and the stars are not pure. There are some things that seem to shine when you look on them in the dark, but if you bring them out and compare them with the sun, they lose all their brightness. So too men who are ignorant of God may make a glistening appearance in their own eyes, but when they come to have a sight of an infinitely holy God and bring themselves out before Him, they lose all their luster. There is no light like the light of God's glory to discover the filthiness of men. We shall know our deformity best when we compare it with the nature of God, the standard of all perfection. The knowledge of God's holiness is the best, the brightest, and the purest light in which we can view ourselves.

§ From "There Is Nothing Like Seeing What God Is to Make Men Sensible to What They Are," pp. 138–39

COUNTERFEIT GRACE

*For what is the hope of the hypocrite, though he hath gained,
when God taketh away his soul?*
— JOB 27:8

False grace is a superficial thing, consisting in mere outward show, or in superficial affections, and not in any change of nature. But true grace reaches to the very bottom of the heart. It consists in a new nature, and therefore it is lasting and enduring. Where there is nothing but counterfeit grace, corruption is unmortified, and whatever wounds may seem to be given it, they are but slight wounds that do not at all reach its life or diminish the strength of its principle, but leave sin in its full strength in the soul, so that it is no wonder that it ultimately prevails and bears down all before it. But true grace really mortifies sin in the heart. It strikes at its vitals and gives it a wound that is mortal, sending its stroke to the very heart. When it first enters the soul, it begins a never-ceasing conflict with sin, and therefore it is no wonder that it keeps possession and finally prevails over its enemy. Counterfeit grace never dispossesses sin of the dominion of the soul nor destroys its reigning power there, and therefore it is no wonder that it does not itself remain. But true grace is of such a nature that it is inconsistent with the reigning power of sin and dispossesses the heart of it as it enters, and takes the throne from it, and therefore is the more likely to keep its seat there, and finally to prevail entirely against it. Counterfeit grace, though it may affect the heart, yet is not founded on any real conviction of the soul. But true grace begins in real and thorough conviction, and, having such a foundation, has so much the greater tendency to perseverance.

§ From "Charity, or True Grace, Not to Be Overthrown by Opposition," pp. 292–93

SUFFER FOR CHRIST'S SAKE

That I may know him, and the power of his resurrection, and the fellowship of his sufferings, being made conformable unto his death.
— PHILIPPIANS 3:10

Lead those who think themselves Christians to examine themselves, whether or not they have the spirit to undergo all sufferings for Christ. It becomes all persons very strictly to examine themselves, whether they are of a suffering spirit or not, seeing such great importance is attached to such a spirit in the Scriptures. Though you never have had the trial of having such great and extreme sufferings laid in the way of your duty, as many others have had, yet you have had enough, in the course of God's providence, to show what your spirit is, and whether you are of a disposition to suffer and to renounce your own comfort, ease, and interest rather than forsake Christ. It is God's manner in His providence, commonly, to exercise all professors of religion, and especially those that may live in times of trial, with trials of this sort, by laying such difficulties in their way as shall make manifest what their spirit is and whether it be a spirit of self-renunciation or not. It is often the case with Christians who are exposed to persecutions that if they will cleave to Christ and be faithful to Him, they must suffer in their good name; and in losing the goodwill of others, or in their outward ease and convenience being exposed to many troubles; or in their estates, being brought into difficulty as to their business; or must do many things that they are exceeding averse to, and that are even dreadful to them. Have you, when you have had such trials, found in yourself a spirit to bear all things that come upon you, rather than in anything be unfaithful to your great Lord and Redeemer? And you have the more need to examine yourselves with respect to this point; for you know not but that before you die you may have such trial of persecutions as other Christians have had.

§ From "Charity, or a Christian Spirit, Willing to Undergo All Sufferings in the Way of Duty," pp. 263–64

THE PURCHASE OF GRACE AND HOLINESS

And for their sakes I sanctify myself, that they also might be sanctified through the truth.
— JOHN 17:19

Christ, by His merits, in the great things that He did and suffered in the world, has purchased grace and holiness for His own people: "For their sakes," He says, "I sanctify myself, that they also might be sanctified through the truth" (John 17:19). And Christ thus redeemed the elect and purchased grace for them, to the end that they might walk in holy practice. He has reconciled them to God by His death, to save them from wicked works, that they might be holy and unblameable in their lives, says the apostle Paul: "And you, that were sometime alienated and enemies in your mind by wicked works, yet now hath he reconciled in the body of his flesh through death, to present you holy, and unblameable, and unreproveable in his sight" (Col. 1:21–22). When the angel appeared to Joseph, he told him that the child that should be born of Mary should be called Jesus, that is, Savior, because He should save His people from their sins (see Matt. 1:21). Holiness of life is declared to be the end of redemption when it is said of Christ that He "gave himself for us, that he might redeem us from all iniquity, and purify unto himself a peculiar people, zealous of good works" (Titus 2:14). And so we are told that Christ "died for all, that they which live should not henceforth live unto themselves, but unto him which died for them, and rose again" (2 Cor. 5:15). For this end, He is said to have offered Himself, through the eternal Spirit, without spot to God, that His blood might purge our conscience from dead works to serve the living God (see Heb. 9:14).

﹩ From "All True Grace in the Heart Tends to Holy Practice in the Life," p. 224

SEEK THOSE THINGS ABOVE

But seek ye first the kingdom of God, and his righteousness; and all these things shall be added unto you. — MATTHEW 6:33

Christians should seek after those things that will be to the honor of their birth, after spiritual wisdom, and after knowledge of the most worthy and noble truths. They should seek more and more an acquaintance with God and to be assimilated to Him, their great progenitor and their immediate Father, that they may have the image of His excellent and divine perfections. They should endeavor to act like God, wherein they are capable of imitation of Him. They should seek heavenly mindedness: those noble appetites after heavenly and spiritual enjoyments, a noble ambition after heavenly glory, a contempt of the trifles and mean things of this world. They should seek after those delights and satisfactions that can be enjoyed by none but heavenly minds. They should exercise a spirit of true, universal, and disinterested love and confidence and Christian charity. They should be much in devotion and divine contemplation. The truly godly are very different in their disposition from others. They hate those things that the rest of the world loves and love those things for which the rest of the world has no relish. They wonder what delight they can take in spending so much time in meditation and prayer and that they do not place happiness in those things that themselves do: "Wherein they think it strange that ye run not with them to the same excess of riot; speaking evil of you" (1 Peter 4:4). But the reason is that Christians are of a different race.

§ From "Christians a Chosen Generation, a Royal Priesthood, a Holy Nation, a Peculiar People," p. 940

REDEEMING MERCY

But God, who is rich in mercy, for his great love wherewith he loved us, even when we were dead in sins, hath quickened us together with Christ (by grace ye are saved).

— EPHESIANS 2:4–5

The redeeming mercy and love of God are highly prized and rejoiced in when discovered. By the discoveries of danger, misery, and helplessness, and desert of wrath, the heart is prepared to embrace a discovery of mercy. When the soul stands trembling at the brink of the pit and despairs of any help from itself, it is prepared joyfully to receive tidings of deliverance. If God is pleased at such a time to make the soul hear His still small voice, His call to Himself and to a Savior, the soul is prepared to give it a joyful reception. The gospel then, if it be heard spiritually, will be glad tidings indeed, the most joyful that the sinner ever heard. The love of God and of Christ to the world, and to him in particular, will be admired, and Christ will be most precious. To remember what danger he was in, what seas surrounded him, and then to reflect how safe he now is in Christ and how sufficient Christ is to defend him and to answer all his wants will cause the greater exultation of soul. God, in this method of dealing with the souls of His elect, consults their happiness, as well as His own glory. It increases happiness for souls to be made sensible of their misery and unworthiness before God comforts them. For then their comfort, when they receive it, is so much the sweeter. The heart is more prepared and disposed to praise God for it. They are ready to say, "How miserable should I have been had not God had pity upon me and provided me a Savior! In what a miserable condition should I have been, had not Christ loved me and given Himself for me!"

§ From "God Makes Men Sensible of Their Misery before He Reveals His Mercy and Love," p. 836

SOVEREIGN OVER ALL

It is he that sitteth upon the circle of the earth, and the inhabitants thereof are as grasshoppers.
— ISAIAH 40:22

The sovereignty of God in His being sovereign over men is more glorious than in His being sovereign over the inferior creatures. For the nobler the creature is, still the greater and higher doth God appear in His sovereignty over it. It is a greater honor to a man to have dominion over men than over beasts; still greater honor to have dominion over princes, nobles, and kings than over ordinary men. So the glory of God's sovereignty appears in that He is sovereign over the souls of men who are so noble and excellent creatures. God, therefore, will exercise His sovereignty over them. The further the dominion of any one extends over another, the greater will be the honor. If a man has dominion over another only in some instances, he is not therein so much exalted as in having absolute dominion over his life and fortune and all he has. So God's sovereignty over men appears glorious, that it extends to everything that concerns them. He may dispose of them with respect to all that concerns them, according to His own pleasure. His sovereignty appears glorious in that it reaches their most important affairs, even the eternal state and condition of the souls of men. Herein it appears that the sovereignty of God is without bounds or limits in that it reaches to an affair of such infinite importance. God, therefore, as it is His design to manifest His own glory, will and does exercise His sovereignty toward men, over their souls and bodies, even in this most important matter of their eternal salvation.

§ From "God's Sovereignty in the Salvation of Men," p. 853

REST OF THE SOUL

O LORD, thou art my God; I will exalt thee, I will praise thy name; for thou hast done wonderful things; thy counsels of old are faithfulness and truth.
— ISAIAH 25:1

Christ's peace is a reasonable peace and rest of soul; it is what has its foundation in light and knowledge, in the proper exercises of reason and a right view of things; whereas the peace of the world is founded in blindness and delusion. The peace that the people of Christ have arises from their having their eyes open and seeing things as they are. The more they consider, and the more they know of the truth and reality of things, the more they know what is true concerning themselves and the state and condition they are in; the more they know of God and what manner of being He is; the more certain they are of another world and future judgment and of the truth of God's threatening and promises; the more their consciences are awakened and enlightened and the brighter and the more searching the light, the more is their peace established. Whereas, on the contrary, the peace that the men of the world have in their worldly enjoyments can subsist no otherwise than by their being kept in ignorance. They must be blindfolded and deceived, otherwise they can have no peace; do but let light in upon their consciences, so that they may look about them and see what they are and what circumstances they are in, and it will at once destroy all their quietness and comfort. Their peace can live nowhere but in the dark. Light turns their ease into torment. The more they know what is true concerning God and concerning themselves, the more they are sensible of the truth concerning those enjoyments that they possess; and the more they are sensible of what things now are, and what things are like to be hereafter, the more will their calm be turned into a storm.

§ From "The Peace Which Christ Gives His True Followers," pp. 91–92

WRATH DIVERTED

For God hath not appointed us to wrath, but to obtain salvation by our Lord Jesus Christ.
— 1 THESSALONIANS 5:9

Those who come to Christ need not be afraid of God's wrath for their sins, for God's honor will not suffer by their escaping punishment and being made happy. The wounded soul is sensible that he has affronted the majesty of God and looks upon God as a vindicator of His honor, as a jealous God that will not be mocked, as an infinitely great God that will not bear to be affronted, that will not suffer His authority and majesty to be trampled on, that will not bear that His kindness should be abused. A view of God in this light terrifies awakened souls. They think how exceedingly they have sinned, how they have sinned against light, against frequent and long-continued calls and warnings, and how they have slighted mercy and been guilty of turning the grace of God into lasciviousness, taking encouragement from God's mercy to go on in sin against him; and they fear that God is so affronted at the contempt and slight that they have cast upon Him that He, being careful of His honor, will never forgive them, but will punish them. But, if they go to Christ, the honor of God's majesty and authority will not be in the least hurt by their being freed and made happy. For what Christ has done has repaired God's honor to the full. It is a greater honor to God's authority and majesty that, rather than it should be wronged, so glorious a person would suffer what the law required.

§ From "Safety, Fullness, and Sweet Refreshment, to Be Found in Christ," p. 930

THE WICKEDNESS OF MEN

God saw that the wickedness of man was great in the earth,
and that every imagination of the thoughts of his heart was
only evil continually.
— GENESIS 6:5

How many sorts of wickedness have you not been guilty of! How manifold have been the abominations of your life! What profaneness and contempt of God has been exercised by you! How little regard have you had to the Scriptures, to the word preached, to Sabbaths, and to sacraments! How profanely have you talked, many of you, about those things that are holy! After what manner have many of you kept God's holy day, not regarding the holiness of the time nor caring what you thought of in it! Yea, you have not only spent the time in worldly, vain, and unprofitable thoughts, but in immoral thoughts, pleasing yourself with the reflection on past acts of wickedness and in contriving new acts. Have not you spent much holy time in gratifying your lusts in your imaginations, yea, not only holy time, but the very time of God's public worship, when you have appeared in God's more immediate presence? How have you not only not attended to the worship, but have in the meantime been feasting your lusts and wallowing yourself in abominable uncleanness! How many Sabbaths have you spent, one after another, in a most wretched manner! Some of you not only in worldly and wicked thoughts, but also in very wicked outward behavior! When you on Sabbath days have got along with your wicked companions, how has holy time been treated among you! What kind of conversation has there been! Yea, how have some of you, by a very indecent carriage, openly dishonored and cast contempt on the sacred services of God's house and holy day! And what you have done some of you alone, what wicked practices there have been in secret, even in holy time, God and your own consciences know.

ⓢ From "The Justice of God in the Damnation of Sinners," p. 671

GOD'S POWER OVER WICKEDNESS

For if, when we were enemies, we were reconciled to God by the death of his Son, much more, being reconciled, we shall be saved by his life.
— ROMANS 5:10

There is no want of power in God to cast wicked men into hell at any moment. Men's hands cannot be strong when God rises up. The strongest have no power to resist Him, nor can any deliver out of His hands. He is not only able to cast wicked men into hell, but He can most easily do it. Sometimes an earthly prince meets with a great deal of difficulty to subdue a rebel who has found means to fortify himself and has made himself strong by the numbers of his followers. But it is not so with God. There is no fortress that is any defense from the power of God. Though hand join in hand and vast multitudes of God's enemies combine and associate themselves, they are easily broken in pieces. They are as great heaps of light chaff before the whirlwind or large quantities of dry stubble before devouring flames. We find it easy to tread on and crush a worm that we see crawling on the earth; so it is easy for us to cut or singe a slender thread that anything hangs by. Thus easy is it for God, when He pleases, to cast His enemies down to hell. What are we that we should think to stand before Him, at whose rebuke the earth trembles and before whom the rocks are thrown down? They deserve to be cast into hell; so that divine justice never stands in the way, it makes no objection against God's using His power at any moment to destroy them. Yea, on the contrary, justice calls aloud for an infinite punishment of their sins. Divine justice says of the tree that brings forth such grapes of Sodom, "Cut it down; why cumbereth it the ground?" (Luke 13:7).

From "Sinners in the Hands of an Angry God," pp. 7–8

THE FOUNTAIN OF ALL GOOD

Which hope we have as an anchor of the soul, both sure and steadfast, and which entereth into that within the veil; whither the forerunner is for us entered, even Jesus, made an high priest for ever after the order of Melchisedec.

— HEBREWS 6:19–20

Whatever changes a godly man passes through, he is happy, because God, who is unchangeable, is his chosen portion. Though he meet with temporal losses and be deprived of many, yea, of all his temporal enjoyments, yet God, whom he prefers before all, still remains and cannot be lost. While he stays in this changeable, troublesome world, he is happy, because his chosen portion, on which he builds as his main foundation for happiness is above the world and above all changes. And when he goes into another world, still he is happy, because that portion yet remains. Whatever he be deprived of, he cannot be deprived of his chief portion; his inheritance remains sure to him. Could worldly minded men find out a way to secure to themselves those earthly enjoyments on which they mainly set their hearts, so that they could not be lost or impaired while they live, how great would they account the privilege, though other things that they esteem in a less degree were liable to the same uncertainty as they now are! Whereas now, those earthly enjoyments, on which men chiefly set their hearts, are often most fading. But how great is the happiness of those who have chosen the Fountain of all good, who prefer Him before all things in heaven or on earth, and who can never be deprived of Him to all eternity!

❧ From "God the Best Portion of the Christian," p. 106

THE PRICE OF DIVINE JUSTICE

I am poured out like water, and all my bones are out of joint: my heart is like wax; it is melted in the midst of my bowels.

— PSALM 22:14

Christ never so eminently appeared for divine justice, and yet never suffered so much from divine justice, as when He offered up Himself a sacrifice for our sins. In Christ's great sufferings did His infinite regard to the honor of God's justice distinguishingly appear; for it was from regard to that that He thus humbled Himself. And yet, in these sufferings, Christ was the mark of the vindictive expressions of that very justice of God. Revenging justice then spent all its force upon Him, on account of our guilt, which made Him sweat blood and cry out upon the cross and probably rent His vitals—and broke His heart, the fountain of blood, or some other blood vessels—and by the violent fermentation turned His blood to water. For the blood and water that issued out of His side, when pierced by the spear, seems to have been extravasated blood; and so there might be a kind of literal fulfillment of Psalm 22:14: "I am poured out like water, and all my bones are out of joint: my heart is like wax; it is melted in the midst of my bowels." And this was the way and means by which Christ stood up for the honor of God's justice, namely by thus suffering its terrible executions. For when He had undertaken for sinners and had substituted Himself in their room, divine justice could have its due honor no other way than by His suffering its revenges. In this the diverse excellencies that met in the person of Christ appeared, namely His infinite regard to God's justice and such love to those that have exposed themselves to it as induced Him thus to yield Himself a sacrifice to it.

ॐ From "The Excellency of Jesus Christ," p. 684

ENJOYMENT RESERVED IN HEAVEN

*An inheritance, incorruptible, and undefiled, and that fadeth
not away, reserved in heaven for you.*
— 1 PETER 1:4

This life ought to be spent by us as to be only a journey or pilgrimage toward
heaven. We ought not to rest in the world and its enjoyments, but should
desire heaven. We should "seek first the kingdom of God" (Matt. 6:33). We
ought above all things to desire a heavenly happiness: to be with God and
dwell with Jesus Christ. Though surrounded with outward enjoyments and
settled in families with desirable friends and relations; though we have companions whose society is delightful, and children in whom we see many
promising qualifications; though we live by good neighbors and are generally
beloved where known; yet we ought not to take our rest in these things as our
portion. We should be so far from resting in them that we should desire to
leave them all in God's due time. We ought to possess, enjoy, and use them,
with no other view but readily to quit them, whenever we are called to it, and
to change them willingly and cheerfully for heaven.

❦ From "The Christian Pilgrim, or the True Christian's Life a Journey toward Heaven," p. 243

PRESS ON

Brethren, I count not myself to have apprehended: but this one thing I do, forgetting those things which are behind, and reaching forth unto those things which are before.

— PHILIPPIANS 3:13

One way to determine whether you truly and sincerely prefer God above all other things is to inquire whether you prefer God to all other things in practice; for example, when you have occasion to manifest by your practice that you prefer—when you must either cleave to one or the other, and must either forsake other things or forsake God—whether then it be your manner practically to prefer God to all other things, even to those earthly things to which your hearts are most wedded. Are your lives those of adherence to God and of serving Him in this manner? He who sincerely prefers God to all other things in his heart will do it in his practice. For when God and all other things come to stand in competition, that is the proper trial a man chooses; and the manner of acting in such cases must certainly determine what the choice is in all free agents or those who act on choice. Therefore there is no sign of sincerity so much insisted on in the Bible as this: that we deny ourselves, sell all, forsake the world, take up the cross, and follow Christ whithersoever He goeth. Therefore, so run, not as uncertainly; so fight, not as those that beat the air; but keep under your bodies, and bring them into subjection. Act not as though you counted yourselves to have apprehended; but this one thing do: "forgetting those things which are behind, and reaching forth unto those things which are before, press toward the mark, for the prize of the high calling of God in Christ Jesus" (Phil. 3:14).

§ From "God the Best Portion of the Christian," pp. 106–7

DISTINCTIVE GRACE

Thou believest that there is one God; thou doest well: the devils also believe, and tremble.
—JAMES 2:19

The devils and damned souls have a great sense of the vast importance of the things of another world. They are in the invisible world, and they see and know how great the things of that world are. Their experience teaches them in the most affecting manner. They have a great sense of the worth of salvation and the worth of immortal souls and the vast importance of those things that concern men's eternal welfare. The parable in the latter end of the sixteenth chapter of Luke teaches this in representing the rich man in hell as entreating that Lazarus might be sent to his five brothers to testify unto them, lest they should come to that place of torment. They who endure the torments of hell have doubtless a most lively and affecting sense of the vastness of an endless eternity and of the comparative momentariness of this life and of the vanity of the concerns and enjoyments of time. They are convinced, effectually, that all the things of this world, even those that appear greatest and most important to the inhabitants of the earth, are despicable trifles, in comparison to the things of the eternal world. They have a great sense of the preciousness of time and of the means of grace and of the inestimable value of the privileges that they enjoy who live under the gospel. They are fully sensible of the folly of those that go on in sin, neglect their opportunities, make light of the counsels and warnings of God, and bitterly lament their exceeding folly in their own sins, by which they have brought on themselves so great and remediless misery. Therefore, however, true godliness is attended with a great sense of the importance of divine things, and it is rare that men who have no grace maintain such a sense in any steady and persevering manner, yet it is manifest those things are no certain evidences of grace.

❧ From "True Grace Distinguished from the Experience of Devils," pp. 44–45

SUPREME JUDGE

*He is wise in heart, and mighty in strength: who hath hard-
ened himself against him, and hath prospered?*
— JOB 9:4

God is the Supreme Judge of the world. He hath power sufficient to vindicate His own right. As He hath a right that cannot be disputed, so He hath
power that cannot be controlled. He is possessed of omnipotence, wherewith
to maintain His dominion over the world; and He doth maintain His dominion in the moral as well as the natural world. Men may refuse subjection to
God as a lawgiver; they may shake off the yoke of His laws by rebellion; yet
they cannot withdraw themselves from His judgment. Although they will
not have God for their lawgiver, yet they shall have Him for their judge. The
strongest of creatures can do nothing to control God or to avoid Him while
acting in His judicial capacity. He is able to bring them to His judgment seat,
and is also able to execute the sentence that He shall pronounce. There was
once a notable attempt made by opposition of power to entirely shake off
the yoke of the moral government of God, both as lawgiver and as judge.
This attempt was made by the angels, the most mighty of creatures, but they
miserably failed in it. God, notwithstanding, acted as their judge in casting
those proud spirits out of heaven and in binding them in chains of darkness
unto a further judgment and in a further execution. "[God] is wise in heart
and mighty in strength; who hath hardened himself against him, and hath
prospered?" (Job 9:4).

From "The Final Judgment, or the World Judged Righteously by Jesus Christ," p. 190

THE EMPTINESS OF MAN

Take ye the spoil of silver, take the spoil of gold: for there is none end of the store and glory out of all the pleasant furniture.

—NAHUM 2:9

We see, in temporal things, that the worth and value of any enjoyment is learned by the want of it. He who is sick knows the worth of health. He who is in pain knows how to prize ease. He who is in a storm at sea knows how to prize safety on shore. People who are subject to the grievances of war know how to value peace. He who endures the hardships of captivity and slavery is thereby taught how to value liberty. And so it is in spiritual things. He who is brought to see his misery in being without hope is prepared to prize hope when obtained. He who is brought into distress, through fear of hell and God's wrath, is the more prepared to prize the comfort that arises from the manifestation of the favor of God and a sense of safety from hell. He who is brought to see his utter emptiness and extreme poverty and necessity, and his perishing condition on that account, is thoroughly prepared to prize and rejoice in the manifestation of a fullness in Christ. And those godly persons who are fallen into corrupt and senseless frames greatly stand in need of something to make them more sensible of their want of spiritual comfort and hope. A sense of the pardon of sin and the favor of God and the hope of eternal life do not afford comfort and joy to the soul any farther than they are valued and prized. So the trouble and darkness that go before comfort serve to render the joy and comfort the greater when obtained, and so are in mercy to those for whom God intends comfort.

🖎 From "Hope and Comfort Usually Follow Genuine Humiliation and Repentance," p. 845

A HIDING PLACE

He that believeth on me, as the scripture hath said, out of his belly shall flow rivers of living water.

—JOHN 7:38

We may here see great reason to admire the goodness and grace of God to us in our low estate that He has so provided for our help and relief. We are, by our own sin against God, plunged into all sorts of evil, and God has provided a remedy for us against every sort of evil; He has left us helpless in no calamity. We, by our sin, have exposed ourselves to wrath, to a vindictive justice, but God has done very great things that we might be saved from that wrath. He has been at infinite cost that the law might be answered without our suffering. We, by our sins, have exposed ourselves to terror of conscience, in expectation of the dreadful storm of God's wrath, but God has provided for us a hiding place from the storm: He bids us enter into His chambers and hide ourselves from indignation. We, by sin, have made ourselves poor, needy creatures, but God has provided for us gold tried in the fire. We, by sin, have made ourselves naked, and when He passed by, He took notice of our want and has provided us white raiment, that we may be clothed. We have made ourselves blind, and God in mercy to us has provided eye salve, that we may see. We have deprived ourselves of all spiritual food; we are like the prodigal son who perished with hunger and would gladly have filled his belly with husks. God has taken notice of our condition and has provided for us a feast of fat things and has sent forth His servants to invite the poor, the maimed, the halt, and the blind. We, by sin, have brought ourselves into a dry and thirsty wilderness; but God was merciful and took notice of our condition and has provided for us rivers of water, water out of the rock.

⟆ From "Safety, Fullness, and Sweet Refreshment, to Be Found in Christ," p. 936

IN THE SCHOOL OF CHRIST

Study to shew thyself approved unto God, a workman that needeth not to be ashamed, rightly dividing the word of truth.
—2 TIMOTHY 2:15

Consider yourselves as scholars or disciples, put into the school of Christ, and, therefore, be diligent to make proficiency in Christian knowledge. Content not yourselves with this, that you have been taught your catechism in your childhood, and that you know as much of the principles of religion as is necessary to salvation. So you will be guilty of what the apostle warns against, going no further than laying the foundation of repentance from dead works. You are all called to be Christians, and this is your profession. Endeavor, therefore, to acquire knowledge in things that pertain to your profession. Let not your teachers have cause to complain that while they spend and are spent to impart knowledge to you, you take little pains to learn. It is a great encouragement to an instructor to have such to teach as make a business of learning, bending their minds to it. This makes teaching a pleasure, when otherwise it will be a very heavy and burdensome task. You all have by you a large treasure of divine knowledge, in that you have the Bible in your hands; therefore, be not contented in possessing but little of this treasure. God hath spoken much to you in the Scripture; therefore, labor to understand as much of what He saith as you can. God hath made you all reasonable creatures; therefore, let not the noble faculty of reason or understanding lie neglected. Content not yourselves with having so much knowledge as is thrown in your way, and as you receive in some sense unavoidably by the frequent inculcation of divine truth in the preaching of the word—of which you are obliged to be hearers—or as you accidentally gain in conversation; but let it be very much your business to search for it, and that with the same diligence and labor with which men are wont to dig in mines of silver and gold.

§ From "The Importance and Advantage of a Thorough Knowledge of Divine Truth," p. 161

OUR MISERY, HIS MERCY

Not unto us, O LORD, not unto us, but unto thy name give glory, for thy mercy, and for thy truth's sake. — PSALM 115:1

They who are not sensible of their misery cannot truly look to God for mercy, for it is the very notion of divine mercy, that it is the goodness and grace of God to the miserable. Without misery in the object, there can be no exercise of mercy. To suppose mercy without supposing misery, or pity without calamity, is a contradiction: therefore men cannot look upon themselves as proper objects of mercy unless they first know themselves to be miserable; and so, unless this be the case, it is impossible that they should come to God for mercy. They must be sensible that they are the children of wrath—that the law is against them and they are exposed to the curse of it; that the wrath of God abideth on them; and that He is angry with them every day while they are under the guilt of sin. They must be sensible that it is a very dreadful thing to be the object of the wrath of God; that it is a very awful thing to have Him for their enemy; and that they cannot bear His wrath. They must be sensible that the guilt of sin makes them miserable creatures, whatever temporal enjoyments they have; that they can be no other than miserable, undone creatures, so long as God is angry with them; that they are without strength and must perish, and that eternally, unless God help them. They must see that their case is utterly desperate for anything that anyone else can do for them; that they hang over the pit of eternal misery; and that they must necessarily drop into it, if God have not mercy on them.

From "Great Guilt No Obstacle to the Pardon of the Returning Sinner," p. 11

EXALTED ABOVE ALL

*The LORD said unto my Lord, Sit thou at my right hand, until
I make thine enemies thy footstool.*
—PSALM 110:1

Christ appears gloriously exalted above all evil in His resurrection and ascension into heaven. When Christ rose from the dead, then it appeared that He was above death, which, though it had taken Him captive, could not hold Him. Then He appeared above the devil. Then this Leviathan that had swallowed Him was forced to vomit Him up again; as the Philistines who had taken captive the ark were forced to return it; Dagon being fallen before it, with his head and hands broken off, and only the stumps left. Then He appeared above our guilt: for He was justified in His resurrection (see Rom. 4:4, 25; 1 Tim. 3:16). In His resurrection He appeared above all affliction. For, though He had been subject to much affliction, and overwhelmed in it, He then emerged out of it, as having gotten the victory, never to conflict with any more sorrow. When He ascended up into heaven, He rose far above the reach of the devil and all his instruments, who had before had Him in their hands. And now has He sat down at the right hand of God, as being made head over all things to the church, in order to a complete and perfect victory over sin, Satan, death, and all His enemies. It was then said to Him, "Sit thou at my right hand, until I make thine enemies thy footstool" (Ps. 110:1). He entered into a state of glory, wherein He is exalted far above all these evils, as the forerunner of His people, and to make intercession for them, until they also are brought to be with Him, in like manner exalted above all evil.

§ From "Christ Exalted," p. 215

CHRIST REJOICES OVER HIS SAINTS

And while they went to buy, the bridegroom came; and they that were ready went in with him to the marriage: and the door was shut.
— MATTHEW 25:10

Christ rejoices over His saints as the bridegroom over the bride at all times, but there are some seasons wherein He doth so more especially. Such a season is the time of the soul's conversion—when the good shepherd finds His lost sheep, brings it home rejoicing, and calls together His friends and neighbors, saying, "Rejoice with me." The day of a sinner's conversion is the day of Christ's espousals, and so is eminently the day of His rejoicing: "Go forth, O ye daughters of Zion, and behold king Solomon with the crown wherewith his mother crowned him in the day of his espousals, and in the day of the gladness of his heart" (Song 3:11). Oftentimes it is remarkably the day of the saints' rejoicing in Christ, for then God turns again the captivity of His elect people, and, as it were, fills their mouth with laughter and their tongue with singing, as in Psalm 126 at the beginning. We read of the jailer in Acts 16, that when he was converted, he "rejoiced, believing in God with all his house" (Acts 16:34). There are other seasons of special communion of the saints with Christ, wherein Christ doth in a special manner rejoice over His saints, and as their bridegroom brings them into His chambers, that they also may be glad and rejoice in Him (see Song 1:4). But this mutual rejoicing of Christ and His saints will be in its perfection at the time of the saints' glorification with Christ in heaven; for that is the proper time of the saints' entering in with the bridegroom into the marriage (see Matt. 25:10).

❧ From "The Church's Marriage to Her Sons, and to Her God," p. 22

ABSENT FROM THE LORD

Whom having not seen, ye love; in whom, though now ye see him not, yet believing, ye rejoice with joy unspeakable and full of glory.

—1 PETER 1:8

When we are absent from our dear friends, they are out of sight, but when we are with them, we have the opportunity and satisfaction of seeing them. So too, while the saints are in the body, and are absent from the Lord, He is in several respects out of sight: "Whom having not seen, ye love; in whom, though now ye see him not, yet believing" (1 Peter 1:8). They have, indeed, in this world, a spiritual sight of Christ, but they see through a glass darkly, and with great interruption; in heaven they see Him face to face (see 1 Cor. 13:12): "Blessed are the pure in heart: for they shall see God" (Matt. 5:8). Their beatifical vision of God is in Christ, who is that brightness or effulgence of God's glory by which His glory shines forth in heaven, to the view of saints and angels there, as well as here on earth. This is the Sun of Righteousness, not only the light of this world, but also the sun that enlightens the heavenly Jerusalem, by whose bright beams it is that the glory of God shines forth there, to the enlightening and making happy all the glorious inhabitants. "The glory of God did lighten it, and the Lamb is the light thereof" (Rev. 21:23). None sees God the Father immediately, who is the King eternal, immortal, invisible; Christ is the image of that invisible God, by which He is seen by all elect creatures.

LABOR FOR HEAVEN

What profit hath a man of all his labour which he taketh under the sun?
— ECCLESIASTES 1:3

Labor to get a sense of the vanity of this world, on account of the little satisfaction that is to be enjoyed here; its short continuance and unserviceableness when we most stand in need of help, namely on a deathbed. All men who live any considerable time in the world might see enough to convince them of its vanity, if they would but consider. Be persuaded to exercise consideration, when you see and hear, from time to time, of the death of others. Labor to turn your thoughts this way. See if you can see the vanity of this world in such a glass. If you were sensible how vain a thing this world is, you would see that it is not worthy that your life should be spent to the purposes thereof, and all is lost that is not some way aimed at heaven. Labor to be much acquainted with heaven. If you are acquainted with it, you will not be likely to spend your life as a journey thither. You will not be sensible of the worth of it, nor will you long for it. Unless you are much conversant in your mind with a better good, it will be exceeding difficult to you to have your hearts loose from these things and to use them only in subordination to something else and to be ready to part with them for the sake of that better good. Labor, therefore, to obtain a realizing sense of a heavenly world, to get a firm belief of the reality of it, and to be very much conversant with it in your thoughts.

§ From "The Christian Pilgrim, or the True Christian's Life a Journey toward Heaven," p. 246

THE ABSENCE OF HOPE

What is the Almighty, that we should serve him? and what profit should we have, if we pray unto him?
— JOB 21:15

I would exhort those who have entertained a hope of their being true converts and who, since their supposed conversion, have left off the duty of secret prayer and ordinarily allow themselves in the omission of it, to throw away their hope. If you have left off calling upon God, it is time for you to leave off hoping and flattering yourselves with an imagination that you are the children of God. It will probably be very difficult for you to do this. It is hard for a man to let go of a hope of heaven on which he hath once allowed himself to lay hold, and that he hath retained for a considerable time. True conversion is a rare thing; but that men should be brought off from a false hope of conversion after they are once settled and established in it, and have continued in it for some time, is much more rare. Those things in men that, if known, would be sufficient to convince others that they are hypocrites, will not convince themselves; and those things that would be sufficient to convince them concerning others will not be sufficient to convince them concerning themselves. They can make larger allowances for themselves than they can for others. They can find out ways to solve objections against their own hope, when they can find none in the like case for their neighbor.

§ From "Hypocrites Deficient in the Duty of Prayer," p. 74

THERE IS NONE LIKE HIM

Now therefore, our God, we thank thee, and praise thy glorious name.
— 1 CHRONICLES 29:13

God is a glorious God. There is none like Him who is infinite in glory and excellency. He is the Most High God, glorious in holiness, fearful in praises, doing wonders. His name is excellent in all the earth, and His glory is above the heavens. Among the gods there is none like unto Him; there is none in heaven to be compared to Him, nor are there any among the sons of the mighty that can be likened unto Him. Their God is the fountain of all good and an inexhaustible fountain; He is an all-sufficient God, able to protect and defend them and do all things for them. He is the King of glory, the Lord strong and mighty, the Lord mighty in battle: a strong rock and a high tower. There is none like the God of Jeshurun, who rideth on the heaven in their help and in His excellency on the sky; the eternal God is their refuge, and underneath are everlasting arms. He is a God who hath all things in His hands and does whatsoever He pleases: He killeth and maketh alive; He bringeth down to the grave and bringeth up; He maketh poor and maketh rich. The pillars of the earth are the Lord's. Their God is an infinitely holy God; there is none holy as the Lord. He is infinitely good and merciful. Many that others worship and serve as gods are cruel beings, spirits that seek the ruin of souls; but this is a God that delighteth in mercy. His grace is infinite and endures forever. He is love itself, an infinite fountain and ocean of it. Such a God is their God!

ᕽ From "Ruth's Resolution," p. 665

READ THE SCRIPTURES

All scripture is given by inspiration of God, and is profitable for doctrine, for reproof, for correction, for instruction in righteousness.
— 2 TIMOTHY 3:16

Be assiduous in reading the Holy Scriptures. This is the fountain whence all knowledge in divinity must be derived. Therefore, let not this treasure lie by you neglected. Every man of common understanding who can read may, if he pleases, become well acquainted with the Scriptures. And what an excellent attainment would this be! Content not yourselves with only a cursory reading, without regarding the sense. This is an ill way of reading; however, many accustom themselves to it all their days. When you read, observe what you read. Observe how things come in. Take notice of the drift of the discourse, and compare one Scripture with another. For the Scripture, by the harmony of its different parts, casts great light upon itself. We are expressly directed by Christ to search the Scriptures; He obviously intends something more than a mere cursory reading. Use means to find out the meaning of the Scripture. When you have it explained in the preaching of the word, take notice of it. If, at any time, a Scripture that you did not understand be cleared up to your satisfaction, mark it, lay it up, and, if possible, remember it. Improve conversation with others to this end. How much might persons promote each other's knowledge in divine things if they would improve conversation as they might; if men that are ignorant were not ashamed to show their ignorance and were willing to learn of others; if those that have knowledge would communicate it, without pride and ostentation; and if all were more disposed to enter on such conversation as would be for their mutual edification and instruction.

๑ From "The Importance and Advantage of a Thorough Knowledge of Divine Truth," p. 162

GRACES DEPENDENT UPON ONE ANOTHER

Tribulation worketh patience; and patience, experience; and experience, hope; and hope maketh not ashamed; because the love of God is shed abroad in our hearts. — ROMANS 5:3–5

The graces of Christianity depend upon one another. There is not only a connection, whereby they are always joined together, but there is also a mutual dependence between them, so that one cannot be without the others. To deny one would, in effect, be to deny another, and so all; just as to deny the cause would be to deny the effect, or to deny the effect would be to deny the cause. Faith promotes love, and love is the most effectual ingredient in a living faith. Love is dependent on faith; for a being cannot be truly loved, and especially loved above all other beings, who is not looked upon as a real being. And then love, again, enlarges and promotes faith; we are more apt to believe and give credit to, and more disposed to trust in, those we love than in those we do not. So faith begets hope; for faith sees and trusts in God's sufficiency to bestow blessings and in His faithfulness to His promises that He will do what He has said. All gracious hope is hope resting on faith; and hope encourages and draws forth acts of faith. And so love tends to hope; for the spirit of love is the spirit of a child, and the more anyone feels in himself this spirit toward God, the more natural it will be to him to look to God and go to God as his father. This childlike spirit casts out the spirit of bondage and fear and gives the Spirit of adoption, which is the spirit of confidence and hope: "Ye have not received the spirit of bondage again to fear; but ye have received the Spirit of adoption, whereby we cry, Abba, Father" (Rom. 8:15); and the apostle John tells us, "There is no fear in love, but perfect love casteth out fear" (1 John 4:18).

§ From "All the Graces of Christianity Connected," pp. 271–72

VICTORIOUS GRACE

Thanks be to God, which giveth us the victory through our Lord Jesus Christ.
— 1 CORINTHIANS 15:57

All the opposition that is or can be made against true grace in the heart cannot overthrow it. The enemies of grace may, in many respects, gain great advantages against it. They may exceedingly oppress and reduce it and bring it into such circumstances that it may seem to be brought to the very brink of utter ruin. But yet it will live. The ruin that seemed impending shall be averted. Though the roaring lion sometimes comes with open mouth, and no visible refuge appears, yet the lamb shall escape and be safe; yea, though it is in the very paw of the lion or the bear, yet it shall be rescued, and not devoured. And though it even seems actually swallowed down, as Jonah was by the whale, yet it shall be brought up again and live. It is with grace in the heart, in this respect, as it was with the ark upon the waters, however terrible the storm may be, yea, though it be such a deluge as overwhelms all things else, yet it shall not overwhelm that. Though the floods rise ever so high, yet it shall be kept above the waters; and though the mighty waves may rise above the tops of the highest mountains, yet they shall not be able to get above this ark, but it shall still float in safety. Or it is with this grace as it was with the ship in which Christ was when there arose a great storm, and the waves ran high, insomuch that it seemed as if the ship would instantly sink; and yet it did not sink, though it was actually covered with water, for Christ was in it. Grace shall not only remain, but at last it shall have the victory. Though it may pass through a long time of sore conflicts and may suffer many disadvantages and depressions, yet it shall live—and not only live, but it will finally prosper and prevail and triumph, and all its enemies shall be subdued under its feet.

§ From "Charity, or True Grace, Not to Be Overthrown by Opposition," pp. 290–91

CARE AT ALL SEASONS

Nevertheless he left not himself without witness, in that he did good, and gave us rain from heaven, and fruitful seasons, filling our hearts with food and gladness.
— ACTS 14:17

How little men, in their dealings with one another, consider their neighbor as well as their own good. All their strife is for themselves. How greatly they resent it if they think themselves wronged; but how easily they hurt others, and how little they are affected by the injuries that others suffer. They are careful to guard themselves, but how little they are concerned for the calamities others are exposed to. How careful of their condition and good name they are, but how freely they make with others' character. How little they are concerned for the honor and reputation of others! But woe to us if God were as careless of our welfare, if God took no more care of our preservation, subsistence, and comfort in the world! God is continually watching over us for our good; otherwise we would be exposed to meet with fatal mischief. Every hour that we live, we would soon stumble, fall, and be ruined. God takes care of us at all seasons. He takes care of us in the summer to give rain to water the earth so that it may bring forth food for us. He takes care of us in the winter and provides us shelter and clothes and fire. He takes care of us every day to feed and nourish us, and every night while we sleep. He takes care of us to keep wicked and carnal spirits from falling upon us to devour us. And woe to us if He did not!

⚘ From "It Is Well for Us That God Is Not as We Are," p. 19

NOTHINGNESS BEFORE GOD

Who hath ascended up into heaven, or descended? who hath gathered the wind in his fists? who hath bound the waters in a garment? who hath established all the ends of the earth? what is his name, and what is his son's name, if thou canst tell?
— PROVERBS 30:4

There is nothing like seeing what God is to make men sensible of what they are. Not that any man ever comes to know what God is, so as to have a comprehensive knowledge of God and to know and understand all the mysteries of His nature. This is what God teaches us, that we do not and cannot ever know what He is. God dwells in an unapproachable light. Yet we may have a true knowledge of God, though not a comprehensive knowledge of Him. There is such a thing as having a right apprehension of God, though this admits of many degrees. It is but little that we know of God, though some know more than others and have great discoveries of God. Those who have some acquaintance with God may grow in acquaintance with Him; and those who know most in this world know but little in comparison of what the saints shall know in heaven when they shall see Him as He is. When men consider themselves by themselves and compare themselves among themselves, they are ready to entertain high thoughts of themselves. They think of themselves something and look big in their own eyes; but when persons come to have a sight of the greatness and majesty of God, it will alter their opinion of themselves. When they see how great and high and glorious God is, then their great imaginations of themselves vanish away and they shrink into nothing in their own eyes. When a man comes to see how great God is, this and this only will make a man sensible of his own nothingness, for there is an infinite distance between God and man. The greatest man is, before God, as nothing, and less than nothing.

§ From "There Is Nothing Like Seeing What God Is to Make Men Sensible to What They Are," pp. 134–35

GIVE HIM YOUR ALL

In him dwelleth all the fullness of the Godhead bodily.
—COLOSSIANS 2:9

If Christ is your all, then give your all to Him. Give to Him all that you are, your body and soul as a living sacrifice, rendering yourself entirely to this glorious person. Give Him all that you have; all your substance, all your enjoyment, let them all be devoted to Him and His glory. In Jesus Christ is all excellency. Everything that is excellent and lovely meets in Christ. It is not possible there should be any lovely qualification but what is in Him. If you see anything truly lovely and excellent in any part of the creation, you may consider that the same is eminently in Christ. It is in Him originally, and He is the fountain of it. There is nothing excellent in God but what is also in Christ. There is no excellency in men but what is also in Him in His human nature. He possesses all human excellency. If you give your all to Christ, you will be exceedingly happy. If you have nothing else, you will need nothing. He is enough; in Him you will have full happiness. He has given Himself and all that He has to you. He gives Himself to those who close with Him and becomes theirs. They may say of Him, "my Beloved is mine" (Song 2:16). He gives Himself wholly, without any reservations. Though He is so great and glorious a person, He gives Himself with all His divine perfections—power, holiness, and so on. He gives Himself in both natures. All that He has—His propitiation, His righteousness, His privileges, His benefits, and all that He possesses—He gives so that you may possess the same, so far as you are capable of it. You, as joint heirs with Christ, may possess all things. So, nothing is Christ's but is yours.

⟡ From "Christ Is the Christian's All," pp. 205–6

THE EXAMPLE OF JOHN THE BAPTIST

He was a burning and a shining light.
—JOHN 5:35

John the Baptist was not only a burning but a shining light. He was so in his doctrine, having more of the gospel in his preaching than the former prophets, or at least the gospel exhibited with greater light and clearness, more plainly pointing forth the person that was to be the great Redeemer and declaring His errand into the world, to take away the sin of the world, as a lamb offered in sacrifice to God, and the necessity that all, even the most strictly moral and religious, stood in front of him, being by nature a generation of vipers. And he was a light in the spiritual nature of his kingdom, consisting not in circumcision or outward baptism or any other external performance or privileges, but in the powerful influences of the Holy Ghost in their hearts. He was a being baptized with the Holy Ghost and with fire. In this clearness with which he gave knowledge of salvation to God's people, John was a bright light, and among them that had been born of women there had not arisen a greater than he. In this brightness this harbinger of the gospel day excelled all the other prophets, as the morning star reflects more of the light of the sun than any other star and is the brightest of all the stars. He also shone bright in his conversation and his eminent mortification and renunciation of the enjoyments of the world; his great diligence and laboriousness in his work, his impartiality in it, declaring the mind and will of God to all sorts without distinction; his great humility, rejoicing in the increase of the honor of Christ, though his honor was diminished, as the brightness of the morning star diminishes as the light of the sun increases; and in his faithfulness and courage, still declaring the mind and will of God, though it cost him his own life. Thus his light shone before men.

§ From "The True Excellency of a Gospel Minister," pp. 955–56

GREATER THAN KINGS

And hath made us kings and priests unto God and his Father.
— REVELATION 1:6

When Christians are called kings, the Scriptures include both what they actually have in this world, and what they have in a future state. The reward that our Lord Jesus promised to His disciples was a kingdom: "And I appoint unto you a kingdom, as my Father hath appointed unto me" (Luke 22:29). The happiness of the saints is far greater than that of the kings and greatest potentates in the world. True Christians will be advanced to honors far above those of earthly kings. They will have a vastly higher dignity than any princes. If these are nobly descended, it is not so great an honor as to be the sons of God. If they are nobly educated and have their minds formed for government and have princely qualifications, these qualifications are not so honorable as those with which God endows His saints, whose minds He fills with divine knowledge, and gives them true and perfect holiness. Princes appear honorable from their outward enjoyment of honor and dignity, their royal robes, and their stately palaces; but these are not so honorable as those white robes, those inherent ornaments, with which the saints shall appear in heaven, with which they shall shine forth as the sun in the kingdom of their Father. What is a king's palace to those mansions in heaven that Christ prepares for His saints? The honor of the creature consists in likeness and nearness to the Creator in heaven. The saints shall be like Him, for they shall see Him as He is. They shall be most near to Him and shall be admitted to a most intimate fellowship.

𝆕 From "Christians a Chosen Generation, a Royal Priesthood, a Holy Nation, a Peculiar People," pp. 940–41

A HOLY AND JEALOUS GOD

And Joshua said unto the people, Ye cannot serve the LORD: *for he is an holy God; he is a jealous God; he will not forgive your transgressions nor your sins.*
—JOSHUA 24:19

There are two reasons God deals with so great a strictness as the lawgiver and judge of the law. First, it is because God is so holy a God. He is an infinitely holy being. Infinite holiness is His very essence. And it is because He is so holy that it is impossible that when He gives a law to men that His law should be any other than exceedingly strict. 'Tis impossible upon this account that His law should allow of any unholiness; 'tis impossible but that He should forbid all unholiness. And as God is infinitely holy, so 'tis necessary that He should infinitely hate all unholiness or that He should not have an infinite enmity against it. And here it is that all sin is threatened in His law with eternal death, which is an infinite punishment; for if God's enmity against sin is infinitely great, it is fitting that the manifestations and testimonies of this enmity should be proportionally great in the punishment of sin. Secondly, it is because God is a jealous God. He is jealous of His own honor and glory. Hence, He will deal with such strictness as the giver and judge of the law. 'Tis hence that God has threatened all sin with so dreadful a punishment as eternal death because that sin is against the honor of His majesty. Their sin is committed against God; it strikes at the honor of God and endeavors to dishonor Him; it is rebellion against the rightful authority of God and has its foundation in a contempt of God. God's jealousy for the honor of His own infinite authority and infinite majesty influences Him so severely to threaten sin, and will influence Him to execute His threatenings for all sin.

§ From "God, as the Giver and Judge of the Law, Deals with the Utmost Strictness," pp. 193–94

THE RESTRAINT OF GOD

But the wicked are like the troubled sea, when it cannot rest,
whose waters cast up mire and dirt.
— ISAIAH 57:20

There are in the souls of wicked men those hellish principles reigning that would presently kindle and flame out into hellfire, if it were not for God's restraints. There is laid in the very nature of carnal men a foundation for the torments of hell. There are those corrupt principles, in reigning power in them and in full possession of them, that are seeds of hellfire. These principles are active and powerful, exceedingly violent in their nature, and if it were not for the restraining hand of God upon them, they would soon break out, they would flame out after the same manner as the same corruptions, the same enmity does in the hearts of damned souls, and would beget the same torments as they do in them. The souls of the wicked are in Scripture compared to the troubled sea (see Isa. 57:20). For the present, God restrains their wickedness by His mighty power, as He does the raging waves of the troubled sea, saying, "Hitherto shalt thou come, but no further" (Job 38:11); but if God should withdraw that restraining power, it would soon carry all before it. Sin is the ruin and misery of the soul; it is destructive in its nature. If God should leave it without restraint there would need nothing else to make the soul perfectly miserable. The corruption of the heart of man is immoderate and boundless in its fury; while wicked men live here, it is like fire pent up by God's restraints: if it were let loose, it would set on fire the course of nature. As the heart is now a sink of sin, so if sin were not restrained it would immediately turn the soul into a fiery oven, or a furnace of fire and brimstone.

§ From "Sinners in the Hands of an Angry God," p. 8

WHAT OTHERS SAY ABOUT YOU

Behold, his soul which is lifted up is not upright in him: but the just shall live by his faith.
— HABAKKUK 2:4

Be advised to consider what others say of you and improve it to this end, to know whether you do not live in some way of sin. Although men are blind to their own faults, yet they easily discover the faults of others and are apt enough to speak of them. Sometimes persons live in ways that do not at all become them, yet are blind to it themselves, not seeing the deformity of their own ways, while it is most plain and evident to others. They themselves cannot see it, yet others cannot shut their eyes against it, cannot avoid seeing it. For instance, some persons are of a very proud behavior and are not sensible of it, but it appears notorious to others. Some are of a very worldly spirit, they are set after the world, so as to be noted for it, so as to have a name for it, yet they seem not to be sensible of it themselves. Some are of a very malicious and envious spirit, and others see it, and to them it appears very hateful, yet they themselves do not reflect upon it. Therefore, since there is no trusting to our own hearts and our own eyes in such cases, we should make our improvement of what others say of us; observe what they charge us with and what fault they find with us, and strictly examine whether there be not foundation for it. If others charge us with being proud; or worldly, close, and niggardly; or spiteful and malicious; or with any other ill temper or practice; we should improve it in self-reflection, to inquire whether it be not so.

§ From "Christian Cautions, or the Necessity of Self-Examination," p. 178

REST FROM AFFLICTIONS

There remaineth therefore a rest to the people of God.
— HEBREWS 4:9

There is in Christ rest for God's people, when exercised with afflictions. If a person labors under great bodily weakness, or under some disease that causes frequent and strong pains, such things will tire out so feeble a creature as man. It may, to such a one, be a comfort and an effectual support to think that he has a Mediator who knows by experience what pain is; who by His pain has purchased eternal ease and pleasure for Him; and who will make His brief sufferings to work out a far more exceeding delight, to be bestowed when he shall rest from his labors and sorrows. If a person be brought into great straits as to outward subsistence, and poverty brings abundance of difficulties and extremities, yet it may be a supporting, refreshing consideration to such a one to think that he has a compassionate Savior, who, when upon earth, was so poor that He had nowhere to lay His head, and who became poor to make him rich, and purchased for him durable riches, and will make His poverty work out an exceeding and eternal weight of glory. If God in His providence calls His people to mourn over lost relations, and if He repeats His stroke and takes away one after another of those that were dear to him; it is a supporting, refreshing consideration to think that Christ has declared that He will be instead of all relations unto those who trust in Him.

⚜ From "Safety, Fullness, and Sweet Refreshment, to Be Found in Christ," p. 935

GOD, THE TRUE REVEALER

Then Agrippa said unto Paul, Almost thou persuadest me to be a Christian.

— ACTS 26:28

Men, by mere principles of nature, are capable of being affected with things that have a special relation to religion as well as other things. A person, by mere nature, for instance, may be liable to be affected with the story of Jesus Christ and the sufferings He underwent, as well as by any other tragic story. He may be the more affected with it from the interest he conceives mankind to have in it. Yea, he may be affected with it without believing it, as well as a man may be affected with what he reads in a romance or sees acted in a stage play. He may be affected with a lively and eloquent description of many pleasant things that attend the state of the blessed in heaven, as well as his imagination be entertained by a romantic description of the pleasantness of fairy land, or the like. A common belief of the truth of such things, from education or otherwise, may help forward their affection with him. We read in Scripture of many that were greatly affected with things of a religious nature, who yet are there represented as wholly graceless, and many of them very ill men. A person, therefore, may have affecting views of the things of religion and yet be very destitute of spiritual light. Flesh and blood may be the author of this: one man may give another an affecting view of divine things with but common assistance, but God alone can give a spiritual discovery of them.

§ From "A Divine and Supernatural Light," p. 13

GOD WILL BE EXALTED

Be still, and know that I am God: I will be exalted among the heathen, I will be exalted in the earth.
—PSALM 46:10

God will be sovereign, and will act as such. He sits on the throne of His sovereignty, and His kingdom rules over all. He will be exalted in His sovereign power and dominion, as He Himself declares in Psalm 46:10: "I will be exalted among the heathen, I will be exalted in the earth." He will have all men to know that He is most high over all the earth. He doeth according to His will in the armies of heaven and among the inhabitants of the earth, and none can stay His hand. There is no such thing as frustrating, or baffling, or undermining His designs, for He is great in counsel and wonderful in working. His counsel shall stand, and He will do all His pleasure. There is no wisdom, nor understanding, nor counsel against the Lord; whatsoever God doeth, it shall be forever; nothing shall be put to it or anything taken from it. He will work, and who shall prevent it? He is able to dash in pieces the enemy. If men join hand-in-hand against Him to hinder or oppose His designs, He breaks the bow, He cuts the spear in sunder, He burneth the chariot in the fire. He kills and He makes alive; He brings down and raises up just as He pleases: "That they may know from the rising of the sun, and from the west, that there is none beside me. I am the LORD, and there is none else: I form the light and create darkness: I make peace and create evil: I the LORD do all these things" (Isa. 45:6–7).

§ From "The Sole Consideration, That God Is God, Sufficient to Still All Objections to His Sovereignty," p. 109

ENTHRONED IN GLORY

For the Son of man shall come in the glory of his Father with his angels; and then he shall reward every man according to his works.
— MATTHEW 16:27

Christ Jesus will, in a most magnificent manner, descend from heaven with all the holy angels. The man Christ Jesus is now in the heaven of heavens, or, as the apostle Paul expresses it, far above all heavens (see Eph. 4:10). And there He hath been ever since His ascension, being there enthroned in glory in the midst of millions of angels and blessed spirits. But when the time appointed for the day of judgment shall have come, notice of it will be given in those happy regions, and Christ will descend to the earth, attended with all those heavenly hosts, in a most solemn, awful, and glorious manner. Christ will come with divine majesty; He will come in the glory of the Father: "For the Son of man shall come in the glory of his Father, with his angels" (Matt. 16:27). We can now conceive but little of the holy and awful magnificence in which Christ will appear, as He shall come in the clouds of heaven, or of the glory of His retinue. How mean and despicable, in comparison with it, is the most splendid appearance that earthly princes can make! A glorious visible light will shine round about Him, and the earth, with all nature, will tremble at His presence. How vast and innumerable will that host be that will appear with Him! Heaven will be for the time deserted of its inhabitants.

⚜ From "The Final Judgment, or the World Judged Righteously by Jesus Christ," p. 194

THE HUMILIATION OF CHRIST

Who, being in the form of God, thought it not robbery to be equal with God: but made himself of no reputation, and took upon him the form of a servant, and was made in the likeness of men: and being found in fashion as a man, he humbled himself, and became obedient unto death, even the death of the cross.

— PHILIPPIANS 2:6–8

It shows wonderful wisdom that our good should be procured by such seemingly unlikely and opposite means as the humiliation of the Son of God. When Christ was about to undertake that great work of redemption, He did not take that method that any creature-wisdom would have thought the most proper. Creature-wisdom would have determined that, in order to His effectually and more gloriously accomplishing such a great work, He should rather have been exalted higher, if it had been possible, rather than humbled so low. Earthly kings and princes, when they are about to engage in any great and difficult work, will put on their strength and will appear in all their majesty and power, that they may be successful. But, when Christ was about to perform the great work of redeeming a lost world, the wisdom of God took an opposite method and determined that He should be humbled and abased to a mean state and appear in low circumstances. He did not deck Himself with glory, but laid it aside. He emptied Himself: "Being in the form of God…he made himself of no reputation, and took upon him the form of a servant, and was made in the likeness of men: and being found in fashion as a man, he humbled himself, and became obedient unto death, even the death of the cross" (Phil. 2:6–8). Creature-wisdom would have thought that Christ, in order to perform this great work, should deck Himself with all His strength; but divine wisdom determined that he should be made weak, or put on the infirmities of human nature.

⸎ From "The Wisdom of God, Displayed in the Way of Salvation," p. 150

INFINITE EXCELLENCY

Looking unto Jesus the author and finisher of our faith; who for the joy that was set before him endured the cross, despising the shame, and is set down at the right hand of the throne of God.
— HEBREWS 12:2

There can be nothing that renders any person deserving of our love, nor any possible degree of it, but what is to be found in Jesus Christ. He has in Him all possible excellency. He has infinite majesty as He is the great God and creator of the world. He has infinite holiness. He has infinite wisdom and boundless grace and goodness. There is nothing that is an excellency but it is in Him in an infinite degree. It is impossible but that it should be so, because all that is excellent, all that is beautiful and desirable in the whole creation, He is the foundation of it. And if it is not enough that He has all divine excellency, which indeed comprehends all possible excellency, He also has in His person all human excellencies, such as charity, meekness, patience, and humility, joined with great wisdom and holiness. We cannot devise any qualification that is endearing in any man but it is in Christ's human nature to an immensely greater degree than it ever was in any other man, and greater than in any other creature. We, in this land of light, have the excellencies of Christ continually set before us from our very infancy by education and by the constant preaching of the word. We have Christ set before our eyes by sensible signs in the sacraments, and we also see the glory of Christ set before us in the many instances of the success of the gospel and the holy lives of His people. God has used an abundance of methods to set before us the excellency of His Son. The light clearly shines all around us and breaks forth from every quarter. God has exercised His infinite wisdom in contriving to set forth His Son's excellency in a glorious light.

§ From "It Is Crime Enough to Render Any Man a Cursed Person Not to Love Jesus Christ," pp. 24–25

SATISFACTION OF CHRIST

But if we walk in the light, as he is in the light, we have fellow-ship one with another, and the blood of Jesus Christ his Son cleanseth us from all sin.

— 1 JOHN 1:7

The satisfaction of Christ is as sufficient for the removal of the greatest guilt as it is for the least: "The blood of Jesus Christ…cleanseth us from all sin" (1 John 1:7); "By him all that believe are justified from all things, from which ye could not be justified by the law of Moses" (Acts 13:39). All the sins of those who truly come to God for mercy, let them be what they will, are satisfied for, if God be true who tells us so; and if they be satisfied for, surely it is not incredible that God should be ready to pardon them. So that Christ having fully satisfied for all sin, or having wrought out a satisfaction that is sufficient for all, it is now no way inconsistent with the glory of the divine attributes to pardon the greatest sins of those who in a right manner come unto Him for it. God may now pardon the greatest sinners without any prejudice to the honor of His holiness. The holiness of God will not suffer Him to give the least countenance to sin, but inclines Him to give proper testimonies of His hatred of it. But Christ having satisfied for sin, God can now love the sinner and give no countenance at all to sin, however great a sinner he may have been. It was a sufficient testimony of God's abhorrence of sin that He poured out His wrath on His own dear Son when He took the guilt of it upon Himself. Nothing can more show God's abhorrence of sin than this. If all mankind had been eternally damned, it would not have been so great a testimony of it.

🔖 From "Great Guilt No Obstacle to the Pardon of the Returning Sinner," p. 111

ONLY STEWARDS

Every man according as he purposeth in his heart, so let him give; not grudgingly, or of necessity: for God loveth a cheerful giver.
— 2 CORINTHIANS 9:7

We are professors of Christianity; we pretend to be the followers of Jesus and to make the gospel our rule. We have the Bible in our houses. Let us not behave ourselves in regard to giving to those who are needy as if we had never seen the Bible, as if we were ignorant of Christianity and knew not what kind of religion it is. What will it signify to pretend to be Christians, and, at the same time, to live in the neglect of those rules of Christianity that are mainly insisted on in it? In regard to giving to the poor, consider that what you have is not your own; you have only a subordinate right. Your goods are only lent to you by God to be improved by you in such ways as He directs. You yourselves are not your own: "Ye are not your own, for ye are bought with a price" (1 Cor. 6:19–20). Your body and your spirit are God's; and if you yourselves are not your own, then neither are your possessions your own. Many of you have, by covenant, given up yourselves and all you have to God. You have disowned and renounced any right in yourselves or in anything that you have and have given God all the absolute right; and if you are true Christians, you have done it from the heart. Your money and your goods are not your own. They are only committed to you as stewards to be used for Him who committed them to you: "Use hospitality one to another… as good stewards of the manifold grace of God" (1 Peter 4:9–10). A steward has no business with his master's goods, to use them any otherwise than for the benefit of his master and his family or according to his master's direction. But he is to give every one of his master's family their portion of meat in due season. Remember that all of us must give account of our stewardship and of how we have disposed of those goods that our Master has put into our hands.

§ From "Christian Charity: The Duty of Charity to the Poor Explained and Enforced," pp. 239–40

TRUE AND INFINITE RICHES

Hearken, my beloved brethren, Hath not God chosen the poor of this world rich in faith, and heirs of the kingdom which he hath promised to them that love him?
— JAMES 2:5

Christians have true and infinite riches. They are the possessors and heirs of something real and substantial and that is worthy to be called by the name of riches. The things they possess are excellent, more precious than gold and than rubies; all the desirable things of this world cannot equal them, and they have enough of it. The riches that they have given them of God are inexhaustible. It is sufficient for them; there is no end of it. They have a fountain of infinite good for their comfort and contentment and joy; for God has given Himself to them to be their portion, and He is a God of infinite glory. There is glory in Him to engage their contemplation forever and ever, without ever being satiated. And He is also an infinite fountain of love; for God is love, yea, an ocean of love without shore or bottom! The glorious Son of God is theirs: that lovely one, who was from all eternity God's delight, rejoicing always before Him. All His beauty is their portion, and His dying love is theirs, His very heart is theirs, and His glory and happiness in heaven are theirs, so far as their capacity will allow them to partake of it; for He has promised it to them and has taken possession of it in their name.

⚬ From "The Portion of the Righteous," p. 889

THE HAPPINESS OF HEAVEN

And there shall be no more curse: but the throne of God and of
the Lamb shall be in it; and his servants shall serve him.
— REVELATION 22:3

The happiness of heaven consists not only in contemplation and a mere passive enjoyment, but also very much in action; particularly in actively serving and glorifying God. This is expressly mentioned as a great part of the blessedness of the saints in their most perfect state: "And there shall be no more curse: but the throne of God and of the Lamb shall be in it; and his servants shall serve him" (Rev. 22:3). The angels are as a flame of fire in their ardor and activity in God's service: the four animals in Revelation 4, which are generally supposed to signify the angels, are represented as continually giving praise and glory to God, and are said not to rest day nor night (v. 8). The souls of departed saints are, doubtless, become as the angels of God in heaven in this respect. And Jesus Christ is the head of the whole glorious assembly; as in other things appertaining to their blessed state, so in this of their praising and glorifying the Father. When Christ, the night before He was crucified, prayed for His exaltation to glory, it was that He might glorify the Father: "These words spake Jesus, and lift up his eyes to heaven, and said, Father, the hour is come; glorify thy Son, that thy Son also may glorify thee" (John 17:1). And this He doubtless does, now He is in heaven, not only in fulfilling the Father's will in what He does as head of the church and ruler of the universe, but also in leading the heavenly assembly in their praises.

§ From "True Saints, When Absent from the Body, Are Present with the Lord," pp. 31–32

CONTRARY TO THE DEVIL

And the great dragon was cast out, that old serpent, called the Devil, and Satan, which deceiveth the whole world: he was cast out into the earth, and his angels were cast out with him.

— REVELATION 12:9

It is unreasonable to suppose that a person's being in any respect as the devil is should be a certain sign that he is very unlike and opposite to him, and hereafter shall not have his part with him. True saints are extremely unlike and contrary to the devil, both relatively and really. They are extremely different relatively in the following ways: The devil is the grand rebel; the chief enemy of God and Christ; the object of God's greatest wrath; a condemned malefactor, utterly rejected and cast off by Him; forever shut out of His presence; the prisoner of His justice; an everlasting inhabitant of the infernal world. The saints, on the contrary, are the citizens of the heavenly Jerusalem; members of the family of the glorious King of heaven; the children of God; the brethren and spouse of His dear Son; heirs of God; joint-heirs with Christ; kings and priests unto God. And they are extremely different really in the following ways: The devil, on account of his hateful nature, and those accursed dispositions that reign in him, is called Satan, the adversary, Abaddon and Apollyon, the great destroyer, the wolf, the roaring lion, the great dragon, the old serpent. The saints are represented as God's holy ones, His anointed ones, the excellent of the earth; the meek of the earth; lambs and doves; Christ's little children; having the image of God, pure in heart; God's jewels; lilies in Christ's garden; plants of paradise; stars of heaven; temples of the living God. The saints, so far as they are saints, are as different from the devil as heaven is from hell and much more contrary than light is to darkness; and the eternal state that they are appointed to is answerably diverse and contrary.

§ From "True Grace Distinguished from the Experience of Devils," p. 42

AVOID THINGS THAT LEAD TO SIN

There was a man in the land of Uz, whose name was Job; and that man was perfect and upright, and one that feared God, and eschewed evil.

—JOB 1:1

It is evident that we ought to avoid things that expose and lead to sin. A due sense of the evil of sin and a just hatred of it will necessarily have this effect upon us, to cause us so to do. If we were duly sensible of the evil and dreadful nature of sin we should have an exceeding dread of it upon our spirits. We should hate it worse than death, fear it worse than the devil himself, and dread it even as we dread damnation. But those things that men exceedingly dread, they naturally shun; and they avoid those things that they apprehend expose to them, just like a child who has been greatly terrified by the sight of any wild beast will by no means be persuaded to go where it apprehends that the beast shall fall in its way. As sin in its own nature is infinitely hateful, so in its natural tendency it is infinitely dreadful. It is the tendency of all sin eternally to undo the soul. Every sin naturally carries hell in it! Therefore, all sin ought to be treated by us as we would treat a thing that is infinitely terrible. If any one sin, yea, the least sin, does not necessarily bring eternal ruin with it, this is owing to nothing but the free grace and mercy of God to us, and not to the nature and tendency of sin itself. But, certainly, we ought not to take the less care to avoid sin or all that tends to it, for the freeness and greatness of God's mercy to us, through which there is hope of pardon, for that would be indeed a most ungrateful and vile abuse of mercy.

From "Temptation and Deliverance," p. 228

RELIGION CONSISTS IN PRACTICE

Be not carried about with divers and strange doctrines. For it is a good thing that the heart be established with grace; not with meats, which have not profited them that have been occupied therein.
— HEBREWS 13:9

There are some who never have come to any determination in their own minds whether to embrace religion in the practice of it. Religion consists not merely, or chiefly, in theory or speculation, but in practice. It is a practical thing; the end of it is to guide and influence us in our practice. Considered in this view, there are multitudes who never have come to a conclusion whether to embrace religion or not. It is probably pretty general for men to design to be religious sometime or other before they die, for none intend to go to hell. But they still keep it at a distance; they put it off from time to time and never come to any conclusion that determines them in their present practice. And some never so much as fix upon any time. They design to be religious sometime before they die, but they know not when. There are many who have always continued unresolved about the necessity of striving and being earnestly engaged for salvation. They flatter themselves that they may obtain salvation, though they are not so earnestly engaged; though they mind the world and their worldly affairs more than their salvation. They are often told how necessary it is that they make haste and not delay, that they do whatever their hand findeth to do with their might; that a dull, slack way of seeking salvation is never likely to be effectual. But of these things they are never thoroughly convinced. Some seem to resolve to be in earnest and seem to set out with some engagedness of mind, but they soon fail, because they have never been fully convinced of its necessity.

🕭 From "The Unreasonableness of Indetermination in Religion," p. 58

THE PRECIOUSNESS OF TIME

Whereas ye know not what shall be on the morrow. For what is your life? It is even a vapour, that appeareth for a little time, and then vanisheth away.
—JAMES 4:14

Time ought to be esteemed by us very precious, because we are uncertain of its continuance. We know that it is very short, but we know not how short. We know not how little of it remains: whether a year, or several years, or only a month, a week, or a day. We are every day uncertain whether that day will not be the last, or whether we are to have the whole day. There is nothing that experience doth more verify than this. If a man had but little provision laid up for a journey or a voyage and at the same time knew that if his provision should fail and he must perish by the way, he would be the more choice of it. How much more would many men prize their time, if they knew that they had but a few months, or a few days more to live! And certainly a wise man will prize his time the more, as he knows not but that it will be so as to himself. This is the case with multitudes now in the world, who at present enjoy health and see no signs of approaching death: many such, no doubt, are to die the next month, many the next week, yea, many probably tomorrow, and some this night; yet these same persons know nothing of it, and perhaps think nothing of it, and neither they nor their neighbors can say that they are more likely soon to be taken out of the world than others. This teaches us how we ought to prize our time and how careful we ought to be, that we lose none of it.

⟐ From "The Preciousness of Time and the Importance of Redeeming It," p. 234

HONOR TO GOD'S AUTHORITY

Therefore as by the offence of one judgment came upon all men to condemnation; even so by the righteousness of one the free gift came upon all men unto justification of life.

— ROMANS 5:18

God saw meet to place man first in a state of trial, and not to give him a title to eternal life as soon as He had made him because it was His will that he should first give honor to His authority by fully submitting to it, in will and act, and perfectly obeying His law. God insisted upon it, that His holy majesty and law should have their due acknowledgment and honor from man, such as became the relation he stood in to that being who created him, before He would bestow the reward of confirmed and everlasting happiness upon him; and therefore God gave him a law that he might have opportunity, by giving due honor to His authority in obeying it, to obtain this happiness. It therefore became Christ—seeing that, in assuming man to Himself, He sought a title to this eternal happiness for him after he had broken the law— that He Himself should become subject to God's authority and be in the form of a servant, that He might do that honor to God's authority for Him, by His obedience, which God at first required of man as the condition of his having a title to that reward. Christ came into the world to render the honor of God's authority and law consistent with the salvation and eternal life of sinners; He came to save them, and yet withal to assert and vindicate the honor of the lawgiver and His holy law.

§ From "Justification by Faith Alone," p. 636

BE WATCHFUL

Watch ye, stand fast in the faith, quit you like men, be strong.
— 1 CORINTHIANS 16:13

In order to persevere in the way of duty to prayer, your own care and watchfulness is necessary. For though it be promised that true saints shall persevere, yet that is no argument that their care and watchfulness is not necessary in order to attain it, because their care to keep the commands of God is the thing promised. If the saints should fail in care, watchfulness, and diligence to persevere in holiness, that failure of their care and diligence would itself be a failure of holiness. They who persevere not in watchfulness and diligence persevere not in holiness of life, for holiness of life very much consists in watchfulness and diligence to keep the commands of God. It is one promise of the covenant of grace that the saints shall keep God's commandments (see Ezek. 11:19–20); yet that is no argument that they have no need to take care to keep these commandments or to do their duty. So, too, the promise of God that the saints shall persevere in holiness is no argument that it is not necessary for them to take heed lest they fall away. Therefore, the Scriptures abundantly warn men to watch over themselves diligently and to give earnest heed lest they fall away: "Watch ye, stand fast in the faith, quit you like men, be strong" (1 Cor. 16:13); "Let him that thinketh he standeth take heed lest he fall" (1 Cor. 10:12); "Take heed, brethren, lest there be in any of you an evil heart of unbelief, in departing from the living God. But exhort one another daily, while it is called To day; lest any of you be hardened through the deceitfulness of sin. For we are made partakers of Christ, if we hold the beginning of our confidence steadfast unto the end" (Heb. 3:12–14).

᪶ From "Hypocrites Deficient in the Duty of Prayer," p. 76

FOLLOW THOSE WHO FOLLOW GOD

So likewise, whosoever he be of you that forsaketh not all that he hath, he cannot be my disciple.

—LUKE 14:33

Our resolutions to cleave to and follow those that are turning to God and joining themselves to His people ought to be fixed and strong because of the great difficulty of it. If we will cleave to them and have their God for our God and their people for our people, we must mortify and deny all our lusts and cross every evil appetite and inclination and forever part with all sin. But our lusts are many and violent. Sin is naturally exceeding dear to us; to part with it is compared to plucking out our right eyes. Men may refrain from wonted ways of sin for a little while and may deny their lusts in a partial degree with less difficulty; but it is heartrending work, finally to part with all sin, to give our dearest lusts a bill of divorce and to utterly send them away. But this we must do, if we would follow those that are truly turning to God; yea, we must not only forsake sin, but must, in a sense, forsake all the world: "Whosoever he be of you that forsaketh not all that he hath, he cannot be my disciple" (Luke 14:33). He must forsake all in his heart, and must come to a thorough disposition and readiness actually to quit all for God and the glorious spiritual privileges of His people, whenever the case may require it. He must do this without any prospect of anything of the like nature or any worldly thing whatsoever, to make amends for it; and all to go into a strange country, a land that has hitherto been unseen, like Abraham, who, being called of God (see Gen. 12:1), went out of his own country, and from his kindred, and from his father's house, for a land that God should show him, not knowing whither he went.

§ From "Ruth's Resolution," pp. 665–66

CHOOSE HEAVEN

Rejoice ye in that day, and leap for joy: for, behold, your reward is great in heaven: for in the like manner did their fathers unto the prophets.

— LUKE 6:23

Labor to obtain such a disposition of mind that you may choose heaven for your inheritance and home, and you may earnestly long for it and be willing to change this world and all its enjoyments for heaven. Labor to have your heart taken up so much about heaven and heavenly enjoyments as that you may rejoice when God calls you to leave your best earthly friends and comforts for heaven, there to enjoy God and Christ. Be persuaded to travel in the way that leads to heaven—namely, in holiness, self-denial, mortification, and obedience to all the commands of God—following Christ's example in a way of a heavenly life, or imitation of the saints and angels in heaven. Let it be your daily work, from morning until night, and hold out in it to the end; let nothing stop or discourage you, or turn you aside from this road. And let all other concerns be subordinated to this. Consider the reasons that have been mentioned why you should thus spend your life: that this world is not your abiding place, that the future world is to be your everlasting abode and that the enjoyments and concerns of this world are given entirely in order to another. How worthy is heaven that your life should be wholly spent as a journey toward it. To what better purpose can you spend your life, whether you respect your duty or your interest? No man is at home in this world, whether he chooses heaven or not; here he is but a transient person. Where can you choose your home better than in heaven?

⚬ From "The Christian Pilgrim, or the True Christian's Life a Journey toward Heaven," p. 246

THE GRACE OF THANKFULNESS

That Christ may dwell in your hearts by faith; that ye, being rooted and grounded in love…might be filled with the fulness of God.
—EPHESIANS 3:17, 19

Love is a principal ingredient in the grace of thankfulness. There is a counterfeit thankfulness in which there is no love; but in all sincere thankfulness there is love in exercise. And the greater any person's love is, the more will he be disposed to praise. Love will cause him to delight in the work. He that loves God proportionally seeks the glory of God and loves to give Him glory. Now, the hearts of the saints in heaven are all, as it were, a pure flame of love. Love is the grace that never fails. Whether there are prophecies, they shall fail; whether there is knowledge, it shall vanish away; faith shall cease in vision and hope in fruition, but love never fails. The grace of love will be exalted to its greatest height and highest perfection in heaven; and love will vent itself in praise. Heaven will ring with praise because it is full of love to God. This is the reason that great assembly, that innumerable host, praise God with such ardency, that their praise is as the voice of many waters and as the mighty thunderings: because they are animated by so ardent, vigorous, and powerful a principle of divine love.

§ From "Praise, One of the Chief Employments of Heaven," p. 915

LOVE YOUR NEIGHBOR

Look not every man on his own things, but every man also on the things of others.

— PHILIPPIANS 2:4

Charity to the poor, very positively and frequently insisted upon by God, is a most reasonable duty, considering the general state and nature of mankind. This renders it most reasonable that we should love our neighbor as ourselves: for men are made in the image of our God and on this account are worthy of our love. Besides, we are all nearly allied one to another by nature. We have all the same nature, like faculties, like dispositions, like desires of good, like needs, like aversion to misery, and are made of one blood; and we are made to subsist by society and union one with another. God hath made us with such a nature that we cannot subsist without the help of one another. Mankind in this respect is as the members of the natural body; one cannot subsist alone without a union with and the help of the rest. Now, this state of mankind shows how reasonable and suitable it is that men should love their neighbors, and that we should not look everyone at his own things, but every man also at the things of others (see Phil. 2:4). A selfish spirit is very unsuitable to the nature and state of mankind. He who is all for himself, and none for his neighbors, deserves to be cut off from the benefit of human society and to be turned out among wild beasts, to subsist by himself as well as he can. A private niggardly spirit is more suitable for wolves and other beasts of prey than for human beings.

§ From "Christian Charity," pp. 164–65

TRUE GODLY PIETY

*Ye are the light of the world. A city that is set on a hill can-
not be hid. Neither do men light a candle, and put it under a
bushel, but on a candlestick; and it giveth light unto all that
are in the house.* —MATTHEW 5:14–15

True grace is no dull, inactive, ineffectual principle. It is a powerful thing.
There is an exceeding energy in it; and the reason is that God is in it. It is a
divine principle, a participation of the divine nature and a communication of
divine life, of the life of a risen Savior who exerts Himself in the hearts of the
saints after the power of an endless life. They that have true grace in them,
they live, but not by their own life, but Christ lives in them. His Holy Spirit
becomes in them a living principle and spring of divine life, the energy and
power of which is in Scripture compared to fire: "I indeed baptize you with
water unto repentance, but he that cometh after me is mightier than I, whose
shoes I am not worthy to bear: he shall baptize you with the Holy Ghost, and
with fire" (Matt. 3:11). True piety is not a thing remaining only in the head or
consisting in any speculative knowledge or opinions or outward morality or
forms of religion. It reaches the heart, is chiefly seated there, and burns there.
There is a holy ardor in everything that belongs to true grace. True faith is an
ardent thing, and so is true repentance. There is a holy power and ardor in
true spiritual comfort and joy; yea, even in true Christian humility, submission, and meekness; and the reason is that divine love or charity is the sum
of all true grace, a holy flame enkindled in the soul. It is by this, therefore,
especially, that a minister of the gospel is a burning light. A minister that is so
has his soul enkindled with the heavenly flame. His heart burns with love to
Christ and fervent desires of the advancement of His kingdom and glory, and
it burns with ardent love to the souls of men and desires for their salvation.

§ From "The True Excellency of a Gospel Minister," p. 957

DESIGNED FOR GLORY

*Ye have seen what I did unto the Egyptians, and how I bare
you on eagles' wings, and brought you unto myself.*

— EXODUS 19:4

God carries His people along through the world to their glory far above the
reach of all their enemies, or anything that might hinder their blessedness.
God designs His people for glory. God had chosen the children of Israel for
His own peculiar treasure. It was His design to bring them out of Egypt to
Himself—to bring them to Mt. Sinai, and to bring them to Canaan, to His
holy habitation—for He was determined and resolved upon it. So it is His
design to bring all His spiritual Israel to the heavenly Canaan and Mt. Zion
so that there they may dwell in glory forever. The glory of the saints consists
in God's bringing them to Himself; His bringing them into the nearest union
to Himself; His bringing them to a perfect and sinless conformity to Himself;
His bringing them to His immediate, glorious presence; His bringing them
to see Him; and His bringing them to the full enjoyment of His love. In these
things consists the highest possible blessedness of the rational creature. And
to this blessedness God is immediately determined to bring all His saints.
'Tis what He purposed in Himself from before the world was, and He has
often declared this purpose and in various ways ever since the world began.
'Tis what He has often promised to them, and He has confirmed His promise
with an oath the more to manifest the immutability of His counsel. Whatever
men designed with respect to God's people, yet this is God's design; their
enemies often design other things. Satan designs quite the contrary; wicked
men often design nothing but their calamity and misery; but God designs
their perfect and immortal glory and blessedness. They are vessels prepared,
foreordained to glory (see Rom. 9:23).

---

§ From "God Carries His People along through the World toward Glory Far Above the Reach
of All Their Enemies or Anything That Might Hinder Their Blessedness," pp. 40–41

INFINITE MERCY EXTENDED TO SINNERS

*Our iniquities are increased over our head, and our trespass is
grown up unto the heavens.*
— EZRA 9:6

If God is a being of such transcendent mercy, then He is a being transcendently amiable. He is worthy that our hearts should ascend to Him in the most ardent flame of love and that we should exalt Him in our praises. In God infinite greatness, infinite goodness, and infinite mercy are joined together. The mercy of God is like a sea or like a deluge. Noah's flood was so great that it was above the tops of the mountains; but the mercy that is in the heart of God is greater: it is above the heavens and over the tops of our sins, which are like great mountains that are grown up to heaven. If God had never manifested any such thing as mercy to the sinful and miserable, if He had executed only His severe justice, all intelligent creatures would have great cause to love Him. Notwithstanding, His holiness and justice are lovely attributes such as deserve our exalted esteem, admiration, and praise; but how sweetly and endearingly does God appear to us, not only as a holy and righteous being, but as the diffusive fountain of all good, having so transcendent a love and mercy. God's goodness and bounty to those who never sinned is very amiable and praiseworthy, but much more so His mercy to the sinful and miserable. God's goodness and bounty to men before the fall with such as our first parents had great cause for which to love and praise God. God's goodness to the angels who never fell is such that they love God with a love that is as a flame of fire, and they praise God for it continually. But such great compassion and kindness to the unworthy is above all attraction and endearment. Why should not God's doing so much to deliver us from everlasting mystery endear Him to our souls, especially considering how God condescended and His divine person suffered to rescue us and bring us from our misery to such great happiness when we were so undeserving?

§ From "God Is a Being of Transcendent Mercy," pp. 282–83

RECONCILED

When we were enemies, we were reconciled to God through the death of his Son.
— ROMANS 5:10

It is well for us that God differs from men with respect to forgiveness and love to enemies. Such is God's grace that He stands ready to forgive the greatest sinners if they will turn from their sins. Though He is so great a God, and to disobey Him is so infinitely heinous, yet He stands ready to forgive, and often does forgive, those who have cast great contempt upon Him and have done it under all aggravations of sinning under clear light and against mercies. God stands ready to pardon those who have gone on in such a way for many years together. He is wholly willing to forgive and blot out all their transgressions so that they shall no more be mentioned—not merely to forgive them but to abate them into His favor and to the enjoyment of Himself. And all this is only upon their turning from their sins and trusting in Him for mercy in His way, without any satisfaction at all made by them or provided by any other than Himself. Christ was ready to forgive His crucifiers, who had treated Him with such indignity and cruelty, He who was the Lord of heaven and earth. How far this is from our manner toward one another. God forgives us ten thousand talents, but how difficult it is for us to forgive a fellow servant who owes us a hundred pence. If one of our fellow creatures has affronted, reproached, and abused us, what a vengeful spirit men have. It is well for us that God is not as we are in this respect. If He was, there would be no hope of us ever being forgiven. God would forever be irreconcilable toward us. God loves us with a transcendent love. Christ set His love upon us and loved us with a dying love. With what difficulty is it that men do a small kindness to their enemies, but Christ so loved us while we were His enemies that He cheerfully laid down His life under the most extreme torments to save us from a deserved hell and to bring us to eternal glory.

§ From "It Is Well for Us That God Is Not as We Are," pp. 23–25

HOLINESS IS THE AIM OF ELECTION

I have chosen you, and ordained you, that ye should go and bring forth fruit, and that your fruit should remain.

—JOHN 15:16

Holy practice is the aim of that eternal election that is the first ground of the bestowment of all true grace. Holy practice is not the ground and reason of election, as is supposed by the Arminians, who imagine that God elects men to everlasting life upon a foresight of their good works, but it is the aim and end of election. God does not elect men because He foresees they will be holy, but that He may make them, and that they may be holy. Thus, in election, God ordained that men should walk in good works, as says the apostle Paul, "for we are his workmanship, created in Christ Jesus unto good works, which God hath before ordained that we should walk in them" (Eph. 2:10). And again it is said that the elect are chosen to this very end: "He hath chosen us in him before the foundation of the world, that we should be holy and without blame before him in love" (Eph. 1:4). And so Christ tells His disciples, "I have chosen you, and ordained you, that ye should go and bring forth fruit, and that your fruit should remain" (John 15:16). Now God's eternal election is the first ground of the bestowment of saving grace. And some have such saving grace, and others do not have it, because some are from eternity chosen of God, and others are not chosen. And seeing that holy practice is the scope and aim of that which is the first ground of the bestowment of grace, this same holy practice is doubtless the tendency of grace itself. Otherwise, it would follow that God makes use of a certain means to attain an end, which is not fitted to attain that end and has no tendency to it.

🔖 From "All True Grace in the Heart Tends to Holy Practice in the Life," p. 223

THE NATURE OF YOUR ANGER

I will therefore that men pray every where, lifting up holy hands, without wrath and doubting. — 1 TIMOTHY 2:8

Our own consciences, if faithfully searched and imperatively inquired of, can best tell us whether we are, or have been, persons of such an angry spirit and wrathful disposition as has been described—whether we are frequently angry or indulge in ill-will or allow the continuance of anger. Have we not often been angry? And if so, is there not reason to think that that anger has been undue, and without just cause, and thus sinful? God does not call Christians into His kingdom that they may indulge greatly in fretfulness and have their minds commonly stirred up and ruffled with anger. Has not most of the anger you have cherished been chiefly, if not entirely, on your own account? Men are often wont to plead zeal for religion and for duty and for the honor of God as the cause of their indignation, when it is only their own private interest that is concerned and affected. It is remarkable how forward men are to appear, as if they were zealous for God and righteousness, in cases wherein their honor, will, or interest has been touched and to make pretense of this in injuring others or complaining of them, and what a great difference there is in their conduct in other cases, wherein God's honor is as much or a great deal more hurt, and their own interest is not specially concerned. In the latter case, there is no such appearance of zeal and engagedness of spirit and no forwardness to reprove, complain, and be angry, but often a readiness to excuse and leave reproof to others, and to be cold and backward in anything like opposition to the sin. And ask, still further, what good has been obtained by your anger, and what have you aimed at in it? Or have you even thought of these things? There has been a great deal of anger and bitterness in things passing in this town on public occasions, and many of you have been present on such occasions; such anger has been manifest in your conduct, and I fear rested in your bosoms. Examine yourselves as to this matter, and ask what has been the nature of your anger.

§ From "The Spirit of Charity, the Opposite of an Angry or Wrathful Spirit," pp. 198–99

CHRISTIAN LOVE

Though I speak with the tongues of men and of angels, and have not charity, I am become as sounding brass, or a tinkling cymbal.
— 1 CORINTHIANS 13:1

All true Christian love is one and the same in its principle. It may be various in its forms and objects and may be exercised either toward God or men, but it is the same principle in the heart that is the foundation of every exercise of a truly Christian love, whatever may be its object. It is not with the holy love in the heart of the Christian as it is with the love of other men. Their love toward different objects may be from different principles and motives, and with different views, but a truly Christian love is different from this. It is one as to its principle, whatever the object about which it is exercised; it is from the same spring or fountain in the heart, though it may flow out in different channels and diverse directions, and therefore it is all fitly comprehended in the one name of charity, as in the text. Christian love is one, whatever the objects toward which it may flow forth. It is all from the same Spirit influencing the heart. It is from the breathing of the same Spirit that true Christian love arises, both toward God and man. The Spirit of God is a Spirit of love, and when the former enters the soul, love also enters with it. God is love, and he that has God dwelling in him by His Spirit will have love dwelling in him also. The nature of the Holy Spirit is love; and it is by communicating Himself, in His own nature, to the saints, that their hearts are filled with divine charity. Hence we find that the saints are partakers of the divine nature.

֍ From "Charity, or Love the Sum of All Virtue," pp. 4–5

SOUL-SATISFYING SWEETNESS

Yet I will rejoice in the LORD, I will joy in the God of my salvation.
—HABAKKUK 3:18

The joy of a Christian does not consist merely in the sense of his own good estate, as natural men often are ready to imagine; but there is an excellent, transcendent, soul-satisfying sweetness that sometimes fills the soul in the apprehension of the excellency of God. The soul dwells upon the thought, fixes on it, and takes complacence in God as the greatest good, the most delightful object of its contemplation. This pleasure is the sweetest pleasure that a Christian ever feels and is a foretaste of the pleasures of heaven itself. Herein sometimes the saints do boast of the clusters of Canaan. This sort of joy is evidence of sincerity above any other joy, a more sure evidence than a rejoicing in our own good estate. From the joy that the Christian has in the view of the glory and excellency of God, the consideration of the love of God to him cannot be excluded. When he rejoices in God as a glorious God, he rejoices in Him the more because He is his God, and in consideration of there being a union between him and this God; otherwise, if there were a separation, the view of God's excellency, though it would raise joy one way, would proportionally excite grief another. God is sometimes pleased to manifest His love to the saints, and, commonly at those times, when a Christian has the greatest views of God's excellency, he has also of His love; the soul is spiritually sensible of God as being present with it, and as manifesting and communicating Himself; and it has sweet communion with God, and tastes the sweetness of His love, and knows a little what is the length, and breadth, and depth, and height of that love that passeth knowledge.

§ From "The Portion of the Righteous," p. 890

THE NATIVE COUNTRY OF THE CHURCH

But ye are come unto mount Sion, and unto the city of the living God, the heavenly Jerusalem, and to an innumerable company of angels, to the general assembly and church of the firstborn, which are written in heaven, and to God the Judge of all, and to the spirits of just men made perfect.

— HEBREWS 12:22–23

The saints are all of the same native country. Heaven is the native country of the church. They are born from above; their Father, of whom they are begotten, is in heaven. The principles that govern their hearts are drawn from heaven, since the Holy Ghost, whose immediate fruits those principles are, is from heaven. The Word of God, which is the seed by which they are begotten, is from heaven. The Bible is a book, as it were, sent down from heaven. The saints in this world are not in their native country, but are pilgrims and strangers on the earth. They are near akin to the inhabitants of the heavenly world and are properly of that society. Heaven is a country that much better suits their natures than this earth, because it is their native climate. When they are in heaven, they breathe their native air; in heaven is their inheritance. Heaven is the proper country of the church, where the greater part of the church is, and where they all will be, and where is their settled abode; from thence all that are now upon earth are derived, and thither they will return again. Though they are for a little while dwelling at a distance from their native country, yet they are of the same nation with those who now dwell there.

§ From "Christians a Chosen Generation, a Royal Priesthood, a Holy Nation, a Peculiar People," pp. 944–45

DEPARTED SOULS WITH CHRIST

Henceforth I call you not servants; for the servant knoweth not what his lord doeth: but I have called you friends; for all things that I have heard of my Father I have made known unto you.

—JOHN 15:15

Departed souls of saints are with Christ, as they enjoy a glorious and immediate intercourse and converse with Him. While we are present with our friends, we have opportunity for that free and immediate conversation with them that we cannot have in absence from them. And therefore, by reason of the vastly more free, perfect, and immediate intercourse with Christ that the saints enjoy when absent from the body, they are fitly represented as present with Him. The most intimate intercourse becomes that relation that the saints stand in to Jesus Christ and especially becomes that most perfect and glorious union they shall be brought into with Him in heaven. They are not merely Christ's servants, but His friends (see John 15:15); His brethren and companions (see Ps. 122:8); yea, they are the spouse of Christ. They are espoused or betrothed to Christ while in the body, but when they go to heaven, they enter into the King's palace, their marriage with Him is come, and the King brings them into His chambers indeed. They then go to dwell with Christ constantly, to enjoy the most perfect converse with Him. Christ conversed in the most friendly manner with His disciples on earth; He admitted one of them to lean on His bosom: but they are admitted much more fully and freely to converse with Him in heaven.

§ From "True Saints, When Absent from the Body, Are Present with the Lord," pp. 28–29

HOW TO GET TO HEAVEN

What must I do to be saved?
— ACTS 16:30

What must I be brought to in order to get to heaven? You must be brought entirely to renounce all hope of obtaining heaven by anything that you can do by your own strength; that you cannot do it either directly or indirectly. Many are sensible that they cannot get to heaven by their own strength directly, but yet they hope to do it indirectly; they hope by their own strength to bring themselves to a disposition to close with Christ and accept of Him for a Savior. They are hoping to bring themselves to a compliance with the terms of salvation. You must be brought off from all confiding in your own strength, and you must also be brought to renounce your own righteousness as the price of heaven. The consideration of what has been said of the glory and happiness of the saints may show us the exceeding folly of those that think to purchase so great happiness by their own righteousness. What a vain thought have men of their performances to think them a sufficient price to offer to God to purchase such glory of Him! How would God dishonor Himself, and dishonor such riches of His own goodness, if He should bestow them on men for their righteousness and should accept their miserable performances as the price of them! Your heart must be brought to close with Him who has purchased heaven. Renouncing all other ways, your heart must entirely close with Him and adhere to Him as the way, the truth, and the life. Your heart must be drawn to Him, and it must be pleasing and sweet to you to have heaven as a free gift, as the fruit of mercy and saving grace, and you must assuredly believe that Christ is a sufficient Savior, and your soul must acquiesce in the way of salvation by Him, by His blood and His righteousness, as a wise, holy, sufficient, and excellent way. Your heart must incline to Jesus Christ as Savior above your own righteousness and all other ways. Your delight must be in this holy way of salvation.

§ From "The Portion of the Righteous," pp. 903–4

WARN OF HELL

The wicked shall be turned into hell.
—PSALM 9:17

I appeal to everyone, whether this is not the very course they would take in case of exposedness to any great temporal calamity? If any of you who are heads of families saw one of your children in a house all on fire and in imminent danger of being soon consumed in the flames, yet who seemed to be very insensible of its danger and neglected to escape after you had often called to it—would you go on to speak to it only in a cold and indifferent manner? Would not you cry aloud and call earnestly to it and represent the danger it was in and its own folly in delaying, in the most lively manner of which you were capable? If you should continue to speak to it only in a cold manner, as you are wont to do in ordinary conversation about indifferent matters, would not those about you begin to think you were bereft of reason yourself? This is not the way of mankind in temporal affairs of great moment that require earnest heed and great haste and about which they are greatly concerned. They are not wont to speak to others of their danger and warn them but a little or in a cold and indifferent manner. Nature teaches men otherwise. If we, who have the care of souls, knew what hell was, had seen the state of the damned, or by any other means had become sensible how dreadful their case was—and at the same time knew that the greater part of men went thither, and saw our hearers not sensible of their danger—it would be morally impossible for us to avoid most earnestly setting before them the dreadfulness of that misery and their great exposedness to it, and even to cry aloud to them.

⧉ From "Distinguishing Marks of a Work of the Spirit of God," p. 266

THE HONOR OF DIVINE MAJESTY

Whom God hath set forth to be a propitiation through faith in his blood, to declare his righteousness for the remission of sins that are past, through the forbearance of God; to declare, I say, at this time his righteousness: that he might be just, and the justifier of him which believeth in Jesus.

— ROMANS 3:25–26

God may, through Christ, pardon the greatest sinner without any prejudice to the honor of His majesty. The honor of the divine majesty indeed requires satisfaction, but the sufferings of Christ fully repair the injury. Let the contempt be ever so great, yet if so honorable a person as Christ undertakes to be a mediator for the offender and suffers so much for him, it fully repairs the injury done to the Majesty of heaven and earth. The sufferings of Christ fully satisfy justice. The justice of God, as the supreme governor and judge of the world, requires the punishment of sin. The Supreme Judge must judge the world according to a rule of justice. God doth not show mercy as a judge, but as a sovereign; therefore His exercise of mercy as a sovereign and His justice as a judge must be made consistent one with another. This is done by the sufferings of Christ, in which sin is punished fully and justice answered: "Whom God hath set forth to be a propitiation through faith in his blood, to declare his righteousness for the remission of sins that are past, through the forbearance of God; to declare, I say, at this time his righteousness: that he might be just, and the justifier of him which believeth in Jesus" (Rom. 3:25–26). The law is no impediment in the way of the pardon of the greatest sin, if men do but truly come to God for mercy, for Christ hath fulfilled the law, and He hath borne the curse of it in His sufferings: "Christ hath redeemed us from the curse of the law, being made a curse for us: for it is written, Cursed is every one that hangeth on a tree" (Gal. 3:13).

ॐ From "Great Guilt No Obstacle to the Pardon of the Returning Sinner," pp. 111–12

MARRIAGE WITH THE LAMB

And there came unto me one of the seven angels which had the seven vials full of the seven last plagues, and talked with me, saying, Come hither, I will shew thee the bride, the Lamb's wife.

— REVELATION 21:9

The time of Christ's last coming is that of the consummation of the church's marriage with the Lamb and the complete and most perfect joy of the wedding. In that resurrection morning, when the Sun of Righteousness shall appear in our heavens, shining in all His brightness and glory, He will come forth as a bridegroom; He shall come in the glory of His Father, with all His holy angels. And at that glorious appearing of the great God and our Savior Jesus Christ, the whole elect church—complete as to every individual member, and each member with the whole man, both body and soul, and both in perfect glory—shall ascend up to meet the Lord in the air, to be thenceforth forever with the Lord. Then the bridegroom will appear in all His glory, without any veil; and then the saints shall shine forth as the sun in the kingdom of their Father, and at the right hand of their Redeemer; and then the church will appear as the bride, the Lamb's wife. Then will come the time when Christ will sweetly invite His spouse to enter in with Him into the palace of His glory, which He had been preparing for her from the foundation of the world, and shall, as it were, take her by the hand, and lead her in with Him. And this glorious Bridegroom and bride shall, with all their shining ornaments, ascend up together into the heaven of heavens, the whole multitude of glorious angels waiting upon them. And this son and daughter of God shall, in their united glory and joy, present themselves together before the Father; and Christ shall say, "Here am I, and the children which thou hast given me." They both shall, in that relation and union, together receive the Father's blessing and shall thenceforward rejoice together, in consummate, uninterrupted, immutable, and everlasting glory, in the love and embraces of each other and in joint enjoyment of the love of the Father.

֍ From "The Church's Marriage to Her Sons, and to Her God," pp. 22–23

SECRETS REVEALED

For there is nothing covered, that shall not be revealed; neither hid, that shall not be known. Therefore whatsoever ye have spoken in darkness shall be heard in the light; and that which ye have spoken in the ear in closets shall be proclaimed upon the housetops.

—LUKE 12:2–3

Let those who live in secret wickedness consider that God will bring them into judgment. Secrecy is your temptation. Promising yourselves this, you practice many things, you indulge many lusts under the cover of darkness and in secret corners that you would be ashamed to do in the light of the sun and before the world. But this temptation is entirely groundless. All your secret abominations are even now perfectly known to God and will also hereafter be made known both to angels and men: "For there is nothing covered, that shall not be revealed; neither hid, that shall not be known. Therefore whatsoever ye have spoken in darkness shall be heard in the light; and that which ye have spoken in the ear in closets shall be proclaimed upon the housetops" (Luke 12:2–3). Before human judges are brought only those things that are known; but before this judge shall be brought the most "hidden things of darkness, and [even the] counsels of the heart" (1 Cor. 4:5). All your secret uncleanness; all your secret fraud and injustice; all your lascivious desires, wishes, and designs; all your inward covetousness, which is idolatry; all your malicious, envious, and revengeful thoughts and purposes; whether brought forth into practice or not, all shall then be made manifest, and you shall be judged according to them. Of these things, however secret, there will be need of no other evidence than the testimony of God and of your own consciences.

§ From "The Final Judgment, or the World Judged Righteously by Jesus Christ," p. 199

THE ENEMY OF GRACE

*For sin, taking occasion by the commandment, deceived me,
and by it slew me.*
— ROMANS 7:11

The natural tendency of sin is to darken the mind and trouble the conscience. There is nothing that wounds a well-informed conscience but sin. Sin is the enemy of grace, and therefore the natural tendency of it is to oppose and keep down the exercises of grace and so to extinguish spiritual comfort; for spiritual comfort comes in no other way than by the exercises of grace. That which prevents the exercises of grace darkens the evidences of a man's good estate. For there are no evidences of this but the exercises of grace. Sin does as much tend to keep out spiritual comfort as do clouds that tend to hide the light of the sun. Therefore it is necessary that this should be removed in order for us to receive light and comfort. It is impossible in its own nature that any should have spiritual light and comfort before sin is mortified. If sinners had comfort while sin is in reigning power, it could not be spiritual comfort; for spiritual comfort is the same with gracious comfort. But how can there be gracious comfort where grace has no place? If there be grace, sin will not be in reigning power, for the nature of grace is to mortify sin. And as there can be no spiritual comfort without a degree of mortification of sin in those in whom sin is mortified, spiritual comfort cannot be any more than in proportion as sin is mortified.

§ From "Hope and Comfort Usually Follow Genuine Humiliation and Repentance," p. 845

THE REMEDY FOR EVIL

*For as many of you as have been baptized into Christ have put
on Christ.*
— GALATIANS 3:27

We should admire the love of Christ to men that He has thus given Himself
to be the remedy for all their evil and a fountain of all good. Christ has given
Himself to us, to be all things to us that we need. We want clothing, and
Christ not only gives us clothing, but He gives Himself to be our clothing,
that we might put Him on: "For as many of you as have been baptized into
Christ have put on Christ" (Gal. 3:27); and "But put ye on the Lord Jesus
Christ, and make not provision for the flesh, to fulfil the lusts thereof" (Rom.
13:14). We want food, and Christ has given Himself to be our food; He has
given His own flesh to be our meat, and His blood to be our drink, to nourish our soul. Thus, Christ tells us that He is the bread that came down from
heaven and the Bread of Life: "I am that bread of life. Your fathers did eat
manna in the wilderness, and are dead. This is the bread which cometh down
from heaven, that a man may eat thereof, and not die. I am the living bread
which came down from heaven: if any man eat of this bread, he shall live
forever: and the bread that I will give is my flesh, which I will give for the life
of the world" (John 6:48–51). In order for us to eat of His flesh, it was necessary that He should be slain, as the sacrifices must be slain before they could
be eaten. Such was Christ's love to us, that He consented to be slain; He went
as a sheep to the slaughter that He might give us His flesh to be food for our
poor, famishing souls.

❧ From "Safety, Fullness, and Sweet Refreshment, to Be Found in Christ," p. 936

UNLEASHED WRATH

Remember, and forget not, how thou provokedst the LORD thy God to wrath in the wilderness: from the day that thou didst depart out of the land of Egypt, until ye came unto this place, ye have been rebellious against the LORD.
— DEUTERONOMY 9:7

The wrath of God is like great waters that are dammed for the present; they increase more and more, and rise higher and higher, until an outlet is given; and the longer the stream is stopped, the more rapid and mighty is its course once it is let loose. It is true that judgment against your evil works has not been executed hitherto; the floods of God's vengeance have been withheld; but your guilt in the meantime is constantly increasing, and you are every day treasuring up more wrath. The waters are constantly rising and waxing more and more mighty; and there is nothing but the mere pleasure of God that holds the waters back; the waters are unwilling to be stopped and press hard to go forward. If God should only withdraw His hand from the flood-gate, it would immediately fly open, and the fiery floods of the fierceness and wrath of God would rush forth with inconceivable fury and would come upon you with omnipotent power; and if your strength were ten thousand times greater than it is, yea, ten thousand times greater than the strength of the stoutest, sturdiest devil in hell, it would be nothing to withstand or endure it. The bow of God's wrath is bent and the arrow made ready on the string, and justice bends the arrow at your heart and strains the bow; it is nothing but the mere pleasure of God, and that of an angry God, without any promise or obligation at all, that keeps the arrow one moment from being made drunk with your blood. Thus all you who never passed under a great change of heart, by the mighty power of the Spirit of God upon your souls; all you who were never born again and made new creatures and raised from being dead in sin to a state of new, and before altogether unexperienced light and life; all you are in the hands of an angry God.

◈ From "Sinners in the Hands of an Angry God," p. 9

THE SUFFERINGS OF CHRIST

Ought not Christ to have suffered these things, and to enter into his glory?

—LUKE 24:26

Christ's holiness never so illustriously shone forth as it did in His last sufferings, and yet He never was to such a degree treated as guilty. Christ's holiness never had such a trial as it had then; and therefore it never had so great a manifestation. When it was tried in this furnace it came forth as gold, or as silver purified seven times. His holiness then, above all, appeared in His steadfast pursuit of the honor of God and in His obedience to Him. His yielding Himself unto death was transcendently the greatest act of obedience that ever was paid to God by anyone since the foundation of the world; and yet, Christ was then in the greatest degree treated as a wicked person would have been. He was apprehended and bound as a malefactor. His accusers represented Him as a most wicked wretch. In His sufferings before His crucifixion He was treated as if He had been the worst and vilest of mankind; then He was put to a kind of death that none but the worst sort of malefactors was wont to suffer, those that were most abject in their persons and guilty of the blackest crimes. He suffered as though guilty from God Himself, by reason of our guilt imputed to Him; for He who knew no sin was made sin for us; He was made subject to wrath as if He had been sinful Himself. He was made a curse for us.

⸭ From "The Excellency of Jesus Christ," pp. 684–85

THE DUTY OF SCRIPTURE READING

This book of the law shall not depart out of thy mouth; but thou shalt meditate therein day and night, that thou mayest observe to do according to all that is written therein: for then thou shalt make thy way prosperous, and then thou shalt have good success.
— JOSHUA 1:8

Inquire of yourself whether you do not live in neglect of the duty of reading the Holy Scriptures. The Holy Scriptures were surely written to be read; and, unless we are popish in our principles, we shall maintain that they were not only given to be read by ministers but by the people too. It doth not answer the design for which they were given that we have once read them, and that we once in a great while read something in them. They were given to be always with us, to be continually conversed with, as a rule of life. As the artificer must always have his rule with him in his work, as the blind man that walks must always have his guide by him, and as he that walks in darkness must have his light with him, so the Scriptures were given to be a lamp to our feet and a light to our path. That we may continually use the Scriptures as our rule of life, we should make them our daily companion and keep them with us continually: "This book of the law shall not depart out of thy mouth, but thou shalt meditate therein day and night." (Josh. 1:8; see also Deut. 6:6–9). Christ also commands us to search the Scriptures (John 5:39). These are the mines wherein we are to dig for wisdom as for hidden treasures. Inquire, therefore, whether you do not live in the neglect of this duty, or neglect it so far, that you may be said to live in a way of sin.

§ From "Christian Cautions, or the Necessity of Self-Examination," p. 180

ARMS OPEN WIDE

Verily, verily, I say unto you, He that heareth my word, and believeth on him that sent me, hath everlasting life, and shall not come into condemnation; but is passed from death unto life.

— JOHN 5:24

Christ's love, compassion, and gracious disposition are such that we may be sure He is inclined to receive all who come to Him. If He should not do it He would fail of His own undertaking and also of His promise to the Father and to us; and His wisdom and faithfulness will not allow of that. He is so full of love and kindness that He is disposed to nothing but to receive and defend us, if we come to Him. Christ is exceedingly ready to pity us; His arms are open to receive us. He delights to receive distressed souls that come to Him and to protect them; He would gather them as a hen gathers her chickens under her wings. It is a work that He exceedingly rejoices in because He delights in acts of love, and pity, and mercy. I shall take occasion from what now has been said to invite those who are afraid of God's wrath to come to Christ Jesus. You are indeed in a dreadful condition. It is dismal to have God's wrath impending over our heads and not to know how soon it will fall upon us. And you are in some measure sensible that it is a dreadful condition; you are full of fear and trouble, and you know not where to flee for help. Your mind is, as it were, tossed with a tempest. But how lamentable is it that you should spend your life in such a condition, when Christ would shelter you, as a hen shelters her chickens under her wings, if you were but willing; and that you should live such a fearful, distressed life, when there is so much provision made for your safety in Christ Jesus!

§ From "Safety, Fullness, and Sweet Refreshment, to Be Found in Christ," p. 931

DEPENDENCE ON GOD'S POWER

When a strong man armed keepeth his palace, his goods are in peace: but when a stronger than he shall come upon him, and overcome him, he taketh from him all his armour wherein he trusted, and divideth his spoils.
—LUKE 11:21–22

Man was dependent on the power of God in his first estate, but he is more dependent on his power now; he needs God's power to do more things for Him and depends on a more wonderful exercise of His power. It was an effect of the power of God to make man holy at the first; but more remarkably so now because there is a great deal of opposition and difficulty in the way. It is a more glorious effect of power to make that holy that was so depraved and under the dominion of sin, than to confer holiness on that which before had nothing of the contrary. It is a more glorious work of power to rescue a soul out of the hands of the devil and from the powers of darkness and to bring it into a state of salvation, than to confer holiness where there was no prepossession or opposition: "When a strong man armed keepeth his palace, his goods are in peace: but when a stronger than he shall come upon him, and overcome him, he taketh from him all his armour wherein he trusted, and divideth his spoils" (Luke 11:21–22). It is a more glorious work of power to uphold a soul in a state of grace and holiness and to carry it on until it is brought to glory when there is so much sin remaining in the heart resisting, and Satan with all his might opposing, than it would have been to have kept man from falling at first, when Satan had nothing in man.

§ From "God Glorified in Man's Dependence," pp. 4–5

OPEN OUR EYES

Open thou mine eyes, that I may behold wondrous things out of thy law.

—PSALM 119:18

Abound in earnest prayer to God, that He would open your eyes that you may behold the glorious and rich provision made for sinners in Jesus Christ. The souls of natural men are so blinded that they see no beauty or excellency in Christ. They do not see His sufficiency. They see no beauty in the work of salvation by Him; and as long as they remain thus blind, it is impossible that they should close with Christ. The heart will never be drawn to an unknown Savior. It is impossible that a man should love, freely choose, and rejoice in that in which he sees no excellency. But if your eyes were opened to see the excellency of Christ, the work would be done. You would immediately believe on Him; and you would find your heart going after Him. It would be impossible to keep it back. But take heed that you do not entertain a wrong notion of what it is to spiritually see Christ. If you do, you may seek that which God never bestows. Do not think that to spiritually see Christ is to have a vision of Him as the prophets had, to see Him in some bodily shape, to see the features of His countenance. Do not pray or seek for any such thing as this. What you are to seek is that you may have a sight of the glorious excellency of Christ, and of the way of salvation through Him, in your heart. This is a spiritual sight of Christ; this is that for which you must cry to God day and night. God is the fountain of spiritual light. He opens the eyes of the blind. He commands the light to shine out of darkness.

✤ From "Natural Man in a Dreadful Condition," p. 829

REDEMPTION

That if thou shalt confess with thy mouth the Lord Jesus, and shalt believe in thine heart that God hath raised him from the dead, thou shalt be saved.
—ROMANS 10:9

When men are fallen and become sinful, God, by His sovereignty, has a right to determine about their redemption as He pleases. He has a right to determine whether He will redeem any or not. He might, if He had pleased, have left all to perish or might have redeemed all. Or, He may redeem some and leave others; and if He doth so, He may take whom He pleases and leave whom He pleases. To suppose that all have forfeited His favor and deserved to perish, and to suppose that He may not leave any one individual of them to perish, implies a contradiction. It supposes that such a one has a claim to God's favor and is not justly liable to perish, which is contrary to the supposition. It is meet that God should order all these things according to His own pleasure. By reason of His greatness and glory, by which He is infinitely above all, He is worthy to be sovereign and that His pleasure should in all things take place. He is worthy that He should make Himself His end and that He should make nothing but His own wisdom His rule in pursuing that end, without asking leave or counsel of any and without giving account of any of His matters. It is fit that He who is absolutely perfect and infinitely wise and the fountain of all wisdom, should determine everything that He effects by His own will, even things of the greatest importance. It is meet that He should be thus sovereign, because He is the first being, the eternal being, whence all other beings are. He is the creator of all things; and all are absolutely and universally dependent on Him. Therefore it is meet that He should act as the sovereign possessor of heaven and earth.

§ From "The Justice of God in the Damnation of Sinners," p. 670

PEACE FOUND IN CHRIST

In that hour Jesus rejoiced in spirit, and said, I thank thee, O Father, Lord of heaven and earth, that thou hast hid these things from the wise and prudent, and hast revealed them unto babes: even so, Father; for so it seemed good in thy sight.
—LUKE 10:21

The peace that Christ has left as a legacy to His true followers is His peace. It is the peace that He Himself enjoys. This is what I take to be principally intended in the expression. It is the peace that He enjoyed while on earth in His state of humiliation. Though He was a man of sorrows and acquainted with grief, and was everywhere hated and persecuted by men and devils and had no place of rest in this world; yet in God, His Father, He had peace. We read of His rejoicing in spirit (see Luke 10:21). So Christ's true disciples, though in the world have tribulation, yet in God have peace. When Christ had finished His labors and sufferings and had risen from the dead and ascended into heaven, He entered into His rest: a state of most blessed, perfect, and everlasting peace, delivered by His own sufferings from our imputed guilt, acquitted and justified of the Father on His resurrection. Having obtained a perfect victory over all His enemies, He was received of His Father into heaven, the rest that He had prepared for Him, there to enjoy His heart's desire fully and perfectly to all eternity. And then were those words in the six first verses of the twenty-first Psalm, which have, in respect to Christ, been fulfilled. This peace and rest of the Messiah is exceeding glorious: "And his rest shall be glorious" (Isa. 11:10). This rest is what Christ has procured not only for Himself, but also His people, by His death. He has bequeathed it to them, that they may enjoy it with Him, imperfectly in this, and perfectly and eternally in another, world.

§ From "The Peace Which Christ Gives His True Followers," p. 91

KINDNESS TO OTHERS

I have been young, and now am old; yet have I not seen the righteous forsaken, nor his seed begging bread. — PSALM 37:25

If ever there should be such a time that you may be in calamity and necessity, your kindness to others now will be but a laying up against such a time. If you yourselves should be brought into calamity and necessity, then would you find what you have given in charity to others, lying ready in store for you. "Cast thy bread upon the waters: for thou shalt find it after many days," says the wise man in Ecclesiastes 11:1, but when shall we find it? Solomon tells us in the next verse: "Give a portion to seven, and also to eight; for thou knowest not what evil shall be upon the earth" (Eccl. 11:2). Then is the time when you shall find it, when the day of evil cometh. You shall again find your bread that you have cast upon the waters when you shall want it most and land in greatest necessity of it. God will keep it for you against such a time. When other bread shall fail, then God will bring to you the bread that you formerly cast upon the waters so that you shall not famish. He that giveth to the poor shall not lack. Giving to the needy is like laying up against winter, or against a time of calamity. It is the best way of laying up for yourselves and for your children. Children in a time of need very often find their fathers' bread, that bread their fathers had cast upon the waters: "I have been young and now am old; yet have I not seen the righteous forsaken, nor his seed begging bread" (Ps. 37:25). Why? What is the reason of it? It follows in the next verse, "He is ever merciful and lendeth, and his seed is blessed."

⸙ From "Christian Charity," p. 168

CREATED IN GOD'S IMAGE

And God said, Let us make man in our image, after our likeness: and let them have dominion over the fish of the sea, and over the fowl of the air, and over the cattle, and over all the earth, and over every creeping thing that creepeth upon the earth.

—GENESIS 1:26

How much God hath bestowed upon you in the endowments of your nature. God hath made you rational, intelligent creatures and hath endued you with noble powers, those endowments wherein the natural image of God consists. You are vastly exalted in your nature above other kinds of creatures here below. You are capable of a thousand times as much as any of the brute creatures. He hath given you a power of understanding that is capable of extending itself, of looking back to the beginning of time, and of considering what was before the world, and of looking forward beyond the end of time. It is capable of extending beyond the utmost limits of the universe and is a faculty whereby you are akin to angels and are capable even of knowing and contemplating the Divine Being, and His glorious perfections, manifested in His works and in His Word. You have souls capable of being the habitation of the Holy Spirit of God and His divine grace. You are capable of the noble employments of angels. How lamentable and shameful it is that such a creature should be altogether useless and live in vain! How lamentable that such a noble and excellent piece of divine workmanship should fail of its end and be to no purpose! Was it ever worthwhile for God to make you such a creature, with such a noble nature, and so much above other kinds of creatures, only for you to eat and drink and gratify your sensual appetites? How lamentable and shameful to you, that such a noble tree should be more useless than any tree of the forest; that man, whom God hath thus set in honor, should make himself more worthless than the beasts that perish!

꧁ From "Wicked Men Useful in Their Destruction Only," p. 128

DO NOT LOOK BACK

And Abraham gat up early in the morning to the place where he stood before the LORD: *and he looked toward Sodom and Gomorrah, and toward all the land of the plain, and beheld, and, lo, the smoke of the country went up as the smoke of a furnace.*

—GENESIS 19:27–28

We ought not to look back when fleeing out of Sodom, because the destruction to which it is appointed is exceedingly dreadful: it is appointed to utter destruction, to be wholly and entirely consumed. It is appointed to suffer the wrath of the great God, which is to be poured down from God upon it, like a dreadful storm of fire and brimstone. This city is to be filled full of the wrath of God. Everyone who remains in it shall have the fire of God's wrath come down on his head and into his soul: he shall be full of fire and full of the wrath of the Almighty. He shall be encompassed with fire without and full of fire within: his head, his heart, his bowels, and all his limbs shall be full of fire, and not a drop of water to cool him. Nor shall he have any place to flee to for relief. Go where he will, there is the fire of God's wrath: his destruction and torment will be inevitable. He shall be destroyed without any pity. He shall cry aloud, but there shall be none to help; there shall be none to regard his lamentations or to afford relief. The decree is gone forth, and the days come when Sodom shall burn as an oven, and all the inhabitants thereof shall be as stubble. As it was in the literal Sodom, the whole city was full of fire: in their houses there was no safety, for they were all on fire; and if they fled out into the streets, they also were full of fire. Fire continually came down out of heaven everywhere. That was a dismal time. What a cry was there then in that city, in every part of it! But there was none to help; they had nowhere to go, where they could hide their heads from fire: they had none to pity or relieve them. If they fled to their friends, they could not help them.

From "The Folly of Looking Back in Fleeing Out of Sodom," p. 65

GLORIFICATION IN REDEMPTION

Christ hath redeemed us from the curse of the law, being made a curse for us: for it is written, Cursed is every one that hangeth on a tree: that the blessing of Abraham might come on the Gentiles through Jesus Christ; that we might receive the promise of the Spirit through faith.

— GALATIANS 3:13–14

The work of redemption is distinguished from all the other works of God. The attributes of God are glorious in His other works, but the three persons of the Trinity are distinctly glorified in no work as in this of redemption. In this work every distinct person has His distinct parts and offices assigned Him. Each one has His particular and distinct concern in it, agreeable to their distinct, personal properties, relations, and economical offices. The redeemed have an equal concern with and dependence upon each person in this affair and owe equal honor and praise to each of them. The Father appoints and provides the Redeemer and accepts the price of redemption. The Son is the Redeemer and the price; He redeems by offering up Himself. The Holy Ghost immediately communicates to us the thing purchased; yea, and He is the good purchased. The sum of what Christ purchased for us is holiness and happiness, but the Holy Ghost is the great principle both of all holiness and happiness. The Holy Ghost is the sum of all that Christ purchased for men. He was "made a curse for us...that we might receive the promise of the Spirit through faith" (Gal. 3:13–14). The blessedness of the redeemed consists in partaking of Christ's fullness, partaking of that Spirit that is given not by measure unto Him. This is the oil that was poured upon the Head of the church, which ran down to the members of His body and to the skirts of His garment. Thus we have an equal concern with and dependence upon each of the persons of the Trinity, distinctly: upon the Father, as He provides the Redeemer and the person of whom the purchase is made; upon the Son, as the purchaser and the price; and upon the Holy Ghost, as the good purchased.

꙳ From "The Wisdom of God, Displayed in the Way of Salvation," p. 145

EARTHLY ENJOYMENT

And the world passeth away, and the lust thereof: but he that doeth the will of God abideth for ever.
— 1 JOHN 2:17

It is not in the power of any earthly enjoyment to drive and shut out all trouble from the heart. If a man has some things in which he takes comfort and pleasure, there are others that yield him uneasiness and sorrow; if he has some things in the world that are sweet, there are others that are bitter; against such things it is not in the power of his pleasures to help him. We never can find anything here below that shall make us so happy but we shall have grief and pleasure mixed together. This world—let us make the best of it—will be spotted with black and white, varied with clouds and sunshine; and to them who yield their hearts to it, it will yield pain as well as pleasure. But this pleasure of seeing God can suffer no mixture; for this pleasure of seeing God is so great and strong that it takes the full possession of the heart; it fills it perfectly full, so that there shall be no room for any sorrow, no room in any corner for anything of an adverse nature from joy. There is no darkness that can bear such powerful light. It is impossible that they who see God face to face, who behold His glory and love so immediately as they do in heaven, should have any such thing as grief or pain in their hearts. Once the saints are come into God's presence, tears shall be wiped from their eyes, and sorrow and sighing shall flee away. The pleasure will be so great as fully and perfectly to employ every faculty; the sight of God's glory and love will be so wonderful, so engaging to the mind, and it shall keep all the powers of it in such strong attention, that the soul will be wholly possessed and taken up.

§ From "The Pure in Heart Blessed," p. 908

THIRST FOR HAPPINESS

That the trial of your faith, being much more precious than of gold that perisheth, though it be tried with fire, might be found unto praise and honour and glory at the appearing of Jesus Christ: whom having not seen, ye love; in whom, though now ye see him not, yet believing, ye rejoice with joy unspeakable and full of glory.

—1 PETER 1:7–8

Man has a natural craving and thirst after happiness, and will thirst and crave until his capacity is filled. His capacity is of vast extent, and nothing but an infinite good can fill and satisfy his desires. But, notwithstanding, provision is made in this way of salvation to answer those needs; there is a satisfying happiness purchased for us that is fully answerable to the capacity and cravings of our souls. Here is food procured to answer all the appetites and faculties of our souls. God has made the soul of man of a spiritual nature, and therefore he needs a corresponding happiness: some spiritual object in the enjoyment of which he may be happy. Christ has purchased the enjoyment of God, who is the great and original Spirit, as the portion of our souls; and He hath purchased the Spirit of God to come and dwell in us as an eternal principle of happiness. God hath made man a rational, intelligent creature, and man needs some good that shall be a suitable object of his understanding for him to contemplate, wherein he may have full and sufficient exercise for his capacious faculties in their utmost extent. Here is an object that is great and noble and worthy of the exercise of the noblest faculties of the rational soul. God Himself should be theirs for them forever to behold and contemplate. His glorious perfections and works are most worthy objects, and there is room enough for improving them and still to exercise their faculties to all eternity.

֍ From "The Wisdom of God, Displayed in the Way of Salvation," p. 145

RETURNING TO FOLLY AND WICKEDNESS

For it had been better for them not to have known the way of righteousness, than, after they have known it, to turn from the holy commandment delivered unto them. But it is happened unto them according to the true proverb, The dog is turned to his own vomit again; and the sow that was washed to her wallowing in the mire.
— 2 PETER 2:21–22

Men are apt to think that if they had lived in Christ's time and had seen and heard Him and had seen His miracles that they would have been effectually convinced and turned from sin. But how was it in fact? How few were there brought to repentance by all His discourses and miracles! How hardhearted were they! Some were very much affected for a little while, but how few constant steady followers had He! He was, notwithstanding His miracles, rejected, despised, and even murdered by the people among whom He dwelt; and they were men of the same natures as sinners in these days. The Scripture is full of instances, sufficient to convince us, that if the word of God will not awaken and convert sinners, nothing will. And we see enough in these days to convince us of it. Men sometimes meet with those things by which we should not imagine if we did not see it and were not used to it, but that they would be thoroughly awakened and reformed. They sometimes hear the warnings of dying men expecting to go to hell. One would think this would be enough to awaken them; and it may be they are affected with it for the present, but it only touches them; it vanishes away and is gone like a puff of wind. Sometimes sinners themselves are laid upon beds of sickness, and their lives hang in doubt before them. They are brought to the sides of the grave and to the very mouth of hell, and their hearts are full of terror and amazement. Yet if they recover, they soon forget it and return to the ways of folly and wickedness.

§ From "The Warnings of Scripture Are in the Best Manner Adapted to the Awakening and Conversion of Sinners," p. 70

TOMORROW MAY NOT COME

Go to now, ye that say, To day or to morrow we will go into such a city, and continue there a year, and buy and sell, and get gain.

— JAMES 4:13

Men behave themselves as those who depend on another day when they neglect anything today that must be done before they die. If there be anything that is absolutely necessary to be done sometime before death, and the necessity of it be sufficiently declared and shown to the person for whom it is thus necessary, and if he neglect setting about it immediately, sincerely, and with all his might, certainly it carries this face with it: that the man depends upon its being done hereafter, and consequently that he shall have opportunity to do it. Because, as to those things that are absolutely necessary to be done, there is need, not only of a possibility of a future opportunity, but of something that is to be depended on, some good ground to conclude that we shall have future opportunity. Therefore, whoever lives under the gospel and does not this day thoroughly reform his life by casting away every abomination and denying every lust, and doth not apply himself to the practice of the whole of his duty toward God and man and begin to make religion his main business, he acts as one who depends on another day. He is abundantly taught that these things must be done before he dies. Those who have been seeking salvation for a great while, in a dull, insincere, and slighty manner, and find no good effect of it, have abundant reason to conclude that, sometime before they die, they must not only seek, but strive to enter in at the strait gate, and must be violent for the kingdom of heaven; and therefore, if they do not begin thus today, they act as those who depend on another day.

§ From "Procrastination, or the Sin and Folly of Depending on Future Time," p. 239

HEIRS OF GOD

Hearken, my beloved brethren; hath not God chosen the poor of this world rich in faith, and heirs of the kingdom which he hath promised to them that love him?
— JAMES 2:5

The saints shall have greater and more extensive possessions than any earthly monarch. One reason for which the state of kings is admired is their wealth. They have the most precious things laid up in their treasures. But the precious treasures of kings are not to be compared to those precious things that Christ will give His saints in another world: the gold tried in the fire that Christ has purchased with His own blood, those precious jewels, those graces and joys of His Spirit, and that beauty of mind with which He will endow them. A king's possessions are very extensive, but these fall short of the extensive possessions of the saints, who possess all things. They are the heirs of God, and all that is God's is theirs so far as it can contribute to their happiness: "He that overcometh shall inherit all things; and I will be his God, and he shall be my son" (Rev. 21:7). Christ has appointed to the saints a kingdom, and in that kingdom they shall reign. They shall reign in fellowship with Christ as joint heirs. They shall reign in the same kingdom with Him, and shall have the happiness of having things done according to their will as much as if their own wills were paramount. Christ wills their will. All things will be disposed in the best manner for them and to promote their happiness.

§ From "Christians a Chosen Generation, a Royal Priesthood, a Holy Nation, a Peculiar People," p. 941

DEPENDENT UPON GOD

But our God is in the heavens: he hath done whatsoever he hath pleased.
— PSALM 115:3

In the great matter of the eternal salvation of our souls, we are dependent on God. We are dependent not only on His wisdom to contrive a way to accomplish it and on His power to bring it to pass, but we are dependent on His mere will and pleasure in the affair. We depend on the sovereign will of God for everything belonging to it, from the foundation to the top-stone. It was of the sovereign pleasure of God that He contrived a way to save any of mankind and gave us Jesus Christ, His only begotten Son, to be our Redeemer. Why did He look on us and send us a Savior? It was from the sovereign pleasure of God. It was of His sovereign pleasure what means to appoint. His giving us the Bible and the ordinances of religion is of His sovereign grace. His giving those means to us rather than to others, His giving the awakening influences of His Spirit, and His bestowing saving grace, are all of His sovereign pleasure. When He says, "Let there be light in the soul of such a one," it is a word of infinite power and sovereign grace. Let us with the greatest humility adore the awful and absolute sovereignty of God. The infinite greatness of God, and His exaltation above us, appears in nothing more than in His sovereignty. Dominion and sovereignty require humble reverence and honor in the subject. The absolute, universal, and unlimited sovereignty of God requires that we should adore Him with all possible humility and reverence.

༺ From "God's Sovereignty in the Salvation of Men," p. 853

FIRMNESS OF RESOLUTION

*One thing have I desired of the L*ORD*, that will I seek after; that*
*I may dwell in the house of the L*ORD *all the days of my life, to*
*behold the beauty of the L*ORD*, and to enquire in his temple.*

— PSALM 27:4

Pressing into the kingdom of heaven denotes earnestness and firmness of resolution. There should be strength of resolution, accompanying strength of desire, as it was in the psalmist: "one thing have I desired, and that will I seek after" (Ps. 27:4). In order to a thorough engagedness of the mind in this affair, both these must meet together. Besides desires after salvation, there should be an earnest resolution in persons to pursue this good as much as lies in their power; to do all that in the use of their utmost strength they are able to do, in an attendance on every duty, and resisting and militating against all manner of sin and to continue in such a pursuit. There are two things needful in a person in order to these strong resolutions: there must be a sense of the great importance and necessity of the mercy sought, and there must also be a sense of opportunity to obtain it or the encouragement there to seek it. The strength of resolution depends on the sense that God gives to the heart of these things. Persons without such a sense may seem, to themselves, to take up resolutions; they may, as it were, force a promise to themselves and say within themselves, "I will seek as long as I live; I will not give up until I obtain," when they do but deceive themselves. Their hearts are not in it; neither do they indeed take up any such resolution as they seem to themselves to do. It is the resolution of the mouth more than of the heart; their hearts are not strongly bent to fulfill what their mouth says. The firmness of the resolution lies in the fullness of the disposition of the heart to do what is resolved to be done. Those who are pressing into the kingdom of God have a disposition of heart to do everything that is required, and that lies in their power to do and to continue in it.

§ From "Pressing into the Kingdom of God," p. 655

HOLY AND JUST

Where there is neither Greek nor Jew, circumcision nor uncir-cumcision, Barbarian, Scythian, bond nor free: but Christ is all, and in all.

—COLOSSIANS 3:11

Infinite justice and infinite grace meet in Jesus Christ. As Christ is a divine person, He is infinitely holy and just, hating sin and disposed to execute condign punishment for sin. He is the judge of the world, and the infinitely just judge of it, and will not at all acquit the wicked or by any means clear the guilty. And, yet, He is infinitely gracious and merciful. Though His justice is so strict with respect to all sin and every breach of the law, yet He has grace sufficient for every sinner, and even the chief of sinners. And His grace is not only sufficient for the most unworthy to show them mercy and bestow some good upon them, but to bestow the greatest good. Yea, it is sufficient to bestow all good upon them and to do all things for them. There is no benefit or blessing that they can receive so great, but the grace of Christ is sufficient to bestow it on the greatest sinner that ever lived. And not only so, but so great is His grace that nothing is too much as the means of this good. It is sufficient not only to do great things, but also to suffer in order to do it; and not only to suffer, but to suffer most extremely—even unto death—the most terrible of natural evils. Not only to suffer unto death, but the most ignominious and tormenting, and every way the most terrible death that men could inflict; yea, and greater sufferings than men could inflict, who could only torment the body. He had sufferings in His soul that were the more immediate fruits of the wrath of God against the sins of those He undertakes for.

꜅ From "The Excellency of Jesus Christ," p. 681

THE AGONY OF CHRIST

And being in an agony he prayed more earnestly, and his sweat was as it were great drops of blood falling down to the ground.
— LUKE 22:44

How dreadful Christ's last sufferings were. We learn it from the dreadful effect that the bare foresight of them had upon Him in His agony. His last sufferings were so dreadful that the view that Christ had of them beforehand overwhelmed Him and amazed Him, as it is said He began to be sore amazed. The very sight of these last sufferings was so very dreadful as to sink His soul down into the dark shadow of death; yea, so dreadful was it, that in the sore conflict His nature had with it, He was all in a sweat of blood, His body all over was covered with clotted blood; and not only His body, but the very ground under Him was covered with the blood that fell from Him, which had been forced through His pores through the violence of His agony. If only the foresight of the cup was so dreadful, how dreadful was the cup itself, how far beyond all that can be uttered or conceived! The sufferings that Christ endured in His body on the cross, though they were very dreadful, were yet the least part of His last sufferings; besides those, He endured sufferings in His soul that were vastly greater. For if it had been only the sufferings that He endured in His body, though they were very dreadful, we cannot conceive that the mere anticipation of them would have such an effect on Christ. Many of the martyrs, for ought we know, have endured as severe tortures in their bodies as Christ did. Many of the martyrs have been crucified, as Christ was, and yet their souls have not been so overwhelmed. There has been no appearance of such amazing sorrow and distress of mind, either at the anticipation of their sufferings or in the actual enduring of them.

᠖ From "Christ's Agony," p. 869

GOD HEARS PRAYERS

O thou that hearest prayer.
— PSALM 65:2

The Most High is a God that hears prayer. Though He is infinitely above all and stands in no need of creatures, yet He is graciously pleased to take a merciful notice of poor worms of the dust. He manifests and presents Himself as the object of prayer and appears as sitting on a mercy seat, that men may come to Him by prayer. When they stand in need of anything, He allows them to come and ask it of Him, and He is wont to hear their prayers. God, in His Word, hath given many promises that He will hear their prayers. The Scripture is full of such examples, and in His dispensations toward His church, He manifests Himself to be a God that hears prayer. Here it may be inquired, what is meant by God's hearing prayer? There are two things implied in it. First, His accepting the supplications of those who pray to Him. Their address to Him is well taken; He is well-pleased with it. He approves of their asking such mercies as they request of Him and approves of their manner of doing it. He accepts of their prayers as an offering to Him. He accepts the honor they do Him in prayer. Second, He acts agreeably to His acceptance. He sometimes manifests His acceptance of their prayers by special discoveries of His mercy and sufficiency, which He makes to them in prayer or immediately after. While they are praying, He gives them sweet views of His glorious grace, purity, sufficiency, and sovereignty and enables them, with great quietness, to rest in Him, to leave themselves and their prayers with Him, submitting to His will and trusting in His grace and faithfulness. He not only inwardly and spiritually discovers His mercy to their souls by His Spirit, but also outwardly, by dealing mercifully with them in His providence, in consequence of their prayers, and by causing an agreeableness between His providence and their prayers.

⟡ From "The Most High a Prayer-Hearing God," p. 114

ABSENT FROM THE BODY, PRESENT WITH THE LORD

We are confident, I say, and willing rather to be absent from the body, and to be present with the Lord. — 2 CORINTHIANS 5:8

The souls of true saints, when absent from the body, go to be with Jesus Christ, as they are brought into a most perfect conformity to and union with Him. Their spiritual conformity is begun while they are in the body. Here beholding, as in a glass, the glory of the Lord, they are changed into the same image. But when they come to see Him as He is, in heaven, then they become like Him in another manner. That perfect sight will abolish all remains of deformity, disagreement, and sinful unlikeness, as all darkness is abolished before the full blaze of the sun's meridian light. As it is impossible that the least degree of obscurity should remain before such light, so it is impossible the least degree of sin and spiritual deformity should remain with such a view of the spiritual beauty and glory of Christ, as the saints enjoy in heaven, when they see that Sun of Righteousness without a cloud. They themselves shall not only shine forth as the Sun, but shall be as little suns, without a spot. For then is come the time when Christ presents His saints to Himself, in glorious beauty: "not having spot, or wrinkle, or any such thing" (Eph. 5:27), and having holiness without a blemish. Then the saints' union with Christ is perfected. This also is begun in this world. The relative union is both begun and perfected at once, when the soul first being quickened by Him closes with Christ by faith. The real union, consisting in the vital union and that of hearts and affections, is begun in this world and perfected in the next. The union of the heart of a believer to Christ is begun when it is drawn to Him by the first discovery of divine excellency, at conversion. When the soul leaves the body, all these clogs and hindrances shall be removed, every separating wall shall be broken down, and every impediment taken out of the way, and all distance shall cease.

§ From "True Saints, When Absent from the Body, Are Present with the Lord," p. 28

THE OWNER AND KING OF HEAVEN

No man hath ascended up to heaven, but he that came down
from heaven, even the Son of man which is in heaven.
— JOHN 3:13

In the fullness of time, Christ united Himself to man by taking upon Himself man's nature. He who is the owner of heaven and who dwells in heaven came down from heaven and was made flesh and dwelt among us: "No man hath ascended up to heaven, but he that came down from heaven, even the Son of man who is in heaven" (John 3:13). That is, no man even ascended there in his own right but He, but He came down from heaven that all who are His might ascend there. Christ, who is the owner and king of heaven, having thus united Himself to man, those to whom He is united cannot fail of ascending to heaven and being where He is. By His death Christ has removed the great thing that separated heaven and earth: guilt. Before man fell, there was a friendly communication between heaven and earth; but when man became a guilty creature, the union was broken and a great separation was made. But Christ, by His death, has removed this, for He has made a complete atonement for sin. So now those obstacles are removed out of the way, the gate of heaven is open, and the way is clear. He has laid down a price for man, sufficient to purchase heaven, as high as heaven. It is as glorious and exalted as its happiness is, and though it is so much above all earthly glory, though it is eternal, yet Christ has paid the price for it, that is, equivalent to the worth of it. His righteousness is a jewel precious enough in the eyes of God to answer to this height of glory. Since His resurrection He has gone into heaven and taken possession of it in His people's name. He ascended into heaven in our nature; the man Christ Jesus has gone to heaven in our name as well as in our nature. He has gone as our forerunner. He now has gone there, and there remains as a public person, as the head of believers.

---

§ From "The Ladder That God Has Set on the Earth for Man to Ascend
to Happiness Reaches Even unto Heaven," pp. 163–64

TIME IS PRECIOUS

Redeeming the time.
—EPHESIANS 5:16

Time is precious because a happy or miserable eternity depends on the good or ill improvement of it. Things are precious in proportion to their importance or to the degree wherein they concern our welfare. Men are wont to set the highest value on those things upon which they are sensible their interest chiefly depends. This renders time so exceedingly precious, because our eternal welfare depends on the improvement of it. Indeed, our welfare in this world depends upon its improvement. If we improve it not, we shall be in danger of coming to poverty and disgrace; but by a good improvement of it, we may obtain those things that will be useful and comfortable. But it is above all things precious, as our state through eternity depends upon it. The importance of the improvement of time upon other accounts is in subordination to this. Gold and silver are esteemed precious by men, but they are of no worth to any man, only as thereby he has an opportunity of avoiding or removing some evil or of possessing himself of some good. And the greater the evil is that any man hath advantage to escape or the good that he hath advantage to obtain by anything that he possesses, by so much the greater is the value of that thing to him, whatever it be. Thus if a man, by anything that he hath, may save his life, which he must lose without it, he will look upon that by which he hath the opportunity of escaping so great an evil as death, to be very precious. Hence it is that time is so exceedingly precious, because by it we have opportunity of escaping everlasting misery and of obtaining everlasting blessedness and glory. On this depends our escape from an infinite evil and our attainment of an infinite good.

From "The Preciousness of Time and the Importance of Redeeming It," p. 233

AN INFINITE REWARD

He that hath mercy on the poor, happy is he.
— PROVERBS 14:21

If you give with a spirit of true charity, you shall be rewarded in what is infinitely more valuable than what you give, even eternal riches in heaven: "Whosoever shall give to drink unto one of these little ones a cup of cold water only in the name of a disciple; verily I say unto you, he shall in no wise lose his reward" (Matt. 10:42). Giving to our needy brethren is in Scripture called laying up treasure in heaven in bags that do not get old: "Sell that ye have, and give alms; provide yourselves bags which wax not old, a treasure in the heavens that faileth not, where no thief approacheth, neither moth corrupteth" (Luke 12:33). When men have laid up their money in their chests, they do not suppose that they have thrown it away. But, on the contrary, they know that it is laid up safely. Much less is treasure thrown away when it is laid up in heaven. What is laid up there is much safer than what is laid up in chests or cabinets. You cannot lay up treasure on earth but it is liable to be stolen, or otherwise fail. But there no thief approaches nor moth corrupts. It is committed to God's care, and He will keep it safely for you. And when you die, you shall receive it with infinite increase. Instead of a part of your earthly substance thus bestowed, you shall receive heavenly riches, on which you may live in the great fullness, honor, and happiness to all eternity, and never be in want of anything. After feeding with some of your bread those who cannot recompense you, you shall be rewarded at the resurrection and eat bread in the kingdom of God: "When thou makest a feast, call the poor, the maimed, the lame, the blind: and thou shalt be blessed; for they cannot recompense thee: for thou shalt be recompensed at the resurrection of the just. And when one of them that sat at meat with him heard these things, he said unto him, Blessed is he that shall eat bread in the kingdom of God" (Luke 14:13–16).

§ From "Christian Charity: The Duty of Charity to the Poor Explained and Enforced," pp. 245–46

SOVEREIGNTY OVER CREATION

Thou hast created all things, and for thy pleasure they are and were created.
                                                        — REVELATION 4:11

God exercises His infinite power and absolute sovereignty toward all the works of His hands. His sovereignty appears in their creation. He created them just as He pleased. He created as many stars as He pleased and fixed them in what places He pleased. He appointed their courses as He pleased. The sun, moon, and stars are constantly true to their Maker's orders, day and night, year after year, and from age to age. And when God pleases, they stop their course, as was true in Joshua's time. God commanded, and the great frame of nature stopped. An arrest was bid on the course of the heavens: "Which commandeth the sun and it riseth not, and sealeth up the stars" (Job 9:7). God created the earth as He pleased. He made a place for the sea where He pleased. He raised the mountains where He pleased and sank the valleys where He pleased. He created what sort of creatures to inhabit the earth and waters as He pleased; and when He pleased, He brought a flood of waters and covered the whole earth, destroying all its inhabitants. And when He is pleased, He will dissolve this curious frame of the world and break all to pieces and set it on fire; then the earth and all the works that are therein shall be burned up and the heavens shall be dissolved and rolled together as a curtain. When God pleases, He will roll all together as a man does when he takes down a tent. In such things as these, relating to the material world, God manifests His sovereignty.

🔖 From "God Does What He Pleases," pp. 153–54

CHRIST: THE GIVER OF HAPPINESS

Thou hast given him power over all flesh, that he should give eternal life to as many as thou hast given him. — JOHN 17:2

All the Christian's happiness is communicated to the Christian by Christ. He is the giver and bestower of it. The Christian does not obtain a right to it by His righteousness, but it comes out of Christ's hands. God the Father has given the glorious reward that Christ purchased into His hands to be bestowed by Him to all for whom He has purchased it (see John 17:2). That spiritual comfort, and those sweet and divine pleasures that Christians sometimes have in this world, they receive at the hands of Christ. They are the dainties with which He feeds them; they are the clusters with which He refreshes them. And the crown of glory hereafter is what they will receive at the hands of Christ. He has bought it, and it is already given into His hands to bestow on His followers. It is Christ who will feed the saints and lead them to living fountains of waters in heaven (see Rev. 7:17). It is He who will take care to carry them along through this world to heaven. He carries them on eagles' wings. He preserves them from their enemies. He saves their souls from death, their eyes from tears, and their feet from falling. He shall send His angels to carry the soul home to Himself when they are departing from this life. It is He who clothes them with the robes of glory and satisfies the soul with rivers of pleasure. He has provided the feast, and His blessed hands deal forth the bountiful provision. It is He who entertains the soul and makes it welcome: "Eat, O friends; drink, yea, drink abundantly, O beloved" (Song 5:1).

§ From "Christ Is the Christian's All," p. 201

FRIENDS OF GOD

In him we live, and move, and have our being.

— ACTS 17:28

Let it be of great comfort to the saints that God is their father and friend and is always present with them and in them; that they live and move and have their being in Him who loves them with a great and everlasting love. Our earthly friends cannot be with us always; we are often called to part with them. But God is a friend who is always at hand, always with and in those who are His. Let those, therefore, who have given themselves to God and have chosen God to be their God consider this: You are in Him and are favorable to Him. He delights in you and always consults your good and seeks your welfare. You are in Him and no one can separate you from Him; wherever you are, you are still with God. This is a matter of consolation to such persons, whatever dangers and difficulties they are brought into, that they are with God. He is nigh at hand, so that they need not be terrified with any amazement; for they are in Him who orders all things and who loves them, so that He will surely take care of them and order all things well for them. If they pray to Him in their difficulty and beg His help, He is present to hear their prayers. They need not go far to seek Him nor cry aloud to make Him hear, but He is in them and hears the silent petitions of their hearts. If they are in solitude and are very much left alone, yet God is with them. None can banish them from the presence and society of God. A Christian never needs to be lonesome as long as he is in the company of such a one.

⟡ From "God Is Everywhere Present," pp. 217–18

UNIVERSAL AND EVANGELICAL OBEDIENCE

Every one that heareth these sayings of mine, and doeth them not, shall be likened unto a foolish man, which built his house upon the sand.

—MATTHEW 7:26

Let your obedience to God's commands be universal. If your obedience is but partial, and you have respect to only some of God's commands and neglect others; if you perform some duties but at the same time live in some certain ways of sin; you cannot expect to have any great matter of comfort from such an obedience. Such obedience will not be acceptable to God, and therefore you will not have the inward testimonies and manifestations of His acceptance. Those ways of sin that you live in will spoil all your obedience and will spoil all the comfort of it. However you obey Him in some things, yet if in others you disobey, you cannot expect any true peace in your own mind, nor can you expect any of the light of God's countenance. Your conscience and the Word of God will accuse you of being a rebel and an enemy and will tell you that the wrath of God abides on you. Let your obedience be evangelical. If you would taste the sweetness of God's commands and have them become a means of your comfort and pleasure, you must obey them from evangelical principles, from a principle of love and not merely from fear. Your obedience must not be slavish and that to which you were merely driven and forced; this is not the way to have much pleasure in obedience. Your obedience must also be performed from a principle of faith and holy confidence in God, trusting in His promises and with hope of that glory that He will bestow on all His faithful servants. If you would have religion be a comfort, a pleasure, and a joy to you, it must not be a dull and dead service, but must be a cheerful, lively, and spiritual obedience.

§ From "There Is Much of the Goodness and Mercy of God Appearing in the Commands He Has Given Us," pp. 258–59

INFINITE MERCY EXTENDED

For thy mercy is great above the heavens.

— PSALM 108:4

God's mercy is transcendent in that it is sufficient to extend itself to the sinful. Herein the mercy of God is infinite, because sin sets the creature at an infinite distance. The mercy of God could not reach a simple object were it not infinite. Every creature is at an infinite distance from God, as he is infinitely unequal to Him; but sin causes a distance between God and the creature that is of quite another kind. It causes an infinite distance in a respect wherein the creature, before it was sinful, was not at any distance from God, but was united; 'tis a distance of opposition and enmity. There is need of infinite mercy to reach a creature separated from God by this kind of distance, for the separation is infinite. God is of a nature that is infinitely opposite to sin, on the account of His infinite holiness. Any degree of holiness would cause a being to hate sin, but infinite holiness must make him infinitely hate sin. God would necessarily have as great a hatred of the sinner as of the sin were not His mercy infinite as well as His holiness. But by reason of His mercy being infinite, it extends itself through this infinite distance and does, as it were, overcome this infinite opposition so as to love an object that is infinitely worthy of His hatred. Therefore, when God, instead of hating, instead of punishing a sinful object, loves it, pities it, and does it good, it argues His mercy to be transcendently great. It is incomprehensible and absolutely infinite.

§ From "God Is a Being of Transcendent Mercy," pp. 272–74

GOD IS LOVE

The love of God is shed abroad in our hearts by the Holy Ghost which is given unto us.
— ROMANS 5:5

The God of love Himself dwells in heaven. Heaven is the palace or presence-chamber of the High and Holy One, whose name is love, and who is both the cause and source of all holy love. God, considered with respect to His essence, is everywhere. He fills both heaven and earth. Yet He is said, in some respects, to be more especially in some places than in others. He was said of old to dwell in the land of Israel, above all other lands; and in Jerusalem, above all other cities of that land; and in the temple, above all other buildings in the city; and in the Holy of Holies, above all other apartments of the temple; and on the mercy seat, over the ark of the covenant, above all other places in the Holy of Holies. But heaven is His dwelling place, above all other places in the universe; and all those places in which He was said to dwell of old were but types of this. Heaven is a part of creation that God has built for this end, to be the place of His glorious presence, and it is His abode forever; and here will He dwell and gloriously manifest Himself to all eternity. This renders heaven a world of love; for God is the fountain of love, as the sun is the fountain of light. Therefore, the glorious presence of God in heaven fills heaven with love, as the sun, placed in the midst of the visible heavens in a clear day, fills the world with light. The apostle John tells us that "God is love" (1 John 4:8); and therefore, seeing He is an infinite being, it follows that He is an infinite fountain of love. Seeing He is an all-sufficient being, it follows that He is a full, overflowing, and inexhaustible fountain of love. And in that He is an unchangeable and eternal being, He is an unchangeable and eternal fountain of love.

❧ From "Heaven, a World of Charity, or Love," pp. 326–27

THE PURCHASED GIFT

And I will pray the Father, and he shall give you another Comforter, that he may abide with you for ever; even the Spirit of truth; whom the world cannot receive, because it seeth him not, neither knoweth him: but ye know him; for he dwelleth with you, and shall be in you.
— JOHN 14:16–17

The Spirit of Christ is given to His church and people everlastingly, to influence and dwell in them. The Holy Spirit is the great purchase, or purchased gift, of Christ. The chief and sum of all the good things that are purchased for the church in this life and in the life to come is the Holy Spirit. And as He is the great purchase, so He is the great promise, or the great thing promised by God and Christ to the church. And this great purchase and promise of Christ is forever to be given to His church. He has promised that His church shall continue, and expressly declared that the gates of hell shall not prevail against it. So it may be preserved, He has given His Holy Spirit to every true member of it and promised the continuance of that Spirit forever. Man, in his first estate in Eden, had the Holy Spirit; but he lost it by his disobedience. But a way has been provided by which it may be restored, and now it is given a second time, never more to depart from the saints. The Spirit of God is so given to His own people as to become truly theirs. It was, indeed, given to our first parents in their state of innocence and dwelt with them, but not in the same sense in which it is given to, and dwells in, believers in Christ. They had no proper right or sure title to the Spirit, and it was not finally and forever given to them, as it is to believers in Christ; for if it had been, they never would have lost it. But the Spirit of Christ is not only communicated to those that are converted, but He is made over to them by a sure covenant, so that He is become their own. Christ is become theirs, and therefore His fullness is theirs, and therefore His Spirit is theirs: their purchased, promised, and sure possession.

§ From "The Holy Spirit Forever to Be Communicated to the Saints, in the Grace of Charity, or Divine Love," pp. 307–8

THE NEW MAN

If any man be in Christ, he is a new creature: old things are passed away; behold, all things are become new.
— 2 CORINTHIANS 5:17

A true convert, the moment he is converted, is possessed not of one or two, but of all holy principles and all gracious dispositions. They may be feeble, indeed, like the faculties and powers of an infant child, but they are all truly there and will be seen flowing out progressively in every kind of holy feeling and behavior toward both God and man. In every real convert there are as many graces as there were in Jesus Christ Himself, which is what the evangelist John means when he says, "The Word was made flesh, and dwelt among us (and we beheld his glory, the glory as of the only begotten of the Father), full of grace and truth.... And of his fullness have all we received, and grace for grace" (John 1:14–16). And, indeed, it cannot be otherwise, for all true converts are renewed in Christ's image, as says the apostle Paul: "And have put on the new man, which is renewed in knowledge after the image of him that created him" (Col. 3:10). But that is no true image or picture of another, which has some parts or features wanting. An exact image has a part answerable to each part in that of which it is an image. The copy answers to the original throughout, in all its parts and features, though it may be obscure in some respects and not represent any part perfectly, as grace answers to grace. Grace in the soul is a reflection of Christ's glory. It is a reflection of His glory, as the image of a man is reflected from a glass that exhibits part for part. It is in the new birth as it is in the birth of the infant child. He has all the parts of a man, though they are as yet in a very imperfect state. Not a part is wanting, but there are as many members as to a man of full stature and strength. And therefore what is wrought in regeneration is called "the new man": not only new eyes or new ears or new hands, but a new man, possessing all the human faculties and members.

From "All the Graces of Christianity Connected," pp. 278–79

TRUST IN GOD

And now, O Lord GOD, thou art that God, and thy words be true, and thou hast promised this goodness unto thy servant.
— 2 SAMUEL 7:28

A trust in God in the way of negligence is what in Scripture is called tempting God; and a trust in Him in the way of sin is what is called presumption, which is a thing terribly threatened in His Word. But he that truly and rightly trusts in God, trusts in Him in the way of diligence and holiness, or, which is the same thing, in the way of holy practice. The very idea of our trusting in another is resting or living in acquiescence of mind and heart in the full persuasion of his sufficiency and faithfulness, so as to be ready fully to venture on him in our actions. But they that do not practice and act upon the persuasion of another's sufficiency and faithfulness do not thus venture. They do not enter on any action or course of action in such a confidence, and so, venture nothing, and therefore cannot be said truly to trust. He that really trusts in another ventures on his confidence. And so it is with those that truly trust in God. They rest in the full persuasion that God is sufficient and faithful, so as to proceed in this confidence to follow God, and, if need be, to undergo difficulties and hardships for Him, because He has promised that they shall be no losers by such a course; and they have such confidence of this that they can and do venture upon His promise, while those who are not willing thus to venture show that they do not trust in Him. They that have the full trust in God that is implied in a living faith will not be afraid to trust God with their estates. It is so with respect to trust in men, that if those we have full confidence in desire to borrow anything of us and promise to pay us again, and to pay us a hundredfold, we are not afraid to venture, and do actually venture it. And so those that feel full confidence in God are not afraid to lend to the Lord.

§ From "All True Grace in the Heart Tends to Holy Practice in the Life," pp. 233–34

THE RUIN OF THE FALL

Charity...seeketh not her own.
— 1 CORINTHIANS 13:4–5

The ruin that the fall brought upon the soul of man consists very much in his losing the nobler and more benevolent principles of his nature and falling wholly under the power and government of self-love. Before, and as God created him, he was exalted, noble, and generous; but now he is debased, ignoble, and selfish. Immediately upon the fall, the mind of man shrank from its primitive greatness and expandedness to an exceeding smallness and contractedness; and, as in other respects, so especially in this. Before, his soul was under the government of that noble principle of divine love, whereby it was enlarged to the comprehension of all his fellow creatures and their welfare. And not only so, but it was not confined within such narrow limits as the bounds of the creation, but went forth in the exercise of holy love to the Creator and abroad upon the infinite ocean of good, and was, as it were, swallowed up by it and became one with it. But so soon as he had transgressed against God, these noble principles were immediately lost, and all this excellent enlargedness of man's soul was gone; and thenceforward he himself shrank, as it were, into a little space, circumscribed and closely shut up within itself to the exclusion of all things else. Sin, like some powerful astringent, contracted his soul to the very small dimensions of selfishness; and God was forsaken and fellow creatures forsaken, and man retired within himself and became totally governed by narrow and selfish principles and feelings. Self-love became absolute master of his soul, and the more noble and spiritual principles of his being took wings and flew away.

§ From "The Spirit of Charity, the Opposite of a Selfish Spirit," pp. 157–58

LOVE YOUR ENEMIES

But I say unto you, Love your enemies, bless them that curse you, do good to them that hate you, and pray for them which despitefully use you, and persecute you. — MATTHEW 5:44

We are to do good both to the good and to the bad. This we are to do, as we would imitate our heavenly Father, for, "he maketh his sun to rise on the evil and on the good, and sendeth rain on the just and on the unjust" (Matt. 5:45). The world is full of various kinds of persons, some good, and some evil; and we should do good to all. We should, indeed, especially "do good to them that are of the household of faith" (Gal. 6:10), or that we have reason, in the exercise of charity, to regard as saints. But though we should most abound in beneficence to them, yet our doing good should not be confined to them, but we should do good to all men, as we have opportunity. While we live in the world we must expect to meet with some men of very evil properties and of hateful dispositions and practices. Some are proud, some immoral, some covetous, some profane, some unjust or severe, and some despisers of God. But any or all of these bad qualities should not hinder our beneficence or prevent our doing them good as we have opportunity. On this very account we should the rather be diligent to benefit them, that we may win them to Christ, and especially should we be diligent to benefit them in spiritual things. We should do good both to friends and enemies. We are obliged to do good to our friends, not only from the obligation we are under to do good to them as our fellow creatures and those that are made in the image of God, but from the obligations of friendship and gratitude and the affection we bear them. And we are also obliged to do good to our enemies, for our Savior says, "But I say unto you, Love your enemies, bless them that curse you, do good to them that hate you, and pray for them which despitefully use you, and persecute you" (Matt. 5:44). To do good to those that do ill to us is the only retaliation that becomes us as Christians.

§ From "Charity Disposes Us to Do Good," pp. 100–101

PERSEVERE IN THE DUTY OF PRAYER

Give us help from trouble: for vain is the help of man.
— PSALM 60:11

To move you to persevere in the duty of prayer, consider how much you always stand in need of the help of God. If persons who have formerly attended this duty leave it off, the language of it is that now they stand in no further need of God's help, that they have no further occasion to go to God with requests and supplications. When, indeed, it is in God we live and move and have our being. We cannot draw a breath without His help. You need His help every day for the supply of your outward wants; and especially you stand in continual need of Him to help your souls. Without His protection they would immediately fall into the hands of the devil, who always stands as a roaring lion, ready, whenever he is permitted, to fall upon the souls of men and devour them. If God should indeed preserve your lives but should otherwise forsake and leave you to yourselves, you would be most miserable; your lives would be a curse to you. Those that are converted, if God should forsake them, would soon fall away totally from a state of grace into a state far more miserable than ever they were in before their conversion. They have no strength of their own to resist those powerful enemies who surround them. Sin and Satan would immediately carry them away, as a mighty flood, if God should forsake them. You stand in need of daily supplies from God. Without God you can receive neither spiritual light nor comfort, can exercise no grace, can bring forth no fruit. Without God your souls will wither and pine away and sink into a most wretched state. You continually need the instructions and directions of God. What can a little child do in a vast, howling wilderness without someone to guide it and to lead it in the right way? Without God you will soon fall into snares, pits, and many fatal calamities.

§ From "Hypocrites Deficient in the Duty of Prayer," p. 76

SING PRAISES TO GOD

*Hear, O ye kings; give ear, O ye princes; I, even I, will sing unto
the* LORD; *I will sing praise to the* LORD *God of Israel.*

—JUDGES 5:3

There is, it may be, not one of us but who hopes to be a saint in heaven, and there continually to sing praises to God and the Lamb; but how disagreeable will it be with such a hope, to live in the neglect of praising God now! We ought now to begin that work that we intend shall be the work of another world; for this life is given us on purpose that therein we might prepare for a future life. The present state is a state of probation and preparation—a state of preparation for the enjoyments and employment of another, future, and eternal state—and no one is ever admitted to those enjoyments and employments but those who are prepared for them here. If ever we would go to heaven, we must be fitted for heaven in this world; we must here have our souls molded and fashioned for that work and that happiness. They must be formed for praise, and they must begin their work here. The beginnings of future things are in this world. The seed must be sown here; the foundation must be laid in this world. Here is laid the foundation of future misery and of future happiness. If it be not begun here, it never will be begun. If our hearts be not in some measure tuned to praise in this world, we shall never do anything at the work hereafter. The light must dawn in this world, or the sun will never rise in the next. As we therefore all of us would be, and hope to be, of that blessed company that praise God in heaven, we should now inure ourselves to the work.

§ From "Praise, One of the Chief Employments of Heaven," p. 916

RESCUE IN CHRIST

He will fulfill the desire of them that fear him: he also will hear their cry, and will save them.
— PSALM 145:19

Christ has undertaken to save all from what they fear, if they come to Him. It is His professional business, the work in which He has engaged since before the foundation of the world. It is what He always had in His thoughts and intentions; He undertook from everlasting to be the refuge of those that are afraid of God's wrath. His wisdom is such that He would never undertake a work for which He is not sufficient. If there were some in so dreadful a case that He was not able to defend them or so guilty that it was not fit that He should save them, then He never would have undertaken for them. Those who are in trouble and distressing fear, if they come to Jesus Christ, have this to ease them of their fears: that Christ has promised them that He will protect them; that they come upon His invitation; that Christ has plighted His faith for their security if they will come to Him; and that He is engaged by covenant to God the Father that He will save those afflicted and distressed souls that come to Him. Christ, by His own free act, has made Himself the surety of such; He has voluntarily put Himself in their stead. If justice has anything against them, He has undertaken to answer for them. Let there be ever so much wrath that they have deserved, they are as safe as if they never had deserved any, because He has undertaken to stand for them, let it be more or less. If they are in Christ Jesus, the storm does, of course, light on Him, and not on them; as when we are under a good shelter, the storm that would otherwise come upon our heads lights upon the shelter.

᭝ From "Safety, Fullness, and Sweet Refreshment, to Be Found in Christ," p. 930

THE DANGER OF FLATTERY

For he flattereth himself in his own eyes, until his iniquity be found to be hateful.
— PSALM 36:2

Sinners, very generally, go on flattering themselves in some or other of these ways, until their punishment actually overtakes them. These are the baits by which Satan catches souls and draws them into his snare. They are such self-flatteries as these that keep men from seeing what danger they are in and that make them go securely on in the way they are in, "as the bird hasteth to the snare, and knoweth not that it is for his life" (Prov. 7:23). Those that flatter themselves with hopes of living a great while longer in the world very commonly continue to do so until death comes. Death comes upon them when they expect it not; they look upon it as a great way off, though there is but a step between them and death. They thought not of dying at that time, nor at anytime near it. When they were young they proposed to live a good while longer; and, if they happen to live until middle age, they still maintain the same thought: they are not yet near death. That thought goes along with them as long as they live, or until they are just about to die. Men often have a dependence on their own righteousness, and as long as they live are never brought off from it. Multitudes uphold themselves with their own intentions until all their prospects are dashed in pieces by death. They put off the work they have to do until such a time; and when that time comes, they put it off to another time; until death, which cannot be put off, overtakes them. There are many also that hold a false hope, a persuasion that they belong to God. As long as they live, by all the marks and signs that are given of a true convert, they never will be persuaded to let go their hope, until it is rent from them by death.

§ From "The Vain Self-Flatteries of the Sinner," p. 219

INFINITE WORTH

Now unto the King eternal, immortal, invisible, the only wise
God, be honour and glory for ever and ever. Amen.

— 1 TIMOTHY 1:17

Our obligation to love, honor, and obey any being is in proportion to his loveliness, honorableness, and authority; for that is the very meaning of these words. When we say anyone is very lovely, it is the same as to say that he is one very much to be loved. Or, if we say such a one is more honorable than another, it is that one that we are more obliged to honor. If we say anyone has great authority over us, it is the same as to say that he has great right to our subjection and obedience. But God is a being infinitely lovely because He has infinite excellency and beauty. To have infinite excellency and beauty is the same thing as to have infinite loveliness. He is a being of infinite greatness, majesty, and glory; therefore He is infinitely honorable. He is infinitely exalted above the greatest rulers of the earth and the highest angels in heaven; therefore He is infinitely more honorable than they. His authority over us is infinite, and the ground of His right to our obedience is infinitely strong. He is infinitely worthy to be obeyed Himself, and we have an absolute, universal, and infinite dependence upon Him.

§ From "The Justice of God in the Damnation of Sinners," p. 669

GOD HAS NOT GIVEN UP ON YOU

Be strong and of a good courage, fear not, nor be afraid of them: for the LORD thy God, he it is that doth go with thee; he will not fail thee, nor forsake thee.
— DEUTERONOMY 31:6

Once God gives a person a truly engaged spirit to wrestle and he resolves that he will not let God go unless He blesses him, it is common to observe that, ordinarily, he doesn't hold on in that way, but let go a little while before he obtains the blessing. You are ready, it may be, to be discouraged and think it in vain for you to seek any longer; you have sought so long and have not obtained. But you have no reason to be discouraged from anything that you have found as of yet; you have no reason to think it will be in vain for you to seek from anything you have found as of yet, for you never have made a trial yet of the right way of seeking, whether it will be in vain or not. You never have made a trial of this way that you have heard of in the text and doctrine. It is not time for you to talk of being discouraged until you have made trial. If you mean that you have reason to be discouraged with the way that you have been seeking in hitherto, that very likely may be true; it may be high time for you to be discouraged with that and to draw the conclusion that it is likely to be in vain to seek any longer in such a slack, dull, remiss, and irresolute manner as you have done, and that it is high time for you to begin in a new method. It may be that you attribute your want of success to God; you say that God will not hear you; you fear that God has given you up. It is quite wrong to lay it on God; 'tis all the while to be laid on yourself, to your own coldness, sloth, and unresolvedness. God is ready to bestow the blessing upon you if you would but seek it with suitable earnestness and resolution.

🙦 From "The Way to Obtain the Blessing of God Is to Resolve Not to Let God Go Unless He Blesses Us," pp. 222–23

THE DUTY OF SECRET PRAYER

But thou, when thou prayest, enter into thy closet, and when thou hast shut thy door, pray to thy Father which is in secret; and thy Father which seeth in secret shall reward thee openly.
— MATTHEW 6:6

Let me direct you to forsake all practices that hinder you in the duty of secret prayer. Examine the things in which you have allowed yourselves, and inquire whether they have had this effect upon you. You are able to look over your past behavior and may, on an impartial consideration, make a judgment of the practices and courses in which you have allowed yourselves. I only desire that you would ask at the mouth of your own consciences what has been the effect of these things with respect to your attendance on the duty of secret prayer. Have you not found that such practices have aided to the neglect of this duty? Have you not found that after them you have been more hindered and less conscientious and careful to attend it? Have they not, from time to time, actually been the means of your neglecting it? If you cannot deny that this is really the case, then, if you seek the good of your souls, forsake these practices. There is no harm in these things themselves, knowing there is a time for all things. Yet, if you find these things to be a hindrance to the duty of secret prayer, it is time for you to forsake them. If you value heaven more than a little worldly diversion, if you set a higher price on eternal glory than on a dance or song, you will forsake them.

§ From "Hypocrites Deficient in the Duty of Prayer," p. 77

MAJESTY AND MEEKNESS

Gird thy sword upon thy thigh, O most mighty, with thy glory and thy majesty.

— PSALM 45:3

In the person of Christ do meet together infinite majesty and transcendent meekness. These are two qualifications that meet together in no other person but Christ. Meekness, properly so called, is a virtue proper only to the creature. We scarcely ever find meekness mentioned as a divine attribute in Scripture, at least not in the New Testament. For thereby seems to be signified a calmness and quietness of spirit, arising from humility in mutable beings that are naturally liable to be put into a ruffle by the assaults of a tempestuous and injurious world. But Christ, being both God and man, has both infinite majesty and superlative meekness. Christ was a person of infinite majesty. It is He that is spoken of in Psalm 45:3: "Gird thy sword upon thy thigh, O most mighty, with thy glory and thy majesty." It is He who is mighty, that rideth on the heavens, and His excellency on the sky. It is He who is terrible out of His holy places, who is mightier than the noise of many waters, yea, than the mighty waves of the sea; before whom a fire goeth and burneth up His enemies round about; at whose presence the earth quakes and the hills melt; who sitteth on the circle of the earth and all the inhabitants thereof are as grasshoppers; who rebukes the sea and maketh it dry and drieth up the rivers; whose eyes are as a flame of fire; from whose presence, and from the glory of whose power, the wicked shall be punished with everlasting destruction; who is the blessed and only Potentate, the King of kings and Lord of lords; who has heaven for His throne and the earth for His footstool and is the high and lofty one who inhabits eternity; whose kingdom is an everlasting kingdom, and of whose dominion there is no end. And yet He was the most marvelous instance of meekness and humble quietness of spirit that ever was, agreeable to what Christ declares of Himself in Matthew 11:29: "I am meek and lowly in heart." He had a wonderful spirit of forgiveness, was ready to forgive His worst enemies, and prayed for them with fervent and effectual prayers. Thus is Christ a lion in majesty and a lamb in meekness.

⟡ From "The Excellency of Jesus Christ," pp. 681–82

DO NOT LOOK BACK

No man, having put his hand to the plough, and looking back,
is fit for the kingdom of God.
— LUKE 9:62

Be directed to forget the things that are behind; that is, do not keep thinking and making much of what you have done, but let your mind be wholly intent on what you have to do. In some sense you ought to look back; you should look back to your sins: "See thy way in the valley, know what thou hast done" (Jer 2:23). You should look back on the wretchedness of your religious performances and consider how you have fallen short in them; how exceedingly polluted all your duties have been, and how justly God might reject and loathe them, and you for them. But you ought not to spend your time in looking back, as many persons do, thinking how much they have done for their salvation; what great pains they have taken, how they have done what they can and do not see how they can do more; how long a time they have been seeking, and how much more they have done than others, and even than such-and-such who has obtained mercy. They think with themselves how hardly God deals with them, that He does not extend mercy to them but turns a deaf ear to their cries, and hence discourage themselves and complain of God. Do not thus spend your time in looking back on what is past, but look forward and consider what is before you; consider what it is that you can do, and what it is necessary that you should do, and what God calls you still to do in order to your own salvation. The apostle, in the third chapter to the Philippians, tells us what things he did while a Jew, how much he had to boast of, if any could boast; but he tells us that he forgot those things, and all other things that were behind, and reached forth toward the things that were before, pressing forward toward the mark for the prize of the high calling of God in Christ Jesus.

⟡ From "Pressing into the Kingdom of God," p. 658

GRACE

For he hath made him to be sin for us, who knew no sin; that
we might be made the righteousness of God in him.

—2 CORINTHIANS 5:21

The redeemed have all from the grace of God. It was of mere grace that God gave us His only begotten Son. The grace is great in proportion to the excellency of what is given. The gift was infinitely precious because it was of a person infinitely worthy, a person of infinite glory, and because it was of a person infinitely near and dear to God. The grace is great in proportion to the benefit we have given us in Him. The benefit is doubly infinite in that in Him we have deliverance from an infinite, because an eternal, misery, and do also receive eternal joy and glory. The grace in bestowing this gift is great in proportion to the unworthiness to whom it is given; instead of deserving such a gift, we merited infinitely ill of God's hands. The grace is great according to the manner of giving or in proportion to the humiliation and expense of the method and means by which a way is made for our having the gift. He gave Him to dwell among us; He gave Him to us incarnate, or in our nature, and in the like though sinless infirmities. He gave Him to us in a low and afflicted state; and not only so, but as slain, that He might be a feast for our souls. The grace of God in bestowing this gift is most free. It was what God was under no obligation to bestow. We never did anything to merit it; it was given while we were yet enemies and before we had so much as repented. Those that are called and sanctified are to attribute it alone to the good pleasure of God's goodness by which they are distinguished.

§ From "God Glorified in Man's Dependence," p. 4

UNSPEAKABLE BLESSEDNESS

According as he hath chosen us in him before the foundation of the world, that we should be holy and without blame before him in love.
— EPHESIANS 1:4

What great love God hath bestowed upon you in choosing you to such unspeakable blessedness before the foundation of the world. How wonderful was the love of God in giving His Son to purchase this blessedness for you, and how wonderful was the love of the Son of God in shedding His own blood to purchase such glory for you! How ought you therefore to live to God's glory! Let me therefore beseech, by those great mercies of God, that you give yourself up a living sacrifice, holy and acceptable to God, which is your reasonable service. And be not slothful in business but fervent in spirit, serving the Lord. Give the utmost diligence, that you may keep all the commandments of God: study that you may prove what is that good, and acceptable, and perfect will of God; study that in all things you may be found approved. Seeing God hath so loved you, strive earnestly that you may bring forth the fruits of the love of God; and seeing Christ hath so loved you, see that you love one another; let love be without dissimulation; be ye kindly affectioned one with another with brotherly love; be of the same mind one toward another, in honor preferring one another; have fervent charity among yourselves. Seeing God hath mercy on you, be ye merciful as your Father who is in heaven is merciful. Look not everyone on his own things; be pitiful, be courteous; be ready to distribute, willing to communicate; be kind one to another, tenderhearted, forgiving one another. Christ hath thus loved you while an enemy; therefore recompense to no man evil for evil, but contrariwise blessing; do good to them that do evil to you. Such things as these become those that are the heirs of the glory of which we have heard.

§ From "The Portion of the Righteous," p. 904

THE DOCTRINES OF RELIGION

Of his own will begat he us with the word of truth, that we should be a kind of firstfruits of his creatures.
— JAMES 1:18

In the things of religion we are to the highest degree interested. The truth or falsehood of the doctrines of religion concerns us to the highest degree possible. It is no matter of indifference to us whether there be a God or not; or whether the Scriptures be the word of God; or whether Christ be the Son of God; or whether there be any such thing as conversion. It makes an infinite difference to us whether these things are so or not. Therefore, we are under the greatest obligation, in point of interest, to resolve in our minds whether they be true or false. They who are undetermined whether there be any truth in religion, and are contented to be so, not inquiring, nor thoroughly using the means to be determined, act very unreasonably. They remain in doubt whether there be any such thing as heaven or hell; are quiet and easy to continue ignorant in this matter; are not engaged in their minds to come to a determination; do not search and inquire what arguments there are to prove any such things, nor diligently weigh and consider the force of them; but busy their minds about other things of infinitely less importance and act as if they thought it did not much concern them whether there be a future and eternal state. If they think that there is not, yet it is a matter of so great importance that no wise man would rest until he had satisfied himself, because if there be such a future state as the Scriptures assert, then we must have our part in it, either in a state of eternal rewards or in a state of eternal punishment.

§ From "The Unreasonableness of Indetermination in Religion," p. 58

PRAISING HIM

For now we see through a glass, darkly; but then face to face: now I know in part; but then shall I know even as also I am known.
— 1 CORINTHIANS 13:12

They that see God cannot but praise Him. He is a being of such glory and excellency that the sight of this excellency of His will necessarily influence them that behold it to praise Him. Such a glorious sight will awaken and rouse all the powers of the soul and will irresistibly impel them and draw them into acts of praise. Such a sight enlarges their souls and fills them with admiration and an unspeakable exultation of spirit. 'Tis from the little that the saints have seen of God and know of Him in this world that they are excited to praise Him in the degree they do here. But here they see but as in a glass darkly; they have only now and then a little glimpse of God's excellency. Then they shall have the transcendent glory and divine excellency of God set in their immediate and full view. They shall dwell in His immediate glorious presence and shall see Him face to face (see 1 Cor. 13:12). Now the saints see the glory of God but by a reflected light, as we in the night see the light of the sun reflected from the moon; but in heaven they shall directly behold the Sun of Righteousness and shall look full upon Him when shining in all His glory. This being the case, it can be no otherwise but that they should very much employ themselves in praising God.

§ From "Praise, One of the Chief Employments of Heaven," p. 914

SAVING GRACE GREATER THAN GIFTS

And though I have the gift of prophecy, and understand all mysteries, and all knowledge; and though I have all faith, so that I could remove mountains, and have not charity, I am nothing.
— 1 CORINTHIANS 13:2

The Spirit of God communicates Himself much more in bestowing saving grace than in bestowing these extraordinary gifts. In the extraordinary gifts of the Spirit, the Holy Ghost does indeed produce effects in men or by men, but not so as properly to communicate Himself, in His own proper nature, to men. A man may have an extraordinary impulse in his mind by the Spirit of God, whereby some future thing may be revealed to him, or he may have an extraordinary vision given him, representing some future event; and yet the Spirit may not at all impart Himself, in His holy nature, by that. The Spirit of God may produce effects in things in which He does not communicate Himself to us. Thus, the Spirit of God moved on the face of the waters, but not so as to impart Himself to the water. When the Spirit, by His ordinary influences, bestows saving grace, He therein imparts Himself to the soul in His own holy nature—that nature of His, on the account of which He is so often called in Scripture the Holy Ghost, or the Holy Spirit. By His producing this effect, the Spirit becomes an indwelling vital principle in the soul, and the subject becomes spiritual, being denominated so from the Spirit of God that dwells in him and of whose nature he is partaker. Yea, grace is, as it were, the holy nature of the Spirit imparted to the soul. But the extraordinary gifts of the Spirit, such as knowing things to come or having power to work miracles, do not imply this holy nature. Not but that God, when He gives the extraordinary gifts of the Spirit, is commonly wont to give the sanctifying influences of the Spirit with them; but one does not imply the other. And if God gives only extraordinary gifts, such as the gift of prophecy or of miracles, these alone will never make their receiver a partaker of the Spirit, so as to become spiritual in Himself, that is to say, in His own nature.

❧ From "Charity, or Love, More Excellent Than the Extraordinary Gifts of the Spirit," pp. 35–36

SINCERE LOVE

Thou shalt not avenge, nor bear any grudge against the children of thy people, but thou shalt love thy neighbour as thyself: I am the LORD.
　　　　　　　　　　　　　　　　　　　　—LEVITICUS 19:18

Whatever men may do or suffer, they cannot, by all their performances and sufferings, make up for the want of sincere love in the heart. If they lay themselves out ever so much in the things of religion and are ever so much engaged in acts of justice and kindness and devotion, and if their prayers and fastings are ever so much multiplied, or if they should spend their time ever so much in the forms of religious worship, giving days and nights to it and denying sleep to their eyes and slumber to their eyelids that they might be the more laborious in religious exercises, and if the things they should do in religion were such as to get them a name throughout the world and make them famous to all future generations, it would all be in vain without sincere love to God in the heart. And so, if a man should give most bounteously to religious or charitable uses, and if, possessing the riches of a kingdom, he should give it all, and from the splendor of an earthly prince should reduce himself to a level of beggars, and if he should not stop there, but when he had done all this, should yield himself to undergo the fiercest sufferings, giving up not only all his possessions but also giving his body to be clothed in rags or to be mangled and burned and tormented as much as the wit of man could conceive, all, even all this, would not make up for the want of sincere love to God in the heart.

❧ From "The Greatest Performances or Sufferings in Vain without Charity," p. 55

AN ENVIOUS SPIRIT

Not that I speak in respect of want: for I have learned, in what-soever state I am, therewith to be content. — PHILIPPIANS 4:11

A Christian spirit not only opposes the exercise and outward expressions of an envious spirit, but it also tends to mortify its principle and disposition in the heart. So far as a Christian spirit prevails, it not only checks the outward acting of envy, but it also tends to mortify and subdue the very principle itself in the heart. So that, just in proportion to the power of the former, the individual will cease to feel any inclination to be grieved at the prosperity of others, and still more, will cease to dislike them, or entertain any ill-will toward them on account of it. A Christian spirit disposes us to feel content with our own condition and with the estate that God has given us among men, and to a quietness and satisfaction of spirit with regard to the allot-ments and distributions of stations and possessions that God, in His wise and kind providence, has made to ourselves and others. Whether our rank be as high as that of the angels, or as low as that of the beggar at the rich man's gate (see Luke 16:20), we shall equally be satisfied with it as the post in which God hath placed us and shall equally respect ourselves if we are endeavor-ing faithfully to serve Him in it. Like the apostle Paul, we shall learn, if we do but have a Christian spirit, "in whatsoever state [we are], therewith to be content" (Phil. 4:11). But, a Christian spirit not only disallows the exercise and expression of envy and tends to mortify its principle and disposition in the heart, but it also disposes us to rejoice in the prosperity of others. Such a spirit of benevolence and goodwill will cast out the evil spirit of envy and enable us to find happiness in seeing our neighbor prospered.

§ From "Charity Inconsistent with an Envious Spirit," pp. 115–16

WILLFUL AND STUBBORN BEHAVIOR

And if any man will sue thee at the law, and take away thy coat, let him have thy cloak also. And whosoever shall compel thee to go a mile, go with him twain. — MATTHEW 5:40–41

Humility tends also to prevent a willful and stubborn behavior. They that are under the influence of a humble spirit will not set up their own will, either in public or private affairs. They will not be stiff and inflexible and insist that everything must go according to what they happen first to propose and manifest a disposition by no means to be easy, but to make all the difficulty they can, and to make others uneasy as well as themselves, and to prevent anything being done with any quietness, if it be not according to their own mind and will. They are not as some that the apostle Peter describes in 2 Peter 2:10, presumptuous and self-willed, always bent on carrying their own points, and, if this cannot be done, then bent on opposing and annoying others. On the contrary, humility disposes men to be of a yielding spirit to others, ready, for the sake of peace and to gratify others, to comply in many things with their inclinations and to yield to their judgments wherein they are not inconsistent with truth and holiness. A truly humble man is inflexible in nothing but the cause of his Lord and Master, which is the cause of truth and virtue. In this he is inflexible, because God and conscience require it. But in things of lesser moment, which do not involve his principles as a follower of Christ, and in things that concern only his own private interests, he is apt to yield to others. And if he sees that others are stubborn and unreasonable in their willfulness, he does not allow that to provoke him to be stubborn and willful in his opposition to them, but rather, he acts on the principles taught in such passages as Matthew 5:40–41: "if any man will sue thee at the law, and take away thy coat, let him have thy cloak also. And whosoever shall compel thee to go a mile, go with him twain."

§ From "The Spirit of Charity Is an Humble Spirit," pp. 141–42

ETERNAL ENJOYMENT

In the midst of the street of it, and on either side of the river, was there the tree of life, which bare twelve manner of fruits, and yielded her fruit every month.
— REVELATION 22:2

The inhabitants of heaven shall know that they shall forever be continued in the perfect enjoyment of each other's love. They shall know that God and Christ shall be forever with them as their God and portion and that His love shall be continued and fully manifested forever and that all their beloved fellow saints shall forever live with them in glory and shall forever keep up the same love in their hearts that they now have. And they shall know that they themselves shall ever live to love God and love the saints, and to enjoy their love in all its fullness and sweetness forever. They shall be in no fear of any end to this happiness or of any abatement from its fullness and blessedness, or that they shall ever be weary of its exercises and expressions or cloyed with its enjoyments, or that the beloved objects shall ever grow old or disagreeable, so that their love shall at last die away. All in heaven shall flourish in immortal youth and freshness. Age will not there diminish anyone's beauty or vigor, and their love shall abide in everyone's heart as a living spring perpetually springing up in the soul or as a flame that never dies away. And the holy pleasure of this love shall be as a river that is forever flowing clear and full and increasing continually. The heavenly paradise of love shall always be kept as in a perpetual spring, without autumn or winter, where no frosts shall blight or leaves decay and fall, but where every plant shall be in perpetual freshness, bloom, fragrance, and beauty, always springing forth and blossoming, and always bearing fruit. The leaf of the righteous shall not wither (see Ps. 1:3). And in the midst of the streets of heaven, and on either side of the river, grows the tree of life, which bears twelve manner of fruits and yields her fruit every month (see Rev. 22:2). Everything in the heavenly world shall contribute to the joy of the saints, and every joy of heaven shall be eternal. No night shall settle down with its darkness upon the brightness of their everlasting day.

From "Heaven, a World of Charity, or Love," pp. 347–48

CONDESCENSION

And the Word was made flesh, and dwelt among us, (and we beheld his glory, the glory as of the only begotten of the Father,) full of grace and truth.

—JOHN 1:14

It would be ill for us if God were no more condescending to us than men are wont to be one to another. Men are commonly very backward to acts of condescension one to another, to stoop and condescend to men of low degree. Men are ready to look upon what hurts their honor and debases themselves. Men are ready to treat inferiors with slight and contempt and to carry along as if they thought themselves too great to take much notice of them. But if God had been as backward to stoop to inferiors as men generally are, what would have become of us? God, though a being infinitely exalted in glory and power, condescends graciously to take notice of such little worms as we are. He condescends to treat us, to converse with us, and to have much to do with us in a way of favor and kindness. He condescended to come down from heaven to dwell with us, to take our nature, to be born one of us, to be one of us, and to take our infirmities upon Him. Christ did not come to be ministered to, but to minister. He came to do the meanest offices for us. He came to wash our feet. He became despised and rejected, was mocked and spat on, and was put to an ignominious death for our sakes. And now God condescends to come to us and make His abode with us and by His Spirit to dwell in us to make us His temples. Thus, God condescends to us, and it is well for us that He does. We would be undone if He did not.

§ From "It Is Well for Us That God Is Not as We Are," p. 21

HOW UNTHANKFUL WE HAVE BEEN

When they knew God, they glorified him not as God, neither were they thankful.
— ROMANS 1:21

Let us reflect and consider of how much ingratitude we have been guilty for the means of grace that God has given. He has been exceedingly kind to us upon this account. Our own consciences may testify whether or not we have been very unthankful. Had we not shown ourselves unthankful in the improvement of these means? How have we improved our Sabbaths, which God has graciously given us? Have we not shown an unthankful spirit for our Sabbaths? Have we not neglected, yea, profaned the Word, and the ordinances, and the calls of the gospel? How have we treated the Lord Jesus Christ, the strivings of God's Spirit in convicting our consciences? Have we not been guilty of grieving the Holy Spirit of God (see Eph. 4:30), repelling and stifling convictions? And then let us consider how God has, notwithstanding all our ungrateful treatment, continued these mercies, continued our Sabbaths, continued giving us the Word and His ordinances, continued the calls of the gospel, and continued to convict our consciences. Let us consider how evil we have been and how unworthy we are of the mercies we have received. What a spirit we have shown toward God, what a spirit of dislike, what a slight of God. We have carried it toward Him as if He was not a being worth regarding, and have made light of His authority. We have preferred a little carnal ease or pleasure, or a small, temporal convenience to Him. How vile we have been in our treatment of the Lord Jesus Christ. Then let us consider how great God's goodness has been to us and how long He has continued it to us, though we have continued our sin and wickedness and have not repented. Let us consider what examples we are of God's kindness to the unthankful. Let us consider how unthankful we have been for the temporal good things we have received.

§ From "God Is Kind to the Unthankful and the Evil," pp. 87–88

KNOWLEDGE OF OURSELVES

Though I were perfect, yet would I not know my soul: I would despise my life.

—JOB 9:21

No man but a godly man has the true knowledge of himself, because God alone has a true knowledge of his filthiness and hatefulness by reason of sin; for only He has the knowledge of the hateful nature of sin. The Spirit of God may teach a sinner much about Himself in conviction. He may teach him his own condemned, lost state and condition by reason of sin. But it is the godly man alone who has seen God's glory, who sees his own hatefulness by reason of sin. He only, who knows God, truly knows himself. Indeed, a godly man has but an imperfect knowledge of himself; the more he knows of God the more he will know of himself. A man may have an imperfect knowledge of himself and yet may have a true knowledge of himself. Indeed, he who does not have the true knowledge of God has no true knowledge of anything. He who does not have the knowledge of God has no true knowledge of the creature, or of the works of God, or of the world or the vanity of it, or of the enemies of God or the friends of God. He who has no knowledge of God knows nothing as he ought to know; he sees nothing in any other way than after the flesh. The apostle expresses it thus in 2 Corinthians 5:16: "Wherefore henceforth know we no man after the flesh: yea, though we have known Christ after the flesh, yet now henceforth know we him no more." But he who only knows things after the flesh does not know them in a right manner. This is one respect wherein, when a man is converted, all things are become new to him, as it follows in verse 17: "Therefore, if any man be in Christ, he is a new creature...all things are become new." God is the being whom our understandings were made to know. He who does not know Him knows nothing else as it really is.

⑤ From "There Is Nothing Like Seeing What God Is to Make Men Sensible to What They Are," pp. 142–43

THE ENJOYMENT OF ALL HAPPINESS

I live; yet not I, but Christ liveth in me.
— GALATIANS 2:20

It is in fellowship with Christ that the Christian enjoys all his happiness. It is not separately or by himself that the Christian is made happy, but it is by partaking with Christ in His happiness and in His members. All that he has is in union with Christ. When the head rejoices and is glorified, all the members rejoice and are glorified in it and with it. Thus it is in fellowship with Christ that the believer is admitted to so honorable a relationship to God as that of children, by being united to Him who is the natural Child of God and partaking in some form of sonship with Him. It is in fellowship with Christ that he enjoys the love of the Father. The Father loves the Son, and those who are in Christ are happy in the enjoyment of God's favor because they, being members of Him, partake of the Father's love to Him. It is in fellowship with Christ that they are advanced to glory and blessedness in heaven, because the members must be with the head and partake with the head, and therefore Christ insisted on this in John 17:24: "Father, I will that they also, whom thou hast given me, be with me where I am." Christ gives this as a reason for the believer's happiness in John 14:19: "Because I live, ye shall live also." And thus, because Christ is an heir with God, they also are heirs of God, because they are joint heirs with Christ. Christ is a divine person; He has all good in Himself. He is all-sufficient and infinitely glorious. He is the brightness of His Father's glory; all look good and happiness is in Him, so that he who has Christ has all and needs no more. He Himself is the Tree of Life that grows in the midst of the paradise of God. He is the glory and darling of heaven, and without Him, heaven is no heaven. He who enjoys Him enjoys all possible happiness.

§ From "Christ Is the Christian's All," pp. 202–3

LONG FOR SPIRITUAL SATISFACTION

Eat, O friends; drink, yea, drink abundantly, O beloved.
— SONG OF SOLOMON 5:1

Endeavor to promote spiritual appetites by keeping yourself out of the way of allurement. We are to avoid being in the way of temptation with respect to our carnal appetites. Job made a covenant with his eyes (see Job 31:1), but we ought to take all opportunities to lay ourselves in the way of enticement with respect to our gracious inclinations. Thus, you should be often with God in prayer, and then you will be in the way of having your heart drawn forth to Him. We ought to be frequent in reading and constant in hearing the Word. And, particularly to this end, we ought to carefully, and with the utmost seriousness and consideration, attend the sacrament of the Lord's Supper, which was appointed to draw forth the longings of our souls toward Jesus Christ. Here are the glorious objects of spiritual desire by visible signs represented to our view. We have Christ evidently set forth as crucified. Here we have that spiritual meat and drink represented and offered to excite our hunger and thirst; here we have all that spiritual feast represented that God has provided for poor souls; and here we have hope, in some measure, to have our longing souls satisfied in this world by the gracious communications of the Spirit of God. Live in the practice of these inclinations. If you long after God and Jesus Christ, then often go to God and Christ and converse with them. If you long to be nearer to God, then draw nearer to Him. If you hunger and thirst after righteousness, then take great care to live in the practice of righteousness, to live a more holy and heavenly life. If you long to be more like Christ, then act like Him and walk as He walked. This is the way to have your holy inclinations increased, and hereby they will in some measure be satisfied.

§ From "Spiritual Appetites Need No Bounds," pp. 234–35

A SOLDIER OF THE CROSS

And from the days of John the Baptist until now the kingdom
of heaven suffereth violence, and the violent take it by force.
—MATTHEW 11:12

There are many things that do greatly oppose the grace that is in the heart of the Christian. This holy principle has innumerable enemies watching and warring against it. The child of God is encompassed with enemies on every side. He is a pilgrim and stranger passing through an enemy's country, exposed to attack at any and every moment. There are thousands of devils—artful, intelligent, active, mighty, and implacable—that are bitter enemies to the grace that is in the heart of the Christian and do all that lies in their power against it. The world is an enemy to this grace, because it abounds with persons and things that make opposition to it and, with various forms of allurement and temptation, attempt to win or drive us from the path of duty. The Christian has not only many enemies without, but also multitudes within his own breast that he carries about with him and from which he cannot get free. Evil thoughts and sinful inclinations cling to him; and many corruptions that still hold their footing in his heart are the worst enemies that grace has and have the greatest advantage of any in their warfare against it. These enemies are not only many, but exceeding strong and powerful and very bitter in their animosity—implacable, irreconcilable, mortal enemies, seeking nothing short of the utter ruin and overthrow of grace. They are unwearied in their opposition, so that the Christian, while he remains in this world, is represented as being in a state of warfare, and his business is that of the soldier, insomuch that he is often spoken of as a soldier of the cross and as one whose great duty it is to fight manfully the good fight of faith.

§ From "Charity, or True Grace, Not to Be Overthrown by Opposition," pp. 287–88

THIS WORLD IS NOT OUR HOME

These all died in faith, not having received the promises, but having seen them afar off, and were persuaded of them, and embraced them, and confessed that they were strangers and pilgrims on the earth.
— HEBREWS 11:13

This world is not our abiding place. Our continuance here is but very short. Man's days on the earth are as a shadow. It was never designed by God that this world should be our home. Neither did God give us these temporal accommodations for that end. If God has given us ample estates and children or other pleasant friends, it is with no such design that we should be furnished here, as for a settled abode, but with a design that we should use them for the present and then leave them in a very little time. When we are called to any secular business or charged with the care of a family, if we improve our lives to any other purpose than as a journey toward heaven, all our labor will be lost. If we spend our lives in the pursuit of a temporal happiness such as riches or sensual pleasures; credit and esteem from men; delight in our children and the prospect of seeing them well brought up and well settled, all these things will be of little significance to us. Death will blow up all our hopes and will put an end to these enjoyments. "The places that have known us, will know us no more:" and "the eye that has seen us, shall see us no more." We must be taken away forever from all these things, and it is uncertain when; it may be soon after we are put into the possession of them. And then, where will be all our worldly employments and enjoyments when we are laid in the silent grave? "So man lieth down and riseth not: till the heavens be no more (Job 14:12)."

꙳ From "The Christian Pilgrim, or the True Christian's Life a Journey toward Heaven," p. 244

RETURNING TO THE WORLD

Yea, thou castest off fear, and restrainest prayer before God.

—JOB 15:4

It is the manner of hypocrites, after a while, to return to sinful practices that will tend to keep them from praying. While they were under convictions, they reformed their lives and walked very exactly. This reformation continues after their supposed conversion, while they are much affected with hope and false comfort. But as these things die away, their old lusts revive, and by degrees they return like the dog to his vomit, like the sow that was washed to her wallowing in the mire. They return to their sensual, worldly, proud, and contentious practices, as before. And no wonder this makes them forsake their closets: sinning and praying agree not well together. If a man be constant in the duty of secret prayer, it will tend to restrain him from willful sinning. So, on the other hand, if he allows himself sinful practices, they will restrain him from praying. It will give quite another turn to his mind, so that he will have no disposition to the practice of such a duty: it will be contrary to him. A man who knows that he lives in sin against God will not be inclined to come daily into the presence of God but will rather be inclined to fly from His presence, as Adam when he had eaten of the forbidden fruit, ran away from God and hid himself among the trees of the garden.

§ From "Hypocrites Deficient in the Duty of Prayer," p. 73

THE OVERTHROW OF SATAN

And he said unto them, I beheld Satan as lightning fall from heaven. Behold, I give unto you power to tread on serpents and scorpions, and over all the power of the enemy: and nothing shall by any means hurt you.
— LUKE 10:18–19

Consider the weak and seemingly despicable means and weapons that God employs to overthrow Satan. Christ poured the greater contempt upon Satan in the victory that He obtained over him by reason of the means of His preparing Himself for it and the weapons He used. Christ chooses to encounter Satan in the human nature, in a poor, frail, afflicted state. He did as David did. David, when going against the Philistine, refused Saul's armor: a helmet of brass, a coat of mail, and his sword. No, he puts them all off. Goliath comes mightily armed against David with a helmet of brass upon his head; a coat of mail, weighing five thousand shekels of brass; greaves of brass upon his legs; a target of brass between his shoulders; and a spear, with a staff like a weaver's beam, and a head weighing six hundred shekels of iron. And besides all this, he had one bearing a shield before him. But David takes nothing but a staff in his hand and a shepherd's bag and a sling, and he goes against the Philistine. So the weapons that Christ made use of were His poverty, afflictions and reproaches, sufferings and death. His principal weapon was His cross: the instrument of His own reproachful death. These were seemingly weak and despicable instruments to wield against such a giant as Satan, and doubtless the devil disdained them as much as Goliath did David's staves and sling; but with such weapons as these has Christ in a human, weak, mortal nature overthrown and baffled all the craft of hell.

🖎 From "The Wisdom of God, Displayed in the Way of Salvation," p. 152

PERFECT SIGHT OF GOD

For God, who commanded the light to shine out of darkness, hath shined in our hearts, to give the light of the knowledge of the glory of God in the face of Jesus Christ.

—2 CORINTHIANS 4:6

We have the true God revealed to us in the Word of God, who is the being in the sight of whom this happiness is to be enjoyed. We have the glorious attributes and perfections of God declared to us. The glory of God in the face of Jesus Christ is discovered in the gospel we enjoy, His beauties and glories are there, as it were, pointed forth by God's own hand to our view; we have those means that God hath provided for our obtaining those beginnings of this sight of Him the saints have in this world, in that spiritual knowledge that they have of God, which is absolutely necessary in order to our having it perfectly in another world. The knowledge that believers have of God and His glory, as appearing in the face of Christ, is the imperfect beginning of this heavenly sight. It is an earnest of it, the dawning of the heavenly light; and this beginning must evermore precede, or a perfect vision of God in heaven cannot be obtained. And all those that have this beginning shall obtain that perfection also. Great, therefore, is our privilege, that we have the means of this spiritual knowledge. We may, in this world, see God as in a glass darkly, in order to our seeing Him hereafter face to face; and surely our privilege is very great, that He has given us that glass from whence God's glory is reflected. We have not only the discoveries of God's glory in the doctrine of His Word, but also abundant directions how to act, so that we may obtain a perfect and beatific sight of God.

From "The Pure in Heart Blessed," p. 909

A BACKSLIDING HEART

I marvel that ye are so soon removed from him that called you into the grace of Christ unto another gospel. —GALATIANS 1:6

The heart of man is a backsliding heart. There is, in the heart, a great love and hankering desire after the ease, pleasure, and enjoyments of Sodom—as there was in Lot's wife—by which persons are continually liable to temptations to look back. The heart is so much toward Sodom that it is a difficult thing to keep the eye from turning that way and the feet from tending thither. When men under convictions are put upon fleeing, it is a mere force, it is because God lays hold on their hands—as He did on Lot's and his wife's—and drags them so far. But the tendency of the heart is to go back to Sodom. Persons are very prone to backsliding also through discouragement. The heart is unsteady, soon tired, and apt to listen to discouraging temptations. A little difficulty and delay soon overcome its feeble resolutions. And discouragement tends to backsliding; it weakens persons' hands, lies as a dead weight on their hearts, and makes them drag heavily; and if it continues long, it very often issues in security and senselessness. Convictions are often shaken off that way: they begin first to go off with discouragement. Backsliding is a disease that is exceeding secret in its way of working. It is a flattering distemper; it works like consumption, wherein persons often flatter themselves that they are not worse, but something better, and in a hopeful way to recover, until a few days before they die. So, backsliding commonly comes on gradually and steals on men insensibly, and they still flatter themselves that they are not backslidden.

From "The Folly of Looking Back in Fleeing Out of Sodom," pp. 67–68

PARDON AND JUSTIFICATION

Being justified freely by his grace through the redemption that is in Christ Jesus.
— ROMANS 3:24

Conversion is the condition of pardon and justification: but if it be so, how absurd is it to say that conversion is one condition of justification and faith another, as though they were two distributively distinct and parallel conditions! Conversion is the condition of justification because it is that great change by which we are brought from sin to Christ and by which we become believers in Him: "And ye, when ye had seen it, repented not afterward, that ye might believe him" (Matt. 21:32). When we are directed to repent, that our sins may be blotted out, it is as much as to say "let your minds and hearts be changed, that your sins may be blotted out." But if it be said "let your hearts be changed, that you may be justified; and believe, that you may be justified"; does it therefore follow, that the heart being changed is one condition of justification, and believing another? Our minds must be changed that we may believe, and so may be justified. And besides, evangelical repentance, being active conversion, is not to be treated as a particular grace, properly and entirely distinct from faith, as by some it seems to have been. What is conversion but the sinful, alienated soul's closing with Christ, or the sinner's being brought to believe in Christ? That exercise of soul in conversion that respects sin cannot be excluded out of the nature of faith in Christ; there is something in faith, or closing with Christ, that respects sin, and that is evangelical repentance.

§ From "Justification by Faith Alone," p. 647

DILIGENCE IN WATCHING

For thus hath the LORD said unto me, Go, set a watchman, let him declare what he seeth.
— ISAIAH 21:6

How strict our lives ought to be. If we have to do with so strict a lawgiver and judge, certainly we need to behave ourselves with the greatest possible strictness. The strict law that He has given us He has given for the rule of our life; and though we are set at liberty by Christ from the threatenings of the law, yet we are still under the law as a rule of life, and we must consider that judgment will proceed according to the law. God will see that the law is fulfilled. How strictly then should we behave ourselves who are to stand before so strict a judge, whose eyes are as a flame of fire and who sees our secret actions and even our thoughts and sees in our hearts and will render to everyone according to the deeds done in the body, whether good or bad. How careful we ought to be, notwithstanding, not to commit the least sin, seeing that every sin is a damning sin. And though Christ has suffered so that we may escape the punishment, we ought not to be less strict for that. The manifestation of God's strictness in the suffering of Christ for our sins ought to have as much influence upon us as if we ourselves must suffer. How ought we to watch ourselves, resist with all diligence, set a watch on things, guard the door of life, and pray that the words of our mouths would be acceptable in His sight.

§ From "God, as the Giver and Judge of the Law, Deals with the Utmost Strictness," pp. 195–96

SEEK THE KINGDOM OF GOD

But seek ye first the kingdom of God, and his righteousness; and all these things shall be added unto you.
— MATTHEW 6:33

If you are fully come to a determination concerning the things of religion, that they are true, they will be of weight with you above all things in the world. If you be really convinced that these things are no fable, but reality, it is impossible but that you must be influenced by them above all things in the world; for these things are so great, and so infinitely exceed all temporal things, that it cannot be otherwise. He that is really convinced that there is a heaven and hell and an eternal judgment; that the soul, as soon as parted from the body, appears before the judgment seat of God; that the happiness and misery of a future state is as great as the Scripture represents it; or that God is as holy, just, and jealous as He hath declared concerning Himself in His Word; I say, he that is really convinced and hath settled it with himself, that these things are certainly true, will be influenced by them above all things in the world. He will be more concerned by far with how he shall escape eternal damnation and have the favor of God and eternal life than in how he shall get the world, gratify the flesh, please his neighbors, get honor, or obtain any temporal advantage whatsoever. His main inquiry will not be "what shall [I] eat," and "what shall [I] drink" (Matt. 6:31), but he will seek "first the kingdom of God, and his righteousness" (Matt. 6:33). Examine yourselves therefore by this: Are not your hearts chiefly set upon the world and the things of it? Is it not more your concern, care, and endeavor to further your outward interest than to secure an interest in heaven?

§ From "The Unreasonableness of Indetermination in Religion," p. 60

THE IMPORTANCE OF DOCTRINE

My doctrine shall drop as the rain, my speech shall distil as the dew, as the small rain upon the tender herb, and as the showers upon the grass.
— DEUTERONOMY 32:2

The things of divinity not only concern ministers but also are of infinite importance to all Christians. It is not with the doctrines of divinity as it is with the doctrines of philosophy and other sciences. Philosophers differ about them; some being of one opinion, and others of another. While they are engaged in warm disputes about them, others may well leave them to dispute among themselves without troubling their heads much about them, it being of little concern to them whether the one or the other is in the right. But it is not thus in matters of divinity. The doctrines nearly concern everyone. They are about those things that relate to every man's eternal salvation and happiness. The common people cannot say, "Let us leave these matters to ministers and divines; let them dispute them among themselves as they can; they concern not us"; for they are of infinite importance to every man. Those doctrines of divinity that relate to the essence, attributes, and subsistencies of God concern all, as it is of infinite importance to common people, as well as to ministers, to know what kind of being God is. For He is the being who hath made us all: "In him we live, and move, and have our being" (Acts 17:28); who is the Lord of all. The Being to whom we are all accountable is the last end of our being and the only fountain of our happiness. The doctrines that also relate to Jesus Christ and His mediation, His incarnation, His life and death, His resurrection and ascension, His sitting at the right hand of the Father, and His satisfaction and intercession infinitely concern common people as well as divines. They stand in as much need of this Savior, and of an interest in His person and offices, and the things that He hath done and suffered, as ministers and divines.

꙳ From "The Importance and Advantage of a Thorough Knowledge of Divine Truth," pp. 159–60

DO NOT LET GOD GO

And he said, Let me go, for the day breaketh. And he said, I will not let thee go, except thou bless me.
— GENESIS 32:26

We have here that remarkable account of Jacob's wrestling with God. It was at a time when Jacob was expecting to meet his brother Esau, who was now coming out with four hundred armed men upon a hostile design against him. Jacob had divided his company and put them into that order in which he would have them meet Esau and sent them away over the ford Jabbok. But he himself stayed behind alone. While he was there alone in the night there came one in a human form and with a human body. It seems to have been the Son of God, the Second Person in the Trinity, who appeared to him. We have an account that this is He who came to Jacob and wrestled with him the remainder of the night. It seems that Jacob did not know it was God until the last. But he doubtless immediately perceived that He was some very extraordinary person, eminent in wisdom and holiness, by His appearance, though it was in the night; also, by His conversation Jacob perceived that He was some very extraordinary person, and not a mere man. Jacob not only wrestled with Him in a figurative sense, as the saints may be said to wrestle with God in prayer, but he wrestled with Him literally, though he did not know then that it was God. The divine person then appeared more resolute to depart and said to Jacob, "Let me go, for the day breaketh." Jacob replied, "I will not let thee go, except thou bless me" (Gen. 32:26). Jacob was resolved upon this that if He would depart, and He could have no more of His company, yet he would, if possible, obtain His blessing before He went. That extraordinary excellency, wisdom, and holiness that appeared in Him made Jacob value His blessing. So too for you, the way to obtain the blessing of God is to resolve not to let God go unless He blesses us.

§ From "The Way to Obtain the Blessing of God Is to Resolve Not to Let God Go Unless He Blesses Us," pp. 211–14

GOD HEARS PRAYER

Be careful for nothing; but in every thing by prayer and sup-
plication with thanksgiving let your requests be made known
unto God.
— PHILIPPIANS 4:6

The Most High God is distinguished from false gods. The true God is the only one of this character; there is no other of whom it may be said that He heareth prayer. Many of those things that are worshiped as gods are idols made by their worshipers; they are mere stocks and stones that know nothing. They are indeed made with ears, but they hear not the prayers of those that cry to them. They have eyes, but they see not. Others, though not the work of men's hands, yet are things without life. Thus, many worship the sun, moon, and stars, which, though glorious creatures, yet are not capable of knowing anything of the wants and desires of those who pray to them. Some worship certain kinds of animals, as the Egyptians were wont to worship bulls, which, though not without life, yet are destitute of that reason whereby they would be capable of knowing the requests of their worshipers. Others worship devils instead of the true God: "But I say, that the things which the Gentiles sacrifice, they sacrifice to devils" (1 Cor. 10:20). But the true God perfectly knows the circumstances of everyone who prays to Him throughout the world. Though millions pray to Him at once, in different parts of the world, it is no more difficult for Him who is infinite in knowledge to take notice of all than of one alone. God is so perfect in knowledge that He doth not need to be informed by us in order to have knowledge of our wants, for He knows what things we need before we ask Him.

§ From "The Most High a Prayer-Hearing God," p. 115

A PECULIAR PEOPLE

But ye are a chosen generation, a royal priesthood, an holy nation, a peculiar people; that ye should shew forth the praises of him who hath called you out of darkness into his marvellous light.

— 1 PETER 2:9

Let God be your peculiar portion. If you are one of His peculiar people, He is so. All who are God's people have chosen Him for their God and portion. Do this more, and more, and more. Let all other things be lightly set by and treated by you with neglect in comparison of God. Let God be the object of your peculiar value and esteem. If God has made you one of those on whom He sets a peculiar value, you who are a poor worthless worm; if He has set such a value upon you as to purchase you with the price of the blood of His Son, you who are in yourself a filthy, despicable creature; how much more reason is there that you should peculiarly value God, who is so great and glorious! It is fitting that this value should be mutual; and it is fitting that it should be in an answerable degree. It will be but a little thing for you to esteem God above all in comparison of what it is for God to so prize His saints. See to it, therefore, that there be nothing that stands in any competition with God in your esteem; value Him more than all riches; value His honor and glory more than all the world; be ready at all times to part with all things else, and cleave to God. Let God be your peculiar friend, and value His friendship more than the respect and love of all the world. When you lose other enjoyments, when you lose earthly friends, let this be a supporting, satisfying comfort to you, that you have not lost God.

§ From "Christians a Chosen Generation, a Royal Priesthood, a Holy Nation, a Peculiar People," p. 948

SIN AGAINST GOD

O Lord, to us belongeth confusion of face, to our kings, to our princes, and to our fathers, because we have sinned against thee.
— DANIEL 9:8

We would have God, in His providence toward us, not to order those things that tend to our hurt or expose our interest; therefore, certainly we ought to avoid those things that lead to sin against Him. We desire and love to have God's providence toward us, that our welfare may be well secured. No man loves to live exposed, uncertain, in dangerous circumstances. While he is so he lives uncomfortably, in that he lives in continual fear. We desire that God would so order things concerning us that we may be safe from fear of evil, and that no evil may come nigh our dwelling because we dread calamity. So we do not love the appearance and approaches of evil and love to have it at a great distance from us. We desire to have God to be to us as a wall of fire round about us, to defend us; and that He would surround us as the mountains do the valleys, to guard us from every danger or enemy; so no evil may come nigh us. Now this plainly shows that we ought, in our behavior toward God, to keep at a great distance from sin and from all that exposes to it: as we desire God, in His providence to us, should keep calamity and misery at a great distance from us, and not to order those things that expose our welfare.

§ From "Temptation and Deliverance," p. 228

AN UNCHANGEABLE SAVIOR

For whom he did foreknow, he also did predestinate to be con-
formed to the image of his Son, that he might be the firstborn
among many brethren. Moreover whom he did predestinate,
them he also called: and whom he called, them he also justi-
fied: and whom he justified, them he also glorified.

— ROMANS 8:29–30

You may consider that you have in Him an unchangeable Savior, who has loved you and undertaken for you from eternity, and in time has died for you before you were born, and has since converted you by His grace and brought you out of a blind, guilty, and undone condition, savingly home to Himself; so He will carry on His work in your heart. He will perfect what is yet lacking in you in order to your complete deliverance from sin, death, and all evil, and to your establishment in complete and unalterable blessedness. From the unchangeableness of your Savior, you may see how He thinks of that chain in Romans 8:29–30: "For whom he did foreknow he also did predestinate…. Whom he did predestinate, them he also called: and whom he called, them he also justified: and whom he justified, them he also glorified." The Savior has promised you very great and precious blessings in this world, and things that eye hath not seen, nor ear heard, nor the heart of man conceived, in the world to come. From His unchangeableness you may be assured that the things that He has promised He will also perform. You may, from this doctrine, see the unchangeableness of His love; and therefore, when you consider how great love He seemed to manifest when He yielded Himself up to God a sacrifice for you, in His agony and bloody sweat in the garden, and when He went out to the place of His crucifixion bearing His own cross, you may rejoice that His love now is the same that it was then.

❧ From "Jesus Christ, the Same Yesterday, Today, and Forever," p. 954

SPIRITUAL DARKNESS

These things I have spoken unto you, that in me ye might have peace. In the world ye shall have tribulation: but be of good cheer; I have overcome the world.
—JOHN 16:33

Some godly persons are the subjects of very great outward afflictions, and some are the subjects of great spiritual darkness; some truly godly persons spend a great part of their lives in the dark, in exercising doubts, anxious thoughts, and distressing fears. Oftentimes God's people make this an argument against themselves. They argue that if God loved them and had made them His children, He would never leave them in such darkness and distress. He would give them more of the light of His countenance. They are ready to say to themselves, if God loves me, why does He not give me more comfort, why does He see me in such darkness and does not comfort me? But what we have heard may solve all the difficulty. If their happiness throughout all eternity be so great, of how little consequence is it what may be their condition for that short moment they continue in this world! What if they are in the dark, what if they walk in darkness and are exercised with great trouble! How little difference will it make, though it is cast into the scales, when weighed against that far more exceeding and eternal weight of glory! It will prove lighter than vanity. If God gives eternal happiness to them, that is evident proof of His love, and all the darkness and sorrow they can meet with in this world are not worthy to be mentioned. All this darkness, however long it continues, if we compare it with future glory, vanishes into nothing.

◈ From "The Portion of the Righteous," p. 903

SALVATION SOUGHT

Wherefore the rather, brethren, give diligence to make your call-
ing and election sure: for if ye do these things, ye shall never fall.
— 2 PETER 1:10

This work, or business, which must be done in order to the salvation of men, is a great undertaking. It often appears so to men upon whom it is urged. Utterly to break off from all their sins and to give up themselves forever to the business of religion, without making a reserve of any one lust, submitting to and complying with every command of God, in all cases, and persevering therein, appears to many so great a thing that they are in vain urged to undertake it. In so doing, it seems to them that they should give up themselves to a perpetual bondage. The greater part of men therefore choose to put it off and keep it at as great a distance as they can. They cannot bear to think of entering immediately on such a hard service and, rather than do it, they will run the risk of eternal damnation by putting it off to an uncertain future opportunity. It is a business of great labor and care. There are many commands to be obeyed, many duties to be done: duties to God, duties to our neighbor, and duties to ourselves. There is much opposition in the way of these duties from without. There is a subtle and powerful adversary laying all manner of blocks in the way. There are innumerable temptations of Satan to be resisted and repelled. There is great opposition from the world, innumerable snares laid on every side, many rocks and mountains to be passed over, many streams to be passed through, and many flatteries and enticements from a vain world to be resisted.

♠ From "The Manner in Which the Salvation of the Soul Is to Be Sought," pp. 53–54

THE WICKED DESTROYED

The same shall drink of the wine of the wrath of God, which is poured out without mixture into the cup of his indignation; and he shall be tormented with fire and brimstone in the presence of the holy angels, and in the presence of the Lamb.

—REVELATION 14:10

The destruction of the unfruitful is of use to give the saints a greater sense of their happiness and of God's grace to them. The wicked will be destroyed and tormented in the view of the saints and other inhabitants of heaven. This we are taught in Revelation 14:10: "The same shall drink of the wine of the wrath of God, which is poured out without mixture into the cup of his indignation; and he shall be tormented with fire and brimstone in the presence of the holy angels, and in the presence of the Lamb." And in Isaiah 66:24: "And they shall go forth, and look upon the carcasses of the men that have transgressed against me: for their worm shall not die, neither shall their fire be quenched, and they shall be an abhorring unto all flesh." When the saints in heaven look upon the damned in hell, it will serve to give them a greater sense of their own happiness. When they see how dreadful the anger of God is, it will make them the more prize His love. They will rejoice the more, that they are not the objects of God's anger, but of His favor; that they are not the subjects of His dreadful wrath, but are treated as His children, to dwell in the everlasting embraces of His love. The misery of the damned will give them a greater sense of the distinguishing grace and love of God to them, that He should from all eternity set His love on them and make so great a difference between them and others who are of the same species and have deserved no worse of God than they. What a great sense will this give them of the wonderful grace of God to them! And how will it heighten their praises! With how much greater admiration and exultation of soul will they sing of the free and sovereign grace of God to them!

☙ From "Wicked Men Useful in Their Destruction Only," p. 127

TIME CANNOT BE RECOVERED

Vanity of vanities, saith the Preacher, vanity of vanities; all is vanity.
— ECCLESIASTES 1:2

Time is very precious, because when it is past, it cannot be recovered. There are many things that men possess that, if they part with, they can obtain them again. If a man have parted with something that he had, not knowing the worth of it or the need he should have of it, he often can regain it, at least with pains and cost. If a man have been overseen in a bargain and have bartered away or sold something, and afterward repent of it, he may often obtain a release and recover that with which he had parted. But it is not so with respect to time; when once that is gone, it is gone forever; no pains, no cost will recover it. Though we repent ever so much that we let it pass and did not improve it while we had it, it will be to no purpose. Every part of it is successively offered to us, that we may choose whether we will make it our own or not, but there is no delay; it will not wait upon us to see whether we will comply with the offer. If we refuse, it is immediately taken away and never offered more. As to that part of time that is gone, however we have neglected to improve it, it is out of our possession and out of our reach. If we have lived fifty, sixty, or seventy years and have not improved our time, now it cannot be helped; it is eternally gone from us; all that we can do is to improve the little that remains.

᛫ From "The Preciousness of Time and the Importance of Redeeming It," p. 234

LONGSUFFERING

What if God, willing to shew his wrath, and to make his power known, endured with much longsuffering the vessels of wrath fitted to destruction: and that he might make known the riches of his glory on the vessels of mercy, which he had afore prepared unto glory.

— ROMANS 9:22–23

It is well for us that God is not toward us as we are toward one another with respect to longsuffering and forbearance. When men look upon themselves as greatly affronted and abused, they have but little patience. They are for speedy revenge. They cannot bear to see their enemy go from day to day without some testimonies of their resentment. It is well for us that it is not so with God. If it were, we would have long ago been destroyed. If God was as we are in this respect, He would have long ago sent His thunder upon our heads, struck us dead, and sent us to hell in a moment; or would have caused the earth to open her mouth to swallow us up quickly, and the earth would never have borne us. But the injuries and affronts we receive are infinitely less heinous and aggravated than those we have offered to God. God bears being affronted and rebelled against by men from day to day. Men disobey Him to His face. When He gives forth His commands in the most solemn manner, attended with all full threatenings, men make nothing of disobeying Him. They give no heed to His will and authority but will presumptuously do the contrary. Though God continues to insist on His commands, they slot them and do the contrary hundreds of times. They do it from day to day, living in direct disobedience and contempt of Him. But God, for all this, allows them to live. He preserves their lives and gives them mercy. He goes on still and loads them with His benefits. He makes His sun to shine upon them and His rain to fall. He causes the earth to bring forth for them. He provides for them and gives them many good things, and this from year to year, when all the while they continue in this way of disobedience. It is well for us that God is infinitely different from us in this respect; for if He were not, our case would have been inexpressibly miserable and utterly desperate long ago.

❧ From "It Is Well for Us That God Is Not as We Are," pp. 22–23

JUDGING OTHERS

Judge not, that ye be not judged.
— MATTHEW 7:1

A forwardness to judge and censure others shows a proud disposition, as though the censorious person thought himself free from such faults and blemishes and therefore felt justified in being busy and bitter in charging others with them and censuring and condemning them for them. This is implied in the language of the Savior: "Judge not, that ye be not judged.... And why beholdest thou the mote that is in thy brother's eye, but considerest not the beam that is in thine own eye? Or how wilt thou say to thy brother, Let me pull out the mote out of thine eye; and, behold, a beam is in thine own eye? Thou hypocrite" (Matt. 7:1, 3–4). And the same is implied in the declaration of the apostle: "Therefore thou art inexcusable, O man, whosoever thou art that judgest: for wherein thou judgest another, thou condemnest thyself; for thou that judgest doest the same things" (Rom. 2:1). If men were humbly sensible of their own failings they would not be very forward or pleased in judging others, for the censure passed upon others would but rest on themselves. There are the same kinds of corruption in one man's heart as in another's; and if those persons that are most busy in censuring others would but look within and seriously examine their own hearts and lives, they might generally see the same dispositions and behavior in themselves, at one time or another, which they see and judge in others, or at least something as much deserving of censure. A disposition to judge and condemn shows a conceited and arrogant disposition. It has the appearance of a person's setting himself up above others, as though he were fit to be the lord and judge of his fellow servants, and he supposed they were to stand or fall according to his sentence.

⟐ From "The Spirit of Charity, the Opposite of a Censorious Spirit," pp. 215–16

ANGER IN TRIVIAL MATTERS

*Wherefore, my beloved brethren, let every man be swift to
hear, slow to speak, slow to wrath.*
—JAMES 1:19

Anger is unsuitable and unchristian as to its occasion, when persons are
angry upon small and trivial occasions, and when, though there is something of blame, yet the fault is very small, and such as is not worth our being
stirred and engaged about. God does not call us to have our spirits ceaselessly engaged in opposition and stirred up in anger, unless it is on some
important occasions. He that is angry at every little fault he may see in others
is certainly one with whom it is otherwise than is expressed in the text. Of
him that is provoked at every little, trifling thing, it surely cannot be said that
he is "not easily provoked" (1 Cor. 13:5). Some are of such an angry, fretful
spirit that they are put out of humor by every little thing and by things in
others—in the family, or in society, or in business—that are no greater faults
than they themselves are guilty of every day. Those that will thus be angry at
every fault they see in others will be sure to be always kept in a fret, and their
minds will never be composed; for it cannot be expected in this world but
that we shall continually be seeing faults in others, as there are continually
faults in ourselves. Therefore, Christians are directed to be "slow to speak,
slow to wrath" (James 1:19); and it is said that "he that is soon angry, dealeth
foolishly" (Prov. 14:17). He who diligently guards his own spirit will not be
very frequently or easily angry. He wisely keeps his mind in a calm, clear
frame and does not suffer it to be stirred with anger, except on extraordinary
occasions, and those that do especially call for it.

§ From "The Spirit of Charity, the Opposite of an Angry or Wrathful Spirit," pp. 192–93

BEAR INJURY FROM OTHERS

And who is he that will harm you, if ye be followers of that which is good?

—1 PETER 3:13

Love to God disposes us meekly to bear injuries from others because it sets us very much above the injuries of men. And it does so in two respects. In the first place, it sets us above the reach of injuries from others because nothing can ever really hurt those that are the true friends of God. Their life is hid with Christ in God, and He, as their protector and friend, will carry them on high as on the wings of eagles. All things shall work together for their good (see Rom. 8:28), and none shall be permitted really to harm them while they are followers of that which is good (see 1 Peter 3:13). In the second place, as love to God prevails, it tends to set persons above human injuries, in that the more they love God, the more they will place all their happiness in Him. They will look to God as their all and seek their happiness and portion in His favor, and that not in the allotments of His providence alone. The more they love God, the less they set their hearts on their worldly interests, which are all that their enemies can touch. Men can injure God's people only with respect to worldly good. But the more a man loves God, the less is his heart set on the things of the world, and the less he feels the injuries that his enemies may inflict, because they cannot reach beyond these things. And so it often is the case that the friends of God hardly think the injuries they receive from men are worthy of the name of injuries, and the calm and quietness of their minds are scarcely disturbed by them. As long as they have the favor and friendship of God, they are not much concerned about the evil work and injuries of men. Love to God will, in these several respects, dispose us to longsuffering under injuries from others.

❧ From "Charity Disposes Us Meekly to Bear the Injuries Received from Others," pp. 80–81

OPEN YOUR HAND TO THE POOR

Thou shalt open thine hand wide unto him, and shalt surely lend him sufficient for his need, in that which he wanteth.
— DEUTERONOMY 15:8

It is the absolute and indispensable duty of the people of God to give bountifully and willingly to supply the wants of the needy. It is commanded: "Thou shalt open thine hand wide unto thy brother, to thy poor, and to thy needy, in thy land" (Deut. 15:11). Merely to give something is not sufficient; it does not answer the rule, nor does it come up to the holy command of God. We must open our hand wide. What we give, considering our neighbor's wants and our ability, should be such as may be called a liberal gift. What is meant in the text by opening the hand wide, with respect to those who are able, is explained in Deuteronomy 15:8: "Thou shalt open thine hand wide unto him, and shalt surely lend him sufficient for his need, in that which he wanteth." By lending, here, as is evident by the two following verses, is not only meant lending to receive again; for the word "lend" in Scripture is sometimes used for giving: "Do good, and lend, hoping for nothing again" (Luke 6:35). We are commanded, therefore, to give our poor neighbor what is sufficient for his need. There ought to be none allowed to live in pinching want among a visible people of God who are able, unless in case of idleness, prodigality, or some such case that the Word of God excepts. It is the duty of the visible people of God to give for the supply of the needy freely, and without grudging. It does not at all answer the rule in the sight of God if it is done with an inward grudging, or if the heart is grieved, and it inwardly hurts the man to give what he gives. God looks at the heart and the hand is not accepted without it: "Every man according as he purposeth in his heart, so let him give; not grudgingly, or of necessity: for God loveth a cheerful giver" (2 Cor. 9:7).

§ From "Christian Charity: The Duty of Charity to the Poor Explained and Enforced," pp. 232–33

CONSISTENT CONDUCT

Which have forsaken the right way, and are gone astray, following the way of Balaam the son of Bosor, who loved the wages of unrighteousness.
— 2 PETER 2:15

How is your conduct consistent with loving God above all? If you have not a spirit to love God above your dearest earthly friends and your most pleasant earthly enjoyments, then the Scriptures are very plain and full in it: you are not true Christians. But if you had indeed such a spirit, would you thus grow weary of the practice of drawing near to Him and become habitually so averse to it as to, in a great measure, cast off so plain a duty that is so much the life of a child of God? It is the nature of love to be averse to absence and to love a near access to those whom we love. We love to be with them; we delight to come often to them and to have much conversation with them. But, when a person, who hath heretofore been wont to converse freely with another, by degrees forsakes him, grows strange, and converses with him but little, and although the other be importunate with him for the continuance of their former intimacy, this plainly shows the coldness of his heart toward him. The neglect of the duty of prayer seems to be inconsistent with supreme love to God also upon another account: it is against the will of God so plainly revealed. True love to God seeks to please Him in everything and universally to conform to His will.

♦ From "Hypocrites Deficient in the Duty of Prayer," p. 75

A DESIGNED HAPPINESS

*Who is this King of glory? The L*ORD *strong and mighty, the* L*ORD mighty in battle.*

— PSALM 24:8

The design of the devil was to gratify his envy in the utter destruction of mankind. But, by the redemption of Jesus Christ, this malicious design of Satan is crossed, because all the elect are brought to their designed happiness. This is much greater than ever Satan thought it was in God's heart to bestow on man. And though some of mankind is left to be miserable, yet that does not answer Satan's end; for this also is ordered for God's glory. No more are left miserable than God saw meet to glorify His justice upon. One reason God suffered Satan to do what he did in procuring the fall of man was that His Son might be glorified in conquering that strong, subtle, and proud spirit and in triumphing over him. How glorious doth Christ Jesus appear in baffling and triumphing over this proud king of darkness and all the haughty confederate rulers of hell. How glorious a sight is it to see the meek and patient Lamb of God leading that proud, malicious, and mighty enemy in triumph! What songs doth this cause in heaven! It was a glorious sight in Israel to see David carrying the head of Goliath in triumph to Jerusalem. It appeared glorious to the daughters of Israel, who came out with timbrels and with dances and sang, "Saul hath slain his thousands, and David his ten thousands" (1 Sam. 18:7). But how much more glorious to see the Son of David, the Son of God, carrying the head of the spiritual Goliath, the champion of the armies of hell, in triumph to the heavenly Jerusalem! It is with a principal view to this, that about Christ is said: "The LORD is a man of war: the LORD is his name" (Ex. 15:3).

§ From "The Wisdom of God, Displayed in the Way of Salvation," p. 148

A SURE AND LASTING FOUNDATION

Through the wrath of the LORD of hosts is the land darkened, and the people shall be as the fuel of the fire: no man shall spare his brother.

— ISAIAH 9:19

God made man to endure forever, and therefore that which is man's true blessedness, we may conclude, has a sure and lasting foundation. As to worldly enjoyments, their foundation is a sandy one that is continually wearing away and certainly will at last let the building fall. If we take pleasure in riches, riches in a little while will be gone; if we take pleasure in gratifying our senses, those objects whence we draw our gratifications will perish with the using. Our senses themselves also will be gone; the organs will be worn out and our whole outward form will turn to dust. If we take pleasure in union with our earthly friends, then that union must be broken; the bonds are not durable, but will soon wear asunder. But he who has the immediate intellectual vision of God's glory and love, and rejoices in that, has his happiness built upon an everlasting rock: "Trust ye in the LORD for ever, for in the LORD JEHOVAH is everlasting strength." In the Hebrew it is, "in the Lord Jehovah is the Rock of ages" (Isa. 26:4). The glory of God is subject to no changes or vicissitudes; it will never cease to shine forth. History gives us an account of the sun's light failing, becoming more faint and dim for many months together; but the glory of God will never be subject to fade. Of the light of that Sun there never will be any eclipse or dimness, but it will shine eternally in its strength.

§ From "The Pure in Heart Blessed," p. 909

THE MEANS OF BESTOWING GRACE

*Teaching us that, denying ungodliness and worldly lusts, we
should live soberly, righteously, and godly, in this present world.*
— TITUS 2:12

God uses certain means to bestow His grace. We shall take notice of what the
appointed means of grace are. The first means God uses to bestow His grace
is reading and hearing the Word of God: "Search the scriptures" (John 5:39);
and "Faith cometh by hearing" (Rom. 10:17). The Word of God is a principle
means, yet how much men fail in reading Scripture. The second means God
uses to bestow His grace is consideration. We should think on death, eternity,
judgment, God, creation, and the like. We should think on our ways and
consider our latter end. God expects that we should exercise our reason and
our powers as men in order to having His grace. The third means God uses
to bestow His grace is prayer in its various kinds: "Praying with all prayer"
(Eph. 6:18); there is secret prayer (see Matt. 6:6) and family prayer. Both
these are recommended by Christ's own example and the common practice
of saints in Scripture. And then there is public prayer. God expects that we
should come to Him for grace, call upon Him for it, and thankfully acknowledge what we have received. The fourth means God uses to bestow His grace
is attending on the sacraments, baptism, and the Lord's Supper. God uses all
manner of means with us. He speaks to us not only by His Word, but also by
sensible figures and representations of spiritual things. The fifth means God
uses to bestow His grace is to carefully and conscientiously avoid all moral
evils and do all moral duties. We must avoid moral evil of thoughts, words,
and deeds. Whatever ordinances are attended, if men go on in a way of wickedness, in indulging any lust whatsoever, it will be to no purpose. The prayers
of such persons, and their attendance on sacraments, is but mockery, and is
not accepted by God. Living soberly, doing justly, and observing the gospel
rules of charity, forgiveness, temperance, meekness, and the like are also a
means of God's appointment of grace.

♦ From "God's Wisdom in His Stated Method of Bestowing Grace," pp. 206–7

CHRIST PLEADS OUR CAUSE

For there is one God, and one mediator between God and men, the man Christ Jesus.
— 1 TIMOTHY 2:5

Christ was justified in the name of all who would believe, of all the elect. He was justified as their head. We may be sure that the covenant of grace will be fulfilled to all believers, seeing that they have such an intercessor at the right hand of God. Christ has gone into heaven with His own blood, there to appear for us, and we may be sure that He is disposed to plead our cause there because He has made us His own cause. Seeing that He has suffered so much for sinners, He doubtless will be concerned that His sufferings should succeed. But they will not succeed unless those who believe on Him are saved, because that is for what He died. We need not doubt but that His intercessions will avail, because He is a person infinitely near and dear to God; He is God's own and only begotten Son, His eternal delight; and because He has so good a plea to make: the Father's own promise to Him in the covenant of redemption and to men in the gospel, and His having fulfilled the condition. The promises are sure, for our Mediator has received them already in our name. Christ, as He is not justified as a private person, but as our head, so He is rewarded as the head of the church. He has gone to receive a kingdom for believers, and He has received it. He has gone to prepare a place for them. When He had answered the law, God the Father did, as it were, give Him the reward into His own hands, to reserve it for those for whom He had bought it; and He has eternal glory naturally in His hands for all those whom the Father has given Him.

⟋ From "The Covenant of Grace Firm and Sure," pp. 90–91

SEEK A HUMBLE SPIRIT

A man's pride shall bring him low: but honour shall uphold the humble in spirit.

— PROVERBS 29:23

Let all be exhorted earnestly to seek much of a humble spirit and to endeavor to be humble in all their behavior toward God and men. Seek for a deep and abiding sense of your comparative meanness before God and man. Know God; confess your nothingness and ill-deservedness before Him. Distrust yourself. Rely only on God; renounce all glory except from Him. Yield yourself heartily to His will and service. Avoid an aspiring, ambitious, ostentatious, assuming, arrogant, scornful, stubborn, willful, leveling, self-justifying behavior, and strive for more and more of the humble spirit that Christ manifested while He was on earth. Consider the many motives to such a spirit. Humility is a most essential and distinguishing trait in all true piety. It is the attendant of every grace and in a peculiar manner tends to the purity of Christian feeling. It is the ornament of the Spirit, the source of some of the sweetest exercises of Christian experience, the most acceptable sacrifice we can offer to God, the subject of the richest of His promises, and the spirit with which He will dwell on earth and that He will crown with glory in heaven hereafter. Earnestly seek, then, and diligently and prayerfully cherish, an humble spirit, and God shall walk with you here below, and when a few more days shall have passed, He will receive you to the honors bestowed on His people at Christ's right hand.

§ From "The Spirit of Charity Is an Humble Spirit," pp. 155–56

THE WAY OF HOLINESS

Wherefore seeing we also are compassed about with so great a cloud of witnesses, let us lay aside every weight, and the sin which doth so easily beset us, and let us run with patience the race that is set before us.
— HEBREWS 12:1

The way that leads to heaven is the way of holiness. We should choose and desire to travel thither in this way and in no other. We should part with all those sins, those carnal appetites that are weights that will tend to hinder us in our traveling toward heaven. We should travel on in a way of obedience to all God's commands: the difficult as well as the easy ones. We should travel on in a way of self-denial, denying all our sinful inclinations and interests. The way to heaven is ascending; we must be content to travel uphill, though it is hard and tiresome, though it is contrary to the natural tendency and bias of our flesh and tends downward to the earth. We should follow Christ in the path that He has gone in. The way that He traveled in was the right way to heaven. We should take up our cross and follow Him. We should travel along in the same way of meekness and lowliness of heart; in the same way of obedience, charity, diligence to do good, and patience under afflictions. The way to heaven is a heavenly life. We must be traveling toward heaven in a way of imitation of those that are in heaven; in imitation of the saints and angels there, in their holy employment, in their way of spending their time, in loving, adoring, serving, and praising God and the Lamb. This is the path that we ought to prefer before all others if we could have any other that we might choose. If we could go to heaven in a way of carnal living, in the way of the enjoyment and gratification of our lusts, we should rather prefer a way of holiness and conformity to the spiritual self-denying rules of the gospel.

⚘ From "The True Christian's Life a Journey toward Heaven," pp. 211–12

THE POWER OF GOD

And what is the exceeding greatness of his power to us-ward who believe, according to the working of his mighty power.

— EPHESIANS 1:19

We receive all from the power of God. Man's redemption is often spoken of as a work of wonderful power as well as grace. The great power of God appears in bringing a sinner from his low state, from the depths of sin and misery, to such an exalted state of holiness and happiness: "And what is the exceeding greatness of his power to us-ward who believe, according to the working of his mighty power" (Eph. 1:19). We are dependent on God's power through every step of our redemption. We are dependent on the power of God to convert us and give faith in Jesus Christ and the new nature. It is a work of creation: "If any man be in Christ, he is a new creature" (2 Cor. 5:17); and "We are…created in Christ Jesus" (Eph. 2:10). The fallen creature cannot attain to true holiness but by being created again: "And that ye put on the new man, which after God is created in righteousness and true holiness" (Eph. 4:24). It is a raising from the dead: "Wherein also ye are risen with him through the faith of the operation of God, who hath raised him from the dead" (Col. 2:12). Yea, it is a more glorious work of power than mere creation, or raising a dead body to life, in that the effect attained is greater and more excellent. That holy and happy being and spiritual life that is produced in the work of conversion is a far greater and more glorious effect than mere being and life.

🕭 From "God Glorified in Man's Dependence," p. 4

THE FOUNDATION OF PEACE AND SAFETY

As the mountains are round about Jerusalem, so the LORD *is round about his people from henceforth even for ever.*
— PSALM 125:2

There is in Christ Jesus an abundant foundation of peace and safety for those who are in fear and danger. The fears and dangers to which men are subject are of two kinds: temporal and eternal. Men are frequently in distress from fear of temporal evils. We live in an evil world, where we are liable to an abundance of sorrows and calamities. A great part of our lives is spent in sorrowing for present or past evils and in fearing those that are future. What poor, distressed creatures are we, when God is pleased to send His judgments among us! If He visits a place with mortal and prevailing sickness, what terror seizes our hearts! If any person is taken sick and trembles for his life, or if our dear friends are at the point of death or in any other dangers, how fearful is our condition! Now, there is sufficient foundation for peace and safety to those exercising with such fears and brought into such dangers. Christ is a refuge in all trouble; there is a foundation for rational support and peace in Him, whatever threatens us. He, whose heart is fixed, trusting in Christ, need not be afraid of any evil tidings. Psalm 125:2 reminds us, "As the mountains are round about Jerusalem, so the LORD is round about his people."

⚘ From "Safety, Fullness, and Sweet Refreshment, to Be Found in Christ," p. 929

GLORY AND HUMILITY

Who, being in the form of God, thought it not robbery to be equal with God.
— PHILIPPIANS 2:6

In the person of Christ do meet together infinite glory and lowest humility. Infinite glory and the virtue of humility meet in no other person but Christ. They meet in no created person, for no created person has infinite glory, and they meet in no other divine person but Christ. For though the divine nature be infinitely abhorrent to pride, yet humility is not properly predicable of God the Father and the Holy Ghost, which exists only in the divine nature, because it is a proper excellency only of a created nature. It consists radically in a sense of a comparative lowness and littleness before God or the great distance between God and the subject of this virtue. But it would be a contradiction to suppose any such thing in God. But in Jesus Christ, who is both God and man, those two diverse excellencies are sweetly united. He is a person infinitely exalted in glory and dignity: "Who, being in the form of God, thought it not robbery to be equal with God" (Phil. 2:6). There is equal honor due to Him with the Father. But however He is thus above all, yet He is lowest of all in humility. There never was so great an instance of this virtue among either men or angels, as Jesus. None ever was so sensible of the distance between God and Him, or had a heart so lowly before God, as the man Christ Jesus. What a wonderful spirit of humility appeared in Him when He was here upon earth in all His behavior: in His contentment in His mean outward condition, contentedly living in the family of Joseph the carpenter and Mary His mother for thirty years together, and afterward choosing outward meanness, poverty, and contempt, rather than earthly greatness; in His washing His disciples' feet; in all His speeches and deportment toward His disciples; in His cheerfully sustaining the form of a servant through His whole life; and in His submitting to such immense humiliation at death!

§ From "The Excellency of Jesus Christ," p. 681

EXALT GOD

That no flesh should glory in his presence. But of him are ye in Christ Jesus, who of God is made unto us wisdom, and righteousness, and sanctification, and redemption: that, according as it is written, He that glorieth, let him glory in the Lord.
— 1 CORINTHIANS 1:29–31

Those who are in a state of salvation are to attribute it to sovereign grace alone and to give all the praise to God. Godliness is no cause for glorying, except it is in God. Such are not, by any means, in any degree to attribute their godliness, their safe and happy state and condition, to any natural difference between them and other men or to any strength or righteousness of their own. They have no reason to exalt themselves in the least degree, but God is the being whom they should exalt. They should exalt God the Father, who chose them in Christ, who set His love upon them, and gave them salvation before they were born and even before the world was. If they inquire why God set His love on them and chose them rather than others, if they think they can see any cause out of God, they are greatly mistaken. They should exalt God the Son, who bore their names on His heart when He came into the world and hung on the cross and in whom alone they have righteousness and strength. They should exalt God the Holy Ghost, who of sovereign grace has called them out of darkness into marvelous light; who has, by His own immediate and free operation, led them into an understanding of the evil and danger of sin and brought them off from their own righteousness and opened their eyes to discover the glory of God and the wonderful riches of God in Jesus Christ and has sanctified them and made them new creatures. The people of God have the greater cause of thankfulness and more reason to love God, who hath bestowed such great and unspeakable mercy upon them of His mere sovereign pleasure.

From "God's Sovereignty in the Salvation of Men," p. 855

WATCH AGAINST PRIDE

Pride goeth before destruction, and an haughty spirit before a fall.

— PROVERBS 16:18

Humility, self-diffidence, and an entire dependence on our Lord Jesus Christ will be our best defense. Let us therefore maintain the strictest watch against spiritual pride, or being lifted up with extraordinary experiences and comforts, and the high favors of heaven that any of us may have received. We had need, after such favors, in a special manner to keep a strict and jealous eye upon our own hearts, lest there should arise self-exalting reflections upon what we have received and high thoughts of ourselves as being now some of the most eminent of saints and peculiar favorites of heaven, and that the secret of the Lord is especially with us. Let us not presume that we above all are fit to be advanced as the great instructors and censors of this evil generation; and, in a high conceit of our own wisdom and discerning, assume to ourselves the airs of prophets or extraordinary ambassadors of heaven. When we have great discoveries of God made to our souls, we should not shine bright in our own eyes. Moses, when he had been conversing with God in the mount, though his face shone so as to dazzle the eyes of Aaron and the people, yet he did not shine in his own eyes: "he wist not that the skin of his face shone" (Ex. 34:29). Let none think themselves out of danger of this spiritual pride, even in their best frames. God saw that the apostle Paul (though probably the most eminent saint that ever lived) was not out of danger of it; no, not when he had just been conversing with God in the third heaven. Pride is the worst viper in the heart; it is the first sin that ever entered into the universe; it lies lowest of all in the foundation of the whole building of sin; and it is the most secret, deceitful, and unsearchable in its ways of working of any lusts whatever.

§ From "Distinguishing Marks of a Work of the Spirit of God," p. 274

ANGRY PASSION

Charity...is not easily provoked.
— 1 CORINTHIANS 13:4–5

Anger may be defined to be an earnest and more or less violent opposition of spirit against any real or supposed evil or in view of any fault or offense of another. All anger is opposition of the mind against real or supposed evil, but it is not all opposition of the mind against evil that is properly called anger. There is an opposition of the judgment that is not anger, for anger is the opposition, not of cool judgment, but of the spirit of the man, that is, of his disposition or heart. But here, again, it is not all opposition of the spirit against evil that can be called anger. There is an opposition of the spirit against natural evil that we suffer, as in grief and sorrow, for instance, which is a very different thing from anger. In distinction from this, anger is opposition to moral evil, or evil real or supposed, in voluntary agents, or at least in agents that are conceived to be voluntary or acting by their own will, and against such evil as is supposed to be their fault. But, yet again, it is not all opposition of spirit against evil or faultiness in voluntary agents that is anger; for there may be a dislike without the spirit being excited and angry, and such dislike is an opposition of the will and judgment, and not always of the feelings. In order to anger, the latter must be moved. In all anger there must be earnestness and opposition of feeling, and the spirit must be moved and stirred within us. Anger is one of the passions or affections of the soul, though; when called an affection, it is, for the most part, to be regarded as an evil affection.

§ From "The Spirit of Charity, the Opposite of an Angry or Wrathful Spirit," pp. 187–88

IMITATE THE FATHER

And the LORD *passed by before him, and proclaimed, The* LORD, *The* LORD *God, merciful and gracious, longsuffering, and abundant in goodness and truth.*
—EXODUS 34:6

Love to God disposes us to imitate Him and therefore disposes us to such longsuffering as He manifests. Longsuffering is often spoken of as one of the attributes of God. In Exodus 34:6, it is said, "And the LORD passed by before him, and proclaimed, The LORD, The LORD God, merciful and gracious, longsuffering." The longsuffering of God is very wonderfully manifest in His bearing innumerable injuries from men, and injuries that are very great and long-continued. If we consider the wickedness that there is in the world, and then consider how God continues the world in existence and does not destroy it, but showers upon it innumerable mercies—the bounties of His daily providence and grace, causing His sun to rise on the evil and on the good, sending rain alike on the just and on the unjust and offering His spiritual blessings ceaselessly and to all—we shall perceive how abundant is His longsuffering toward us. If we consider His longsuffering to some of the great and populous cities of the world and think how constantly the gifts of His goodness are bestowed on and consumed by them, and then consider how great the wickedness of these very cities is, it will show us how amazingly great is His longsuffering. And the same longsuffering has been manifest to very many particular persons, in all ages of the world. He is longsuffering to the sinners that He spares and to whom He offers His mercy, even while they are rebelling against Him. Now, it is the nature of love, at least in reference to a superior, that it always inclines and disposes to imitation of him. A child's love to his father disposes him to imitate his father, and especially does the love of God's children dispose them to imitate their heavenly Father.

❧ From "Charity Disposes Us Meekly to Bear the Injuries Received from Others," pp. 76–77

ATONEMENT BY SUFFERING

And they sung a new song, saying, Thou art worthy to take the book, and to open the seals thereof: for thou wast slain, and hast redeemed us to God by thy blood out of every kindred, and tongue, and people, and nation. — REVELATION 5:9

To suppose that all Christ does is make atonement for us by suffering is to make Him our Savior but in part. It is to rob Him of half His glory as a Savior. For, if all that He does is to deliver us from hell, He does not purchase heaven for us. The adverse scheme supposes that He purchases heaven for us, in that He satisfies for the imperfections of our obedience; and so purchases that our sincere imperfect obedience might be accepted as the condition of eternal life; and so purchases an opportunity for us to obtain heaven by our own obedience. But to purchase heaven for us only in this sense is to purchase it in no sense at all; for all of it comes to no more than a satisfaction for our sins, or removing the penalty by suffering in our stead. For all the purchasing they speak of, that our imperfect obedience should be accepted, is only to pay a debt for us; there is no positive purchase of any good. We are taught in Scripture that heaven is purchased for us; it is called the purchased possession in Ephesians 1:14. The gospel proposes the eternal inheritance, not to be acquired, as the first covenant did, but as already acquired and purchased. But he that pays a man's debt for him, and so delivers him from slavery, cannot be said to purchase an estate for him merely because he sets him at liberty, so that henceforward he has an opportunity to get an estate by his own hand-labor. According to this scheme, the saints in heaven have no reason to thank Christ for purchasing heaven for them or redeeming them to God and making them kings and priests, as we have an account that they do in Revelation 5:9.

✎ From "Justification by Faith Alone," p. 638

OUR LITTLENESS BEFORE GOD

Though he slay me, yet will I trust in him.

—JOB 13:15

Humility disposes a person heartily and freely to acknowledge his meanness or littleness before God. He sees how fit and suitable it is that he should do this, and he does it willingly, even with delight. He freely confesses his own nothingness and vileness and owns himself unworthy of any mercy and deserving of all misery. It is the disposition of the humble soul to lie low before God and to humble himself in the dust in His presence. Humility also disposes one to be distrustful of himself and to depend only on God. The proud man, who has a high opinion of his own wisdom, strength, or righteousness is self-confident. But the humble are not disposed to trust in themselves but are diffident of their own sufficiency. It is their disposition to rely on God and with delight to cast themselves wholly on Him as their refuge, righteousness, and strength. The humble man is further disposed to renounce all the glory of the good he has or does, and to give it all to God. If there be anything that is good in him, or any good done by him, it is not his disposition to glory or vaunt himself in it before God, but to ascribe all to God, and in the language of the psalmist to say, "Not unto us, O LORD, not unto us, but unto thy name give glory, for thy mercy and for thy truth's sake" (Ps. 115:1). It is the disposition, again, of the humble person, wholly to subject himself to God. His heart is not opposed to a full and absolute subjection to the divine will, but inclined to it. He is disposed to be subject to the commands and laws of God, for he sees it to be right and best that he who is so infinitely inferior to God should be thus subject, and that it is an honor that belongs to God, to reign over and give laws to him.

ᔥ From "The Spirit of Charity Is an Humble Spirit," pp. 137–38

FLEE FROM SODOM

Remember Lot's wife.
—LUKE 17:32

You that are seeking an interest in Christ, you are to flee out of Sodom. Sodom is the place of your nativity, and the place where you have spent your lives. You are citizens of a city that is full of filthiness and an abomination before God, a polluted and accursed city. You belong to that impure society. You not only live among them, but you are of them, you have committed those abominations and have so provoked God as you have heard. It is you that I have all this while been speaking of under this doctrine; you are the inhabitants of Sodom. Perhaps you may look on your circumstances as not very dreadful, but you dwell in Sodom. Though you may be reformed, and appear with a clean outside and a smooth face to the world, yet, as long as you are in a natural condition, you are impure inhabitants of Sodom. The world of mankind is divided into two companies, or, as I may say, into two cities: there is the city of Zion, the church of God, the holy and beloved city; and there is Sodom, that polluted and accursed city that is appointed to destruction. You belong to the latter of these. However much you may look upon yourselves as better than some others, you are of the same city: the same company with fornicators, drunkards, adulterers, common swearers, highwaymen, pirates, and Sodomites. However much you may think yourselves distinguished, as long as you are out of Christ you belong to the very same society; you are of the company—you join with them and are no better than they, any otherwise than as you have greater restraints. You are considered in the sight of God as fit to be ranked with them.

§ From "The Folly of Looking Back in Fleeing Out of Sodom," p. 66

HUMILITY PREVENTS ARROGANCE

Let nothing be done through strife or vainglory; but in lowliness of mind let each esteem other better than themselves.
— PHILIPPIANS 2:3

Humility tends to prevent an arrogant and assuming behavior. He that is under the influence of a humble spirit is not forward to take too much upon him, and when he is among others, he does not carry it toward them as if he expected and insisted that a great deal of regard should be shown to himself. His behavior does not carry with it the idea that he is the best among those about him and that he is the one to whom the chief regard should be shown and whose judgment is most to be sought and followed. He does not carry it as if he expected that everybody should bow and truckle to him and give place to him, as if no one was of as much consequence as himself. He does not put on assuming airs in his common conversation or in the management of his business or in the duties of religion. He is not forward to take upon himself that which does not belong to him, as though he had power where indeed he has not, as if the earth ought to be subject to his bidding, and must comply with his inclination and purposes. On the contrary, he gives all due deference to the judgment and inclinations of others, and his behavior carries with it the impression that he sincerely receives and acts on that teaching of the apostle Paul: "Let nothing be done through strife or vainglory; but in lowliness of mind let each esteem other better than themselves" (Phil. 2:3). In talking of the things of religion, he has not the air—either in his speech or behavior—of one who esteems himself one of the best saints in the whole company, but he rather carries himself as if he thought, in the expression of the apostle Paul, that he was "less than the least of all saints" (Eph. 3:8).

§ From "The Spirit of Charity Is an Humble Spirit," pp. 139–40

EXALT GOD ALONE

For we are his workmanship, created in Christ Jesus unto good works, which God hath before ordained that we should walk in them.
— EPHESIANS 2:10

Let us be exhorted to exalt God alone and to ascribe to Him all the glory of redemption. Let us endeavor to obtain, and increase in, a sensibleness of our great dependence on God, to have our eye to Him alone, to mortify a self-dependent and self-righteous disposition. Man is naturally exceeding prone to exalt himself and depend on his own power or goodness, as though from himself he must expect happiness. He is prone to have respect to enjoyments alien from God and His Spirit, as those in which happiness is to be found. This doctrine should teach us to exalt God alone: as by trust and reliance, so by praise. Let him that glorieth, glory in the Lord. Hath any man hope that he is converted and sanctified and that his mind is endowed with true excellency and spiritual beauty; that his sins are forgiven and he is received into God's favor, and he is exalted to the honor and blessedness of being His child and an heir of eternal life? Let him give God all the glory; God alone makes him to differ from the worst of men in this world or the most miserable of the damned in hell. Hath any man much comfort and strong hope of eternal life, let not his hope lift him up but dispose him the more to abase himself, to reflect on his own exceeding unworthiness of such a favor, and to exalt God alone. Is any man eminent in holiness and abundant in good works; let him take nothing of the glory of it to himself, but ascribe it to him whose workmanship we are: "created in Christ Jesus unto good works" (Eph. 2:10).

§ From "God Glorified in Man's Dependence," p. 7

GOD IS PRECIOUS TO THE BELIEVER

For a day in thy courts is better than a thousand. I had rather be a doorkeeper in the house of my God, than to dwell in the tents of wickedness.

— PSALM 84:10

The saint prefers what he hath already of God before anything in this world. That which was infused into his heart at his conversion is more precious to him than anything the world can afford. The views that are sometimes given him of the beauty and excellency of God are more precious to him than all the treasures of the wicked. The relation of a child in which he stands to God, the union that there is between his soul and Jesus Christ, he values more than the greatest earthly dignity. The image of God that is stamped on his soul he values more than any earthly ornaments. It is, in his esteem, better to be adorned with the graces of God's Holy Spirit than to be made to shine in jewels of gold and the most costly pearls, or to be admired for the greatest external beauty. He values the robe of Christ's righteousness, which he hath on his soul, more than the robes of princes. The spiritual pleasures and delights that he sometimes has in God, he prefers far before all the pleasures of sin: "A day in thy courts is better than a thousand. I had rather be a doorkeeper in the house of my God, than to dwell in the tents of wickedness" (Ps. 84:10).

JOY IN THE LOVE OF CHRIST

As the apple tree among the trees of the wood, so is my beloved among the sons. I sat down under his shadow with great delight, and his fruit was sweet to my taste.

— SONG OF SOLOMON 2:3

Christ gives to those who come to Him such comfort and pleasure as are enough to make them forget all their former labor and travail. A little of true peace, a little of the joys of the manifested love of Christ, and a little of the true and holy hope of eternal life are enough to compensate for all that toil and weariness, and to erase the remembrance of it from the mind. That peace that results from true faith passes understanding, and that joy is joy unspeakable. There is something peculiarly sweet and refreshing in this joy that is not in other joys, and what can more effectually support the mind or give a more rational ground of rejoicing than a prospect of eternal glory in the enjoyment of God from God's own promise in Christ? If we come to Christ, we may not only be refreshed by resting in His shadow, but also by eating His fruit. These things are the fruits of this tree: "I sat down under his shadow with great delight, and his fruit was sweet to my taste" (Song 2:3).

᪥ From "Safety, Fullness, and Sweet Refreshment, to Be Found in Christ," p. 934

A JEALOUS EYE ON OURSELVES

Take heed, brethren, lest there be in any of you an evil heart of unbelief, in departing from the living God. But exhort one another daily, while it is called To day; lest any of you be hardened through the deceitfulness of sin. — HEBREWS 3:12–13

Men are very apt to bring their principles to their practices, and not their practices to their principles, as they ought to. They, in their practice, comply not with their consciences, but all their strife is to bring their consciences to comply with their practice. On the account of this deceitfulness of sin, and because we have so much sin dwelling in our hearts, it is a difficult thing to pass a true judgment on our own ways and practices. On this account we should make diligent search and be much concerned to know whether there be not some wicked way in us: "Take heed, brethren, lest there be in any of you an evil heart of unbelief, in departing from the living God. But exhort one another daily, while it is called To day; lest any of you be hardened through the deceitfulness of sin" (Heb. 3:12–13). Men can more easily see faults in others than they can in themselves. When they see others out of the way, they will presently condemn them; when perhaps they do, or have done, the same, or the like, themselves, and in themselves justify it. Men can discern motes in others' eyes, better than they can beams in their own: "Every way of man is right in his own eyes" (Prov. 21:2). The heart, in this matter, is exceedingly deceitful: "The heart is deceitful above all things, and desperately wicked: who can know it?" (Jer. 17:9). We ought not therefore to trust in our own hearts in this matter, because "he that trusteth in his own heart is a fool" (Prov. 28:26). We must keep a jealous eye on ourselves, to pry into our own hearts and ways and to cry to God that He would search us.

§ From "Christian Cautions, or the Necessity of Self-Examination," p. 176

THE FORBEARANCE OF GOD

He that believeth on the Son hath everlasting life: and he that believeth not the Son shall not see life; but the wrath of God abideth on him.

— JOHN 3:36

God has laid Himself under no obligation, by any promise, to keep any natural man out of hell one moment. God certainly has made no promises either of eternal life or of any deliverance or preservation from eternal death but what are contained in the covenant of grace, the promises that are given in Christ, in whom all the promises are yea and amen. But surely they have no interest in the promises of the covenant of grace who are not the children of the covenant, who do not believe in any of the promises, and have no interest in the Mediator of the covenant. So that, whatever some have imagined and pretended about promises made to natural men's earnest seeking and knocking, it is plain and manifest that whatever pains a natural man takes in religion, whatever prayers he makes, until he believes in Christ, God is under no manner of obligation to keep him a moment from eternal destruction. Thus it is that natural men are held, in the hand of God, over the pit of hell; they have deserved the fiery pit and are already sentenced to it. And God is dreadfully provoked; His anger is as great toward them as to those that are actually suffering the executions of the fierceness of His wrath in hell, and they have done nothing in the least to appease or abate that anger. Neither is God in the least bound by any promise to hold them up one moment. The devil is waiting for them, hell is gaping for them, the flames gather and flash about them and would fain lay hold on them and swallow them up. The fire pent up in their own hearts is struggling to break out, and they have no interest in any mediator; there are no means within reach that can be any security to them. In short, they have no refuge, nothing to take hold of; all that preserves them every moment is the mere arbitrary will and uncovenanted, unobliged forbearance of an incensed God.

§ From "Sinners in the Hands of an Angry God," p. 9

MUTUAL JOY

Thou whom I have taken from the ends of the earth, and called thee from the chief men thereof, and said unto thee, Thou art my servant; I have chosen thee, and not cast thee away.

—ISAIAH 41:9

The mutual joy of Christ and His church is like that of bridegroom and bride: they rejoice in each other, as those whom they have chosen above others, for their nearest, most intimate and everlasting friends and companions. The church is Christ's chosen: "I have chosen thee, and not cast thee away" (Isa. 41:9); and "I have chosen thee in the furnace of affliction" (Isa. 48:10). How often are God's saints called His elect or chosen ones! He has chosen them, not to be mere servants, but friends: "I call you not servants;…but I have called you friends" (John 15:15). Though Christ is the Lord of glory, infinitely above men and angels, yet He has chosen the elect to be His companions and has taken upon Him their nature. So, in some respect, as it were, He leveled Himself with them, that He might be their brother and companion. Christ, as well as David, calls the saints His brethren and companions: "For my brethren and companions' sakes, I will now say, Peace be within thee" (Ps. 122:8); and, in the book of Song of Solomon, He calls His church His sister and spouse. Christ hath loved and chosen His church as His peculiar friend, above others: "The LORD hath chosen Jacob unto himself, and Israel for his peculiar treasure" (Ps. 135:4). As the bridegroom chooses the bride for His peculiar friend, above all others in the world, so Christ has chosen His church for a peculiar nearness to Him, as His flesh and His bone, and the high honor and dignity of espousals above all others.

§ From "The Church's Marriage to Her Sons, and to Her God," p. 21

BESTOWING SALVATION

But God hath chosen the foolish things of the world to confound the wise; and God hath chosen the weak things of the world to confound the things which are mighty.

— 1 CORINTHIANS 1:27

God exercises His sovereignty in sometimes bestowing salvation upon the low and mean and denying it to the wise and great. Christ, in His sovereignty, passes by the gates of princes and nobles and enters some cottage and dwells there and has communion with its obscure inhabitants. God, in His sovereignty, withheld salvation from the rich man, who fared sumptuously every day, and bestowed it on poor Lazarus, who sat begging at his gate. In this way God pours contempt on princes and on all their glittering splendor. So God sometimes passes by wise men, men of great understanding, learned and great scholars, and bestows salvation on others of weak understanding, who only comprehend some of the plainer parts of Scripture and the fundamental principles of the Christian religion. Yea, there seem to be fewer great men called than others. In ordering it thus God manifests His sovereignty: "For ye see your calling, brethren, how that not many wise men after the flesh, not many mighty, not many noble, are called: but God hath chosen the foolish things of the world to confound the wise; and God hath chosen the weak things of the world to confound the things which are mighty; and base things of the world, and things which are despised, hath God chosen, yea, and things which are not, to bring to nought things that are" (1 Cor. 1:26–28).

♦ From "God's Sovereignty in the Salvation of Man," p. 852

CHRIST CAN NEVER FAIL

*For I am the L*ORD*, I change not; therefore ye sons of Jacob are not consumed.*

— MALACHI 3:6

From the unchangeableness of your Savior you may be assured of your continuance in a state of grace. As to yourself, you are so changeable that, if left to yourself, you would soon fall utterly away. There is no dependence on your unchangeableness. But Christ is the same, and therefore, when He has begun a good work in you He will finish it; as He has been the author, He will be the finisher of your faith. Your love to Christ is in itself changeable; but His to you is unchangeable, and therefore He will never suffer your love to Him utterly to fail. The apostle Paul gives this reason why the saints' love to Christ cannot fail: namely, that His love to them never can fail. From the unchangeableness of Christ you may learn the unchangeableness of His intercession, how He will never cease to intercede for you; and from this you may learn the unalterableness of your heavenly happiness. Once you have entered on the happiness of heaven it never shall be taken from you, because Christ, your Savior and friend, who bestows it on you and in whom you have it, is unchangeable. He will be the same forever and ever, and therefore so will be your happiness in heaven. As Christ is an unchangeable Savior, so He is your unchangeable portion. That may be your rejoicing, that however your earthly enjoyments may be removed, Christ can never fail. Your dear friends may be taken away and you may suffer many losses; and at last you must part with all those things. Yet you have a portion, a precious treasure, more worth—ten thousand times more—than all these things. That portion cannot fail you, for you have it in Him, who is the same yesterday, today, and forever.

⸎ From "Jesus Christ, the Same Yesterday, Today, and Forever," p. 954

THE DARKNESS OF THE HEART

Know ye not, that to whom ye yield yourselves servants to obey, his servants ye are to whom ye obey; whether of sin unto death, or of obedience unto righteousness?
—ROMANS 6:16

Men come into the world with many strong and violent lusts in their hearts and are exceeding prone of themselves to transgress, even in the safest circumstances in which they can be placed. And surely, so much the nearer they are to that sin to which they are naturally strongly inclined, so much the more are they exposed. If any of us who are parents should see our children near the brink of some deep pit or close by the edge of the precipice of a high mountain, and not only so, but the ground upon which the child stood slippery, and steeply descending directly toward the precipice, should we not reckon a child exposed in such a case? Should we not be in haste to remove the child from its very dangerous situation? It was the manner among the Israelites to build their houses with flat roofs so that persons might walk on the tops of their houses. Therefore, God took care to make it a law among them that every man should have battlements upon the edges of their roofs, lest any person should fall off and be killed. We ought to take the like care that we do not fall into sin, which carries in it eternal death. We should, as it were, fix a battlement, a guard, to keep us from the edge of the precipice. Much more ought we to take care that we do not go upon a roof that is not only without battlements, but also is steep, and we shall naturally incline to fall. Men's lusts are like strong enemies, endeavoring to draw them into sin. If a man stood upon a dangerous precipice and had enemies about him, pulling and drawing him, endeavoring to throw him down, would he, in such a case, choose or dare to stand near the edge?

§ From "Temptation and Deliverance," pp. 229–30

DETERMINATION IN THE MIND

Verily, verily, I say unto you, He that heareth my word, and believeth on him that sent me, hath everlasting life, and shall not come into condemnation; but is passed from death unto life.

—JOHN 5:24

There are some persons who have never come to a settled determination in their own minds as to whether or not there is any truth in religion. They hear of the things of religion from their childhood all their days, but never come to a conclusion in their own minds as to whether they are real or fabulous. Particularly, some have never come to any determination in their own minds as to whether there is any such thing as conversion. They hear much talk about it and know that many pretend to be the subjects of it, but they are never resolved as to whether all is not merely designed hypocrisy and imposture. Some never come to any determination as to whether the Scriptures are the Word of God, or whether they are the invention of men and whether the story concerning Jesus Christ is anything but a fable. They fear it is true, but sometimes they very much doubt of it. Sometimes when they hear arguments for it, they assent that it is true; but upon every little objection or temptation arising, they call it in question and are always wavering and never settled about it. So it seems to have been with many of the Jews in Christ's time; they were always at a loss what to make of Him, whether He were indeed the Christ, or whether He were Elias, or one of the old prophets, or a mere impostor: "Then came the Jews round about him, and said unto him, How long dost thou make us to doubt? If thou be the Christ, tell us plainly. Jesus answered them, I told you, and ye believed not" (John 10:24–25). Some have never so much as come to a resolution in their own minds as to whether there is a God or not. They know not that there is, and oftentimes they very much doubt of it.

⟡ From "The Unreasonableness of Indetermination in Religion," pp. 57–58

POUR OUT YOUR SOUL

And the prayer of faith shall save the sick, and the Lord shall raise him up; and if he have committed sins, they shall be forgiven him.

—JAMES 5:15

It is natural to one who is truly born from above to pray to God and to pour out his soul in holy supplications before his heavenly Father. This is as natural to the new nature and life as breathing is to the nature and life of the body. But hypocrites have not this new nature. Those illuminations and affections that they had went away and left no change of nature. Therefore, prayer naturally dies away in them, having no foundation laid in the nature of the soul. It is maintained awhile only by a certain force put upon nature. But force is not constant; and as that declines, nature will take place again. The spirit of a true convert is a spirit of true love to God, and that naturally inclines the soul to those duties wherein it is conversant with God and makes it to delight in approaching Him. A hypocrite hath no such spirit. He is left under the reigning power of enmity against God, which naturally inclines him to shun His presence. The spirit of a true convert is a spirit of faith and reliance on the power, wisdom, and mercy of God, and such a spirit is naturally expressed in prayer. True prayer is nothing else but faith expressed. Hence we read of the prayer of faith (see James 5:15). True Christian prayer is the faith and reliance of the soul breathed forth in words.

§ From "Hypocrites Deficient in the Duty of Prayer," p. 73

GOD'S PEOPLE ARE HAPPY PEOPLE

Thus saith the LORD of hosts; In those days it shall come to pass, that ten men shall take hold out of all languages of the nations, even shall take hold of the skirt of him that is a Jew, saying, We will go with you: for we have heard that God is with you.
— ZECHARIAH 8:23

The people of God are the most excellent and happy society in the world. That God whom they have chosen for their God is their Father; He has pardoned all their sins, and they are at peace with Him. He has admitted them to all the privileges of His children. As they have devoted themselves to God, so He has given Himself to them. He is become their salvation and their portion. His power and mercy and all His attributes are theirs. They are in a safe state, free from all possibility of perishing; Satan has no power to destroy them. God carries them on eagle's wings, far above Satan's reach, and above the reach of all the enemies of their souls. God is with them in this world; they have His gracious presence. God is for them; who then can be against them? As the mountains are round about Jerusalem, so Jehovah is round about them. God is their shield and their exceeding great reward. Their fellowship is with the Father and with His Son Jesus Christ, and they have the divine promise and oath that in the world to come they shall dwell forever in the glorious presence of God. It may well be sufficient to induce us to resolve to cleave to those that forsake their sins and idols to join themselves with this people, to know that God is with them (see Zech. 8:23). So should persons, as it were, take hold of the skirt of their neighbors and companions that have turned to God, and resolve that they will go with them, because God is with them.

♦ From "Ruth's Resolution," p. 665

A RESTING PLACE

I am the living bread which came down from heaven: if any man eat of this bread, he shall live for ever: and the bread that I will give is my flesh, which I will give for the life of the world.

—JOHN 6:51

They who come to Christ do not only come to a resting place after they have been wandering in a wilderness, but they also come to a banqueting house where they may rest and feast. They may cease from their former troubles and toils, and they may enter upon a course of delights and spiritual joys. Christ not only delivers from fears of hell and of wrath, but He also gives hopes of heaven and the enjoyment of God's love. He delivers from inward tumults and inward pain, from that guilt of conscience that is as a worm gnawing within, and He gives delight and inward glory. He brings us out of a wilderness of pits and drought and fiery flying spirits; and He brings us into a pleasant land, a land flowing with milk and honey. He delivers us out of prison and lifts us off from the dunghill, and He sets us among princes and causes us to inherit the throne of glory. Wherefore, if anyone is weary, if any is in prison, if anyone is in captivity, if anyone is in the wilderness, let Him come to the blessed Jesus, who is as the shadow of a great rock in a weary land. Delay not, arise and come away.

§ From "Safety, Fullness, and Sweet Refreshment, to Be Found in Christ," p. 935

EXTERNAL WORK AND LOVE

Every beast of the forest is mine, and the cattle upon a thousand hills.... If I were hungry, I would not tell thee: for the world is mine, and the fulness thereof.
— PSALM 50:10, 12

It is not the external work done or the suffering endured that is, in itself, worth anything in the sight of God. The motions and exercise of the body, or anything that may be done by it, if considered separately from the heart—the inward part of the man—is of no more consequence or worth in the sight of God than the motions of anything without life. If anything be offered or given, though it is silver, or gold or the cattle on a thousand hills; though it is a thousand rams or ten thousands of rivers of oil; there is nothing of value in it, as an external thing, in God's sight. If God were in need of these things they might be of value to Him in themselves considered, independently of the motives of the heart that led to their being offered. We often stand in need of external good things, and therefore such things, offered or given to us, may and do have a value to us, in themselves considered. But God stands in need of nothing. He is all-sufficient in Himself. He is not fed by the sacrifices of beasts, or enriched by the gift of silver, or gold, or pearls: "All things come of thee, and of thine own have we given thee.... O LORD our God, all this store that we have prepared to build thee an house for thine holy name cometh of thine hand, and is all thine own" (1 Chron. 29:14, 16). And as there is nothing profitable to God in any of our services or performances, so there can be nothing acceptable in His sight in a mere external action without sincere love in the heart, "for the Lord seeth not as man seeth; for man looketh on the outward appearance, but God looketh on the heart." The heart is just as naked and open to Him as the external actions. Therefore, He sees our actions and all our conduct, not merely as the external motions of a machine but as the actions of rational, intelligent creatures and voluntary free agents. Therefore, there can be, in His estimation, no excellence or amiableness in anything we can do, if the heart be not right with Him.

§ From "The Greatest Performances or Sufferings in Vain without Charity," pp. 55–56

THE GRACE OF HUMILITY

*Who humbleth himself to behold the things that are in heaven,
and in the earth!*

— PSALM 113:6

Humility is a grace proper for beings that are glorious and excellent in very many respects. Thus, the saints and angels in heaven excel in humility, and humility is proper and suitable in them, though they are pure, spotless, and glorious beings, perfect in holiness and excelling in mind and strength. Though they are thus glorious, yet they have a comparative meanness before God, of which they are sensible; for He is said to humble Himself to behold the things that are in heaven (see Ps. 113:6). So the man Christ Jesus, who is the most excellent and glorious of all creatures, is yet meek and lowly of heart and excels all other beings in humility. Humility is one of the excellencies of Christ because He is not only God but man, and as a man He was humble. For humility is not, and cannot be, an attribute of the divine nature. God's nature is indeed infinitely opposite to pride, and yet humility cannot properly be predicated of Him. If it could this would argue imperfection, which is impossible in God. God, who is infinite in excellence and glory and infinitely above all things, cannot have any comparative meanness, and, of course, cannot have any such comparative meanness to be sensible of, and therefore cannot be humble. Humility is an excellence proper to all created intelligent beings, for they are all infinitely little and mean before God, and most of them are in some way mean and low in comparison with some of their fellow creatures. Humility implies a compliance with the rule of the apostle Paul that we think not of ourselves more highly than we ought to think, but that we think soberly, according as God hath dealt to everyone of us the measure, not only of faith, but of other things (see Rom. 12:3). And this humility, as a virtue in men, implies a sense of their own comparative meanness, both as compared with God and as compared with their fellow creatures.

§ From "The Spirit of Charity Is an Humble Spirit," pp. 130–31

LOVE OF HAPPINESS

Thou shalt love thy neighbour as thyself.
— MATTHEW 19:19

The inordinateness of self-love does not consist in our love of our own happiness being, absolutely considered, too great in degree. I do not suppose it can be said of any that their love to their own happiness—if we consider that love absolutely and not comparatively—can be in too high a degree, or that it is a thing that is liable either to increase or diminution. For I apprehend that self-love, in this sense, is not a result of the fall, but is necessary, and what belongs to the nature of all intelligent beings, and that God has made it alike in all. Saints and sinners, and all alike, love happiness and have the same unalterable and instinctive inclination to desire and seek it. The change that takes place in a man when he is converted and sanctified is not that his love for happiness is diminished, but only that it is regulated with respect to its exercises and influence and the courses and objects it leads to. Who will say that the happy souls in heaven do not love happiness as truly as the miserable spirits in hell? If their love of happiness is diminished by their being made holy, then that will diminish their happiness itself; for the less anyone loves happiness, the less he relishes it and, consequently, is the less happy. When God brings a soul out of a miserable state and condition into a happy state, by conversion, He gives him happiness that before he had not, but He does not at the same time take away any of his love of happiness. And so, when a saint increases in grace, he is made still more happy than he was before; but his love of happiness, and his relish of it, do not grow less as his happiness itself increases, for that would be to increase his happiness one way, and to diminish it another.

§ From "The Spirit of Charity, the Opposite of a Selfish Spirit," pp. 161–62

THE FAITHFULNESS OF GOD

It is of the LORD's mercies that we are not consumed, because his compassions fail not. They are new every morning: great is thy faithfulness.
— LAMENTATIONS 3:22–23

It is well for us that God is not as unfaithful to us as we are to Him. We who are professing Christians are under solemn vows and engagements to be the Lord's and to serve Him; every time we come to the Lord's Supper we renew those vows in a most solemn manner. But how much unfaithfulness there is among professors toward God. And of those who do sincerely give themselves to God at their conversion, how often they fail in point of faithfulness to their covenant God. God is not so toward those who are godly. God is engaged to them by promise: to keep them through faith to salvation, not to suffer them to be tempted above what they are able, to carry them on in a way of grace, and to deliver them from all their enemies. He has promised that He will evermore take care of them and watch over them for good; that He will keep them from the power of the devil; that He will keep them out of hell and at last bring them to glory. God never fails in any one instance. The word has gone out of His mouth, and heaven and earth shall pass away before one jot or tittle of it shall fail. If we were not sure but that God's faithfulness toward us might fail, and was as liable to fail as men's toward Him, what a poor, doubtful case we would all be in!

⟡ From "It Is Well for Us That God Is Not as We Are," p. 31

COMMUNICATIONS OF GOD'S LIGHT

Whatsoever doth make manifest is light.
— EPHESIANS 5:13

Christ's design in the appointment of the order and office of ministers of the gospel was that they might be lights to the souls of men. Satan's kingdom is a kingdom of darkness; the devils are the rulers of the darkness of this world. Christ's kingdom is a kingdom of light; the designs of His kingdom are carried on by light. His people are not of the night or of darkness, but are the children of the light, as they are the children of God, who is the Father of lights, and, as it were, a boundless fountain of infinite pure and bright light (see 1 John 1:5; James 1:17). Man, by the fall, extinguished the divine light that shone in this world in its first estate. The Scripture represents the wickedness of man as reducing the world to that state wherein it was when it was yet without form and void, and darkness filled it: "For my people is foolish, they have not known me; they are sottish children, and they have none understanding: they are wise to do evil, but to do good they have no knowledge…. I beheld the earth, and lo, it was without form and void; and the heavens, and they had no light" (Jer. 4:22, 23). God, in infinite mercy, has made glorious provision for the restoration of light to this fallen, dark world. He has sent Him who is the brightness of His own glory into the world, to be the light of the world. "He is the true light that lighteth every man that cometh into the world," that is, every man in the world that ever has any true light. In His wisdom and mercy, He is pleased to convey His light to men by means and instruments. He has sent forth His messengers and appointed ministers in His church to be subordinate lights and to shine with the communications of His light and to reflect the beams of His glory on the souls of men.

From "The True Excellency of a Gospel Minister," p. 956

GUILTY IN SIN

Repent ye therefore, and be converted, that your sins may be blotted out, when the times of refreshing shall come from the presence of the Lord. And he shall send Jesus Christ, which before was preached unto you. — ACTS 3:19–20

God makes men be sensible of and consider of what sin they are guilty. Before, it may be, they were very regardless of this. They went on sinning and never reflected upon what they did, never considered or regarded what or how many sins they committed. They saw no cause why they should trouble their minds about it. But, when God convinces them, He brings them to reflect upon themselves; He sets their sins in order before their eyes. He brings their old sins to their minds so that they are fresh in their memory— things they had almost forgotten. Many things that they used to regard as light offenses, which were not wont to be a burden to their consciences or to appear worthy to be taken notice of, they are now made to reflect upon. Thus, they discover of what a multitude of transgressions they have been guilty, of which they have heaped up until they are grown up to heaven. There are some sins especially of which they have been guilty that are ever before them, so that they cannot get them out of their minds. Sometimes, when men are under conviction, their sins follow them and haunt them like a specter. God makes men sensible of the sin of their hearts and of how corrupt and depraved their hearts are.

⟋ From "God Makes Men Sensible of Their Misery before He Reveals His Mercy and Love," pp. 831–32

SATISFIED IN CHRIST

His branches shall spread, and his beauty shall be as the olive tree, and his smell as Lebanon.

— HOSEA 14:6

Worldly men imagine that there is true excellency and true happiness in those things they are pursuing. They think that if they could but obtain them, they should be happy; and when they obtain them, and cannot find happiness, they look for happiness in something else and are still upon the pursuit. Christ Jesus has true excellency, and so great excellency that when they come to see it they look no further, but the mind rests there. It sees a transcendent glory and an ineffable sweetness in Him; it sees that, until now, it has been pursuing shadows, but now it has found the substance; that before it had been seeking happiness in the stream, but now it has found the ocean. The excellency of Christ is an object adequate to the natural cravings of the soul and is sufficient to fill the capacity. It is an infinite excellency, such an one as the mind desires, in which it can find no bounds; and the more the mind is used to it, the more excellent it appears. Every new discovery makes this beauty appear more ravishing, and the mind sees no end; here is room enough for the mind to go deeper and deeper and never come to the bottom. The soul is exceedingly ravished when it first looks on this beauty, and it is never weary of it. The mind never has any satiety, but Christ's excellency is always fresh and new and tends as much to delight, after it has been seen a thousand or ten thousand years, as when it was seen the first moment. The excellency of Christ is an object suited to the superior faculties of man; it is suited to entertain the faculty of reason and understanding, and there is nothing so worthy about which the understanding can be employed as this excellency. No other object is so great, noble, and exalted.

⑤ From "Safety, Fullness, and Sweet Refreshment, to Be Found in Christ," pp. 932–33

THE DANGER OF SIN

My little children, these things write I unto you, that ye sin not. And if any man sin, we have an advocate with the Father, Jesus Christ the righteous.

— 1 JOHN 2:1

If we live in any way of sin, we shall thereby provoke God to anger and bring guilt upon our own souls. Neither will it excuse us that we were not sensible how evil that way was in which we walked; that we did not consider it; that we were blind as to any evil in it. We contract guilt not only by living in those ways that we know, but also in those that we might know to be sinful, if we were but sufficiently concerned to know what is sinful and what is not and to examine ourselves and search our own hearts and ways. If we walk in some evil way, and know it not for want of watchfulness and consideration, that will not excuse us; for we ought to have watched and considered and made the most diligent inquiry. If we walk in some evil way, it will be a great prejudice to us in this world. We shall thereby be deprived of that comfort we otherwise might enjoy and shall expose ourselves to a great deal of soul trouble, sorrow, and darkness, from which otherwise we might have been free. A wicked way is the original way of pain or grief. In it we shall expose ourselves to the judgments of God, even in this world; and we shall be great losers by it in respect to our eternal interest; and that though we may not live in a way of sin willfully, and with a deliberate resolution, but carelessly, and through the deceitfulness of our corruptions. However, we shall offend God, and prevent the flourishing of grace in our hearts, if not the very being of it.

᧥ From "Christian Cautions, or the Necessity of Self-Examination," p. 175

HELPLESS IN OURSELVES

When he came to himself, he said, How many hired servants of my father's have bread enough and to spare, and I perish with hunger! I will arise and go to my father, and will say unto him, Father, I have sinned against heaven, and before thee.

—LUKE 15:17–18

God oftentimes makes use of men's own experience to convince them that they are helpless in themselves. When they first set out in seeking salvation, it may be they thought it an easy thing to be converted. They thought they should presently bring themselves to repent of their sins and believe in Christ, and accordingly they strove in their own strength with hopes of success; but they were disappointed. God suffers them to go on striving to open their own eyes and mend their own hearts, but they find no success. They have been striving to see for a long time, yet they are as blind as ever and can see nothing. It is all Egyptian darkness. They have been striving to make themselves better, but they are bad as ever. They have often striven to do something that is good, to be in the exercise of good affections that should be acceptable to God, but they have no success. It seems to them that, instead of growing better, they grow worse and worse; their hearts are fuller of wicked thoughts than they were at first and they see no more likelihood of their conversion than there was at first. God suffers them to strive in their own strength until they are discouraged and despair of helping themselves. The prodigal son first strove to fill his belly with the husks that the swine did eat, but, when he despaired of being helped in that way, he came to himself and entertained thoughts of returning to his father's house.

§ From "God Makes Men Sensible of Their Misery before He Reveals His Mercy and Love," p. 834

TRUE PEACE

For unto us a child is born, unto us a son is given: and the government shall be upon his shoulder: and his name shall be called Wonderful, Counsellor, The mighty God, The everlasting Father, The Prince of Peace.
—ISAIAH 9:6

Our Lord Jesus Christ has obtained true peace and comfort upon His followers. Christ is called the Prince of Peace in Isaiah 9:6. When He was born into the world, the angels on that joyful and wonderful occasion sang, "Glory to God in the highest, on earth peace" (Luke 2:14), because of that peace that He should procure for and bestow on the children of men: peace with God, and peace with one another, and tranquility and peace within themselves. Christ has obtained for them peace and reconciliation with God and His favor and friendship, in that He satisfied for their sins and laid a foundation for the perfect removal of the guilt of sin and the forgiveness of all their trespasses and wrought out for them a perfect and glorious righteousness, most acceptable to God and sufficient to recommend them to God's full acceptance, to the adoption of children and to the eternal fruits of His fatherly kindness. The true followers of Christ have not only ground of rest and peace of soul, by reason of their safety from evil, but on account of their sure title and certain enjoyment of all that good of which they stand in need, living, dying, and through all eternity. They are on a sure foundation for happiness, are built on a rock that can never be moved, and have a foundation that is sufficient and can never be exhausted.

꙳ From "The Peace Which Christ Gives His True Followers," p. 90

FULL REFRESHMENT IN CHRIST

Thus saith the LORD, *Stand ye in the ways, and see, and ask for the old paths, where is the good way, and walk therein, and ye shall find rest for your souls. But they said, We will not walk therein.*
— JEREMIAH 6:16

There is quiet rest and full refreshment in Christ for sinners who are weary and heavy-laden with sin. Sin is the most evil and odious thing, as well as the most mischievous and fatal; it is the most mortal poison; it, above all things, hazards life and endangers the soul, exposes it to the loss of all happiness and to the suffering of all misery, and brings the wrath of God. All men have this dreadful evil hanging about them, and cleaving fast to the soul, and ruling over it, and keeping it in possession and under absolute command. It hangs like a viper to the heart or, rather, holds it as a lion does its prey. Yet there are multitudes who are not sensible of their misery. They are in such a sleep that they are not very unquiet in this condition; it is not very burdensome to them. They are so foolish that they do not know what is their state and what is likely to become of them. But, there are others who have their sense so far restored to them that they feel the pain and see the approaching destruction, and sin lies like a heavy load upon their hearts; it is a load that lies upon them day and night. They cannot lay it down to rest themselves, but it continually oppresses them. It is bound fast unto them and is ready to sink them down; it is a continual labor of heart to support itself under this burden. Thus we read of them "that labour, and are heavy laden" (Matt. 11:28).

꙳ From "Safety, Fullness, and Sweet Refreshment, to Be Found in Christ," pp. 933–34

WATCH AND PRAY

Watch unto prayer.
—1 PETER 4:7

Let me earnestly exhort such to give diligent heed to themselves to avoid all errors, misconduct, and whatever may darken and obscure the work, and to give no occasion to those who stand ready to reproach it. The apostle Paul was careful to cut off occasion from those that desired occasion. The same apostle exhorts Titus to maintain a strict care and watch over himself, that both his preaching and behavior might be such as "cannot be condemned; that he that is of the contrary part may be ashamed, having no evil thing to say of them" (Titus 2:8). We had need to be wise as serpents and harmless as doves. It is of no small consequence that we should, at this day, behave ourselves innocently and prudently. We must expect that the great enemy of this work will especially try his utmost with us; and he will especially triumph if he can prevail in anything to blind and mislead us. He knows it will do more to further his purpose and interest than if he prevailed against a hundred others. We had need to watch and pray, for we are but little children; this roaring lion is too strong for us, and this old serpent too subtle for us.

§ From "Distinguishing Marks of a Work of the Spirit of God," pp. 273–74

THE SWEETNESS OF THE LOVE OF CHRIST

Keep yourselves in the love of God, looking for the mercy of our Lord Jesus Christ unto eternal life.
—JUDE 1:21

The manifestation of the love of Christ gives the soul abundant contentment. This love of Christ is exceedingly sweet and satisfying; it is better than life, because it is the love of a person of such dignity and excellency. The sweetness of His love depends very much upon the greatness of His excellency; so much the more lovely the person, so much the more desirable is His love. How sweet must the love of that person be who is the eternal Son of God, who is of equal dignity with the Father! How great a happiness must it be to be the object of the love of Him who is the creator of the world and by whom all things consist; who is exalted at God's right hand and made head over principalities and powers in heavenly places; who has all things put under His feet; who is King of kings and Lord of lords; and who is the brightness of the Father's glory! Surely, to be beloved by Him is enough to satisfy the soul of a worm of the dust. This love of Christ is also exceedingly sweet and satisfying from the greatness of it; it is a dying love. Such love as never was before seen, and such as no other can parallel. There have been instances of very great love between one earthly friend and another—there was a surpassing love between David and Jonathan—but there never was any such love as Christ has toward believers. The satisfying nature of this love arises also from the sweet fruits of it. Those precious benefits that Christ bestows upon His people, and those precious promises that He has given them, are the fruit of this love; joy and hope are the constant streams that flow from this fountain, from the love of Christ.

᭡ From "Safety, Fullness, and Sweet Refreshment, to Be Found in Christ," p. 933

MADE AWARE OF SIN

The sinners in Zion are afraid; fearfulness hath surprised the hypocrites. Who among us shall dwell with the devouring fire? who among us shall dwell with everlasting burnings?

—ISAIAH 33:14

God convinces sinners of the dreadful danger they are in by reason of their sin. Having their sins set before them, God makes them sensible of the relation their sin has to misery. God makes them sensible that His displeasure is very dreadful. Before, they heard often about the anger of God and the fierceness of His wrath, but they were not moved by it. Now they are made sensible that it is a dreadful thing to fall into the hands of the living God. They are made, in some measure, sensible of the dreadfulness of hell. They are led with fixedness and impression to think what a dismal thing it will be to have God an enraged enemy, setting to work the misery of a soul, and how dismal it will be to dwell in such torment forever without hope: "The sinners in Zion are afraid; fearfulness hath surprised the hypocrites. Who among us shall dwell with the devouring fire? who among us shall dwell with everlasting burnings?" (Isa. 33:14). Other sinners are told of hell, but convinced sinners often have hell, as it were, in their view. Their being impressed with a sense of the dreadfulness of its misery is the cause why it works upon their imagination oftentimes; and it will seem as though they saw the dismal flames of hell; as though they saw God in implacable wrath exerting His fury upon them; as though they heard the cries and shrieks of the damned.

⑤ From "God Makes Men Sensible of Their Misery before He Reveals His Mercy and Love," p. 832

LONGING FOR CHRIST

I am the door: by me if any man enter in, he shall be saved,
and shall go in and out, and find pasture.
— JOHN 10:9

There is provision for the satisfaction and contentment of the thirsty, longing soul in Christ, as He is the way to the Father, not only from the fullness of excellency and grace that He has in His own person, but as by Him we may come to God, may be reconciled to Him, and may be made happy in His favor and love. The poverty and want of the soul in its natural state consist in its being separated from God, for God is the riches and the happiness of the creature. We naturally are alienated from God, and God is alienated from us, and our Maker is not at peace with us. But, in Christ, there is a way for a free communication between God and us—for us to come to God and for God to communicate Himself to us by His Spirit: "Jesus saith unto him, I am the way, the truth, and the life: no man cometh unto the Father, but by me" (John 14:6); and "But now in Christ Jesus, ye who sometimes were far off are made nigh by the blood of Christ…. For through him we both have access by one Spirit unto the Father…. Now therefore ye are no more strangers and foreigners, but fellow citizens with the saints, and of the household of God" (Eph. 2:13, 18, 19). Christ, by being thus the way to the Father, is the way to true happiness and contentment: "I am the door: by me if any man enter in, he shall be saved, and shall go in and out, and find pasture" (John 10:9).

⚘ From "Safety, Fullness, and Sweet Refreshment, to Be Found in Christ," p. 933

THE GODLY MOVE UPWARD

But we all, with open face beholding as in a glass the glory of the Lord, are changed into the same image from glory to glory, even as by the Spirit of the Lord. — 2 CORINTHIANS 3:18

Have you in any measure gotten above the world? Is your heart in some good measure above earthly things? This way of salvation by Jesus Christ is upward; the ascent of the ladder in salvation is away from the earth and toward heaven. Those who ascend this ladder do not stay upon the earth; they get off from it and get up above it. And the more they ascend, so much the further are they separated from the earth. Are you one who has in your heart, in some measure, left the earth and ascended up above it? Are you one who chooses your portion in this life, or do you see something above the world that is better than the world? Is your heart as knit to the world and earthly things as it ever was? Are not your appetites and inclinations as eager and violent as they used to be after the things of this world? A godly man may have great remains of worldliness and earthly enjoyments for charitable uses. But when the world and your duty to God or Christ's honor and glory stand in competition, is it not your manner or practice to give the preference to worldly enjoyments? Do you not stick faster to the world than to God in such cases? Is it not your manner in such cases to excuse yourself from duty when it is cross to your worldly interests? And so, by one means or another, worldly men will cleave to the world. They will not forsake it. Because it is the character of a godly man that he must be ready to part with other things for God, he will labor to invent arguments to satisfy his case that such things are not his duty. When God and the world come into competition, do you stick to the world? Do you find arguments to satisfy your conscience and blind your own eyes to duty? Do not be the one who finds out some way or another to keep the world close by.

§ From "The Ladder That God Has Set on the Earth for Man to Ascend to Happiness Reaches Even unto Heaven," pp. 168–69

SELECTED SERMONS
OF JONATHAN EDWARDS

Sermon excerpts were taken from the following publications:

Charity and Its Fruits: Christian Love as Manifested in the Heart and Life. Edited by Tryon Edwards. London: Banner of Truth Trust, 1969, 2000.

Jonathan Edwards: Containing 16 Sermons Unpublished in Edwards' Lifetime. Compiled and edited by Don Kistler. Morgan, Pa.: Soli Deo Gloria, 2004.

A Just and Righteous God: 18 Sermons. Compiled and edited by Don Kistler. Orlando, Fla.: Soli Deo Gloria Publications, 2006.

Selected Sermons of Jonathan Edwards. Edited by H. Norman Gardiner. New York: The MacMillian Company, 1904.

The Works of Jonathan Edwards. Edited by Edward Hickman. 2 vols. Edinburgh: Banner of Truth Trust, 1997.

The Works of President Edwards, in Eight Volumes. Worcester, Mass.: Isaac Sturtevant, 1809.

Sermons:

"All the Graces of Christianity Connected." In *Charity and Its Fruits: Christian Love as Manifested in the Heart and Life*, 386–409.

"All True Grace in the Heart Tends to Holy Practice in the Life." In *Charity and Its Fruits: Christian Love as Manifested in the Heart and Life*, 318–60.

"The Character of Paul an Example to Christians." In vol. 2 of *The Works of Jonathan Edwards*, 855–66.

"Charity Disposes Us to Do Good." In *Charity and Its Fruits: Christian Love as Manifested in the Heart and Life*, 139–60.

"Charity Disposes Us Meekly to Bear the Injuries Received from Others." In *Charity and Its Fruits: Christian Love as Manifested in the Heart and Life*, 96–138.

"Charity Inconsistent with an Envious Spirit." In *Charity and Its Fruits: Christian Love as Manifested in the Heart and Life*, 161–84.

"Charity, or a Christian Spirit Willing to Undergo all Sufferings in the Way of Duty." In *Charity and Its Fruits: Christian Love as Manifested in the Heart and Life*, 361–85.

"Charity, or Love the Sum of All Virtue." In *Charity and Its Fruits: Christian Love as Manifested in the Heart and Life*, 1–37.

"Charity, or Love, More Excellent Than the Extraordinary Gifts of the Spirit." In *Charity and Its Fruits: Christian Love as Manifested in the Heart and Life*, 38–72.

"Charity, or True Grace, Not to be Overthrown by Opposition." In *Charity and Its Fruits: Christian Love as Manifested in the Heart and Life*, 38–72.

"Christ Exalted." In vol. 2 of *The Works of Jonathan Edwards*, 213–17.

"Christ the Example of Ministers." In vol. 2 of *The Works of Jonathan Edwards*, 960–65.

"Christian Cautions, or the Necessity of Self-Examination." In vol. 2 of *The Works of Jonathan Edwards*, 173–85.

"Christian Charity." In vol. 2 of *The Works of Jonathan Edwards*, 163–73.

"Christian Charity: The Duty of Charity to the Poor Explained and Enforced." In *A Just and Righteous God: 18 Sermons*, 224–69.

"Christian Knowledge." In vol. 2 of *The Works of Jonathan Edwards*, 157–63.

"The Christian Pilgrim, or the True Christian's Life a Journey toward Heaven." In vol. 2 of *The Works of Jonathan Edwards*, 243–46.

"Christians a Chosen Generation, a Royal Priesthood, a Holy Nation, a Peculiar People." In vol. 2 of *The Works of Jonathan Edwards*, 936–49.

"Christ Is the Christian's All." In *Jonathan Edwards: Containing 16 Sermons Unpublished in Edwards' Lifetime*, 192–206.

"The Church's Marriage to Her Sons, and to Her God." In vol. 2 of *The Works of Jonathan Edwards*, 17–26.

"The Covenant of Grace, Firm and Sure." In *A Just and Righteous God: 18 Sermons*, 78–96.

"Distinguishing Marks of a Work of the Spirit of God." In vol. 2 of *The Works of Jonathan Edwards*, 257–77.

"A Divine and Supernatural Light." In vol. 2 of *The Works of Jonathan Edwards*, 12–17.

"The Excellency of Jesus Christ." In vol. 1 of *The Works of Jonathan Edwards*, 680–89.

"The Final Judgment, or the World Judged Righteously by Jesus Christ." In vol. 2 of *The Works of Jonathan Edwards*, 190–201.

"The Folly of Looking Back in Fleeing Out of Sodom." In vol. 2 of *The Works of Jonathan Edwards*, 64–68.

"The Future Punishment of the Wicked Unavoidable and Intolerable." In vol. 2 of *The Works of Jonathan Edwards*, 78–89.

"God, as the Giver and Judge of the Law, Deals with the Utmost Strictness." In *A Just and Righteous God: 18 Sermons*, 174–94.

"God the Best Portion of the Christian." In vol. 2 of *The Works of Jonathan Edwards*, 104–7.

"God Carries His People Along through the World toward Glory Far Above the Reach of All Their Enemies, or Anything That Might Hinder Their Blessedness." In *A Just and Righteous God: 18 Sermons*, 35–49.

"God Doesn't Thank Men for Doing Those Things He Commands." In *Jonathan Edwards: Containing 16 Sermons Unpublished in Edwards' Lifetime*, 39–55.

"God Does What He Pleases." In *Jonathan Edwards: Containing 16 Sermons Unpublished in Edwards' Lifetime*, 147–75.

"God Glorified in Man's Dependence." In vol. 2 of *The Works of Jonathan Edwards*, 3–7.

"God Is a Being of Transcendent Mercy." In *Jonathan Edwards: Containing 16 Sermons Unpublished in Edwards' Lifetime*, 271–85.

"God Is a Just and Righteous God." In *A Just and Righteous God: 18 Sermons*, 1–16.

"God Is Everywhere Present." In *Jonathan Edwards: Containing 16 Sermons Unpublished in Edwards' Lifetime*, 207–22.

"God Is Kind to the Unthankful and the Evil." In *Jonathan Edwards: Containing 16 Sermons Unpublished in Edwards' Lifetime*, 69–92.

"God Makes Men Sensible of Their Misery before He Reveals His Mercy and Love." In vol. 2 of *The Works of Jonathan Edwards*, 830–38.

"God Never Changes His Mind." In *Jonathan Edwards: Containing 16 Sermons Unpublished in Edwards' Lifetime*, 1–13.

"God's Sovereignty in the Salvation of Men." In vol. 2 of *The Works of Jonathan Edwards*, 849–54.

"God's Wisdom in His Stated Method of Bestowing Grace." In *A Just and Righteous God: 18 Sermons*, 195–207.

"God Will Deal with Men According to Their Own Temper and Practice." In *A Just and Righteous God: 18 Sermons*, 123–46.

"The Greatest Performances or Sufferings in Vain without Charity." In *Charity and Its Fruits: Christian Love as Manifested in the Heart and Life*, 73–95.

"Great Guilt No Obstacle to the Pardon of the Returning Sinner." In vol. 2 of *The Works of Jonathan Edwards*, 110–13.

"A Heart to Do the Will of God." In *A Just and Righteous God: 18 Sermons*, 113–22.

"Heaven, a World of Charity, or Love." In *Charity and Its Fruits: Christian Love as Manifested in the Heart and Life*, 463–530.

"The Holy Spirit Forever to Be Communicated to the Saints, in the Grace of Charity, or Divine Love." In *Charity and Its Fruits: Christian Love as Manifested in the Heart and Life*, 433–62.

"Hope and Comfort Usually Follow Genuine Humiliation and Repentance." In vol. 2 of *The Works of Jonathan Edwards*, 838–49.

"Hypocrites Deficient in the Duty of Prayer." In vol. 2 of *The Works of Jonathan Edwards*, 71–77.

"The Importance and Advantage of a Thorough Knowledge of Divine Truth." In vol. 2 of *The Works of Jonathan Edwards*, 157–63.

"It Is Crime Enough to Render Any Man a Cursed Person Not to Love Jesus Christ." In *A Just and Righteous God: 18 Sermons*, 17–34.

"It Is Well for Us That God Is Not as We Are." In *Jonathan Edwards: Containing 16 Sermons Unpublished in Edwards' Lifetime*, 14–38.

"Jesus Christ, the Same Yesterday, Today, and Forever." In vol. 2 of *The Works of Jonathan Edwards*, 949–54.

"The Justice of God in the Damnation of Sinners." In vol. 1 of *The Works of Jonathan Edwards*, 668–79.

"Justification by Faith Alone." In vol. 1 of *The Works of Jonathan Edwards*, 622–53.

"The Ladder That God Has Set on the Earth for Man to Ascend to Happiness Reaches Even unto Heaven." In *A Just and Righteous God: 18 Sermons*, 147–73.

"The Manner in Which the Salvation of the Soul Is to Be Sought." In vol. 2 of *The Works of Jonathan Edwards*, 51–57.

"Men's Addiction to Sin Is No Excuse, but an Aggravation." In *Jonathan Edwards: Containing 16 Sermons Unpublished in Edwards' Lifetime*, 56–68.

"The Many Mansions." In *Selected Sermons of Jonathan Edwards*, 64–77.

"Men Naturally Are God's Enemies." In vol. 2 of *The Works of Jonathan Edwards*, 130–41.

"The Most High a Prayer-Hearing God." In vol. 2 of *The Works of Jonathan Edwards*, 113–18.

"Natural Men in a Dreadful Condition." In vol. 2 of *The Works of Jonathan Edwards*, 817–29.

"The Peace Which Christ Gives His True Followers." In vol. 2 of *The Works of Jonathan Edwards*, 89–93.

"The Perpetuity and Change of the Sabbath." In vol. 2 of *The Works of Jonathan Edwards*, 93–96.

"The Portion of the Righteous." In vol. 2 of *The Works of Jonathan Edwards*, 888–905.

"Praise, One of the Chief Employments of Heaven." In vol. 2 of *The Works of Jonathan Edwards*, 913–17.

"The Preciousness of Time and the Importance of Redeeming It." In vol. 2 of *The Works of Jonathan Edwards*, 233–36.

"Pressing into the Kingdom of God." In vol. 1 of *The Works of Jonathan Edwards*, 634–63.

"Procrastination, or the Sin and Folly of Depending on Future Time." In vol. 2 of *The Works of Jonathan Edwards*, 237–42.

"The Pure in Heart Blessed." In vol. 2 of *The Works of Jonathan Edwards*, 905–17.

"Ruth's Resolution." In vol. 1 of *The Works of Jonathan Edwards*, 664–68.

"Safety, Fullness, and Sweet Refreshment, to Be Found in Christ." In vol. 2 of *The Works of Jonathan Edwards*, 929–36.

"Sinners in the Hands of an Angry God." In vol. 2 of *The Works of Jonathan Edwards*, 7–12.

"The Sin of Theft and of Injustice." In vol. 2 of *The Works of Jonathan Edwards*, 220–26.

"The Sole Consideration, That God Is God, Sufficient to Still All Objections to His Sovereignty." In vol. 2 of *The Works of Jonathan Edwards*, 107–10.

"Some Men Shall Never Be Saved." In *A Just and Righteous God: 18 Sermons*, 97–112.

"The Sorrows of the Bereaved Spread before Jesus." In vol. 2 of *The Works of Jonathan Edwards*, 965–69.

"The Spirit of Charity Is an Humble Spirit." In *Charity and Its Fruits: Christian Love as Manifested in the Heart and Life*, 185–225.

"The Spirit of Charity, the Opposite of a Censorious Spirit." In *Charity and Its Fruits: Christian Love as Manifested in the Heart and Life*, 294–317.

"The Spirit of Charity, the Opposite of an Angry or Wrathful Spirit." In *Charity and Its Fruits: Christian Love as Manifested in the Heart and Life*, 268–93.

"The Spirit of Charity, the Opposite of a Selfish Spirit." In *Charity and Its Fruits: Christian Love as Manifested in the Heart and Life*, 226–67.

"Spiritual Appetites Need No Bounds." In *Jonathan Edwards: Containing 16 Sermons Unpublished in Edwards' Lifetime*, 223–35.

"Temptation and Deliverance." In vol. 2 of *The Works of Jonathan Edwards*, 226–33.

"There Is Nothing Like Seeing What God Is to Make Men Sensible to What They Are." In *Jonathan Edwards: Containing 16 Sermons Unpublished in Edwards' Lifetime*, 131–46.

"'Tis the Spirit of a Truly Godly Man to Prefer God before All Other Things Either in Heaven or on Earth." In *Jonathan Edwards: Containing 16 Sermons Unpublished in Edwards' Lifetime*, 176–91.

"The True Christian's Life a Journey toward Heaven," In vol. 7 of *The Works of President Edwards, in Eight Volumes*, 208–27.

"The True Excellency of a Gospel Minister." In vol. 2 of *The Works of Jonathan Edwards*, 955–60.

"True Grace Distinguished from the Experience of Devils." In vol. 2 of *The Works of Jonathan Edwards*, 41–50.

"True Saints, When Absent from the Body, Are Present with the Lord." In vol. 2 of *The Works of Jonathan* Edwards, 26–36

"Unbelievers Condemn the Glory and Excellency of Christ." In vol. 2 of *The Works of Jonathan Edwards*, 61–64.

"The Unreasonableness of Indetermination in Religion." In vol. 2 of *The Works of Jonathan Edwards*, 57–61.

"The Vain Self-Flatteries of the Sinner." In vol. 2 of *The Works of Jonathan Edwards*, 217–20.

"A Warning to Professors." In vol. 2 of *The Works of Jonathan Edwards*, 185–90.

"The Warnings of Scripture Are in the Best Manner Adapted to the Awakening and Conversion of Sinners." In vol. 2 of *The Works of Jonathan Edwards*, 68–71.

"The Way to Obtain the Blessing of God Is to Resolve Not to Let God Go Unless He Blesses Us." In *A Just and Righteous God: 18 Sermons*, 208–23.

"Wicked Men Useful in Their Destruction Only." In vol. 2 of *The Works of Jonathan Edwards*, 125–29.

"The Wisdom of God, Displayed in the Way of Salvation." In vol. 2 of *The Works of Jonathan Edwards*, 141–56.

"Wrath upon the Wicked to the Uttermost." In vol. 2 of *The Works of Jonathan Edwards*, 122–25.